CGI for Commerce

A Complete Web-Based Selling Solution

CGI for Commerce

A Complete Web-Based Selling Solution

Gunther Birznieks
Selena Sol

A Subsidiary of Henry Holt and Company
New York

M&T Books
A Division of MIS:Press, Inc.
A Subsidiary of Henry Holt and Company, Inc.
115 West 18th Street
New York, New York 10011
http://www.mispress.com

Copyright © 1997 by M&T Books

Printed in the United States of America

First Edition—1997

MIS:Press and M&T Books are available at special discounts for bulk purchases for sales promotions, premiums, and fundraising. Special editions or book excerpts can also be created to specification. For details contact the Special Sales Director at the above address.

10 9 8 7 6 5 4 3 2 1

```
Library of Congress Cataloging-in-Publication Data
Sol, Selena
   CGI for commerce: a complete web-based selling solution/by Selena
Sol, Gunther Birznieks.
     p. cm.
   ISBN 1-55851-559-3
1. Electronic commerce.  2. Web sites--Design and construction.
3. CGI (Computer network protocol)  4. Perl (Computer program lan-
guage)  5. Web--servers--Computer programs.  I. Birznieks, Gunther.
II. Title
HF5548.32.S65  1997                              97-5728
004.67'8--dc21                                       CIP
```

Associate Publisher: *Paul Farrell*
Managing Editor: *Shari Chappell*
Editor: *Michael Sprague*

Production Editor: *Gay Nichols*
Copy Edit Manager: *Karen Tongish*
Copy Editor: *Winifred Davis*

CONTENTS

INTRODUCTION

The Web Store

Shopping cart applications are some of the most popular, interesting to customize, and technically demanding CGI applications currently in use on the Web. Such applications allow companies to display their inventories online so that clients can quickly and easily browse through and order items of interest (Figure I.1).

Some of the more famous and groundbreaking examples include Virtual Vineyards (http://www.virtualvin.com/) and CD-Now (http://www.cdnow.com/). Both of these sites generate large sums of money from virtual clients through their user-friendly interfaces and sleek design. Because the warehouses are virtual and the sales staff are automated, the virtual store is a profitable option for many small and midsize businesses that want to gain instant access to a global market. Web stores can also provide larger, established companies with alternative outlets for their products, as well as a continued presence in emerging markets.

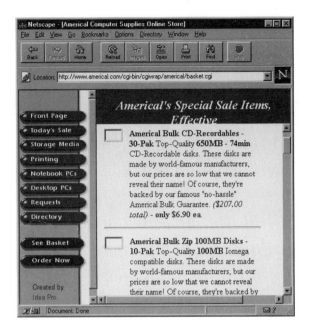

Figure I.1 Americal Web store customized by IDEA PRO Online Marketing at http://www.silicon.net/~tbond.

In addition, the customers receive the benefits of dynamic, customizable browsing tools. Rather than deal with mail-order catalogs, 1-800 numbers, or fax (or worse yet, snail mail–based) order forms, a customer need only navigate over to their favorite store on the World Wide Web, click to their section of interest, add some items to their virtual shopping cart, type in some shipping information, and submit the information over a secure channel of the Internet. As David Cook writes in *Launching a Business on the Web*, "The idea of a virtual shopping system is to make the job of picking products as painless as possible. In essence, we want the user to do no more than simply point to a picture or word to purchase an item."

And yet, however invisible and seamless the application is to the customer, an online store is a demanding application to program, customize, and install because it integrates many Web/CGI functions into one system. Consider the complexity for a programmer. A shopping cart application must be able to manage *every* function of shopping, not only from the perspective of the customer but from that of the vendor as well.

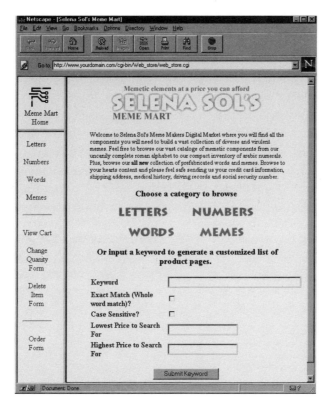

Figure I-2 Image of the Web store.

Store Management from the Vendor's Perspective

For one thing, the application must be able to manage and display the stores inventory. That is, the application must be able to keep track of every item in the store and to present those items in an efficient and sensible way. Think of this function as that of the store employee who must continually restock the shelves of the store with new items, change some prices here, remove some items there, introduce "specials," and generally make sure that aisles are clean, current, and organized for the convenience of customers.

In terms of the Web Store application, the program must be able to generate and display HTML "product pages" that can be browsed according to the needs of the client. There are many different ways these product pages can be displayed to the user. For example, they might be organized hierarchically, according to categories and subcategories of products or they might be generated dynamically based on the customer's search criteria. Further, depending on the desires of the vendor and the demands of the inventory itself, the inventory might be physically stored as a simple ASCII text flat file, in an SQL database, or as a series of predesigned HTML pages. The shopping cart system must be flexible and intelligent enough to produce a consistent look and feel while the specific display of items is changing based on the customer's desires.

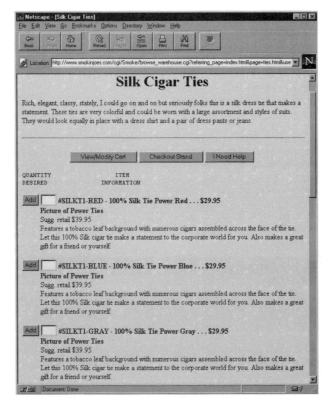

Figure I.3   Product page from the Smokin' Joe Web store.

A further complication lies in the fact that every item must be uniquely identified and may have unique qualities that differentiate it from other items, even within the same category. One good example of this is the application of options. Many items, even within the same category may have different options available. For example, in an online music shop, certain albums might come in CD format only, in both tape and CD format, or even LP only. The Web store application must have a means for interpreting such unique qualities for every item and incorporating them into the logic of the process. In a store with 1000 items, there may be up to a 1000 special cases.

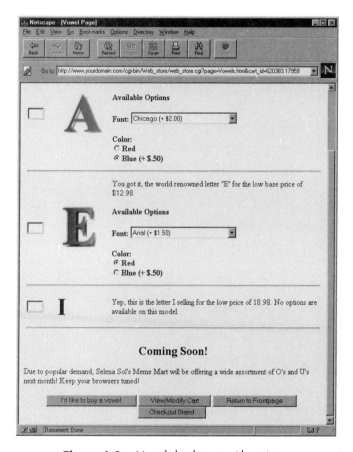

Figure I.4   Vowels.html page with options.

The Web store must also be able to keep track of many customers simultaneously, all of whom are at different points in the shopping process. Some of those clients might be just entering the store, some might be at the virtual cash register, and others might be browsing the shelves casually or with a specific product in mind. The Web store must be able to handle each of these situations so seamlessly that each customer feels as if he or she is the only customer in the store. Speed and consistency are paramount.

Keeping track of visitors also involves administrative functions. For example, just as someone must constantly keep track of used shopping carts in the parking lot of your local supermarket, so must the Web store application deal with its own old, used shopping carts. After all, it would not do to continually save all the carts used by all the customers. If all goes well and your products attract droves of browsing clients, you might generate hundreds of carts per day. Though each cart will occupy only a small amount of space on your server, when combined, the set of all carts could cause your server's hard disk to fill up quickly. Thus, the application must be responsible for pruning old carts at a regular interval.

Another administrative function is that of logging accesses and errors. Every new client will bring a set of valuable data that if gathered and interpreted wisely, could yield insights crucial to your continued success. How many of your clients are international? How many are repeat visitors? Which pages do clients most often request? Which items do they most often buy? What percent of your visitors use Netscape? When are your daily peak hours? These are the kinds of data that should be available in your access logs for analysis.

Similarly, you should have a complete error log. Have there been any attempted hacks? Are there errors in your configuration that slipped by you? Has some environment variable on your server changed that demands your attention, such as a change in permissions? The error log can be used to quickly diagnose problems with the application as it evolves. In some cases, a well-analyzed error log can save you from having to hire a programming consultant to do troubleshooting.

Finally, the Web store must be your cashier, totaling up shopping carts full of items and accepting payment from customers. In doing so, it must be able to handle your local taxes, shipping costs, discounts, specials, and any number of surprise price modifications on the fly for every customer.

More crucially, the Web store must do this flawlessly and securely. Not only must the connection between the browser and server be secure (an issue between you and your ISP), but orders must then be sent securely from the server to the person handling order processing. What good is a powerful and expensive SSL account if the customer's credit card and personal information are sent via unprotected email to the store owner? A secure store is only as secure as its weakest link. The Web store must be able to support SSL technology and provide a secure method of getting that information from the secure server to the store owner or administrator for processing.

Whatever the case, the application must be able to quickly provide a virtual store environment with seamless access to products. At this infant stage of the Web, there are already enough barriers between the clients and vendors: speed, ignorance, unfamiliarity, and more; the Web store technology must not add another barrier. It must be an interface that makes the user want to come back.

Shopping from the Customer's Perspective

The Web store is also responsible for handling the needs of the customer. It must follow each client through the store, even if there are dozens of clients shopping simultaneously, and act as his or her personal shopping servant. When the customer says "grab this item," the Web store must do so. It must also be able to get more than one item or to put all the items back on the virtual shelves if so instructed. The shopping cart itself is actually a database file that is built and modified on the fly based on the client's needs. The maintenance of the cart, therefore, requires a database management system capable of handling the addition, modification, and deletion of items in the cart.

However, the script must do more than just display and modify the shopping cart. It must also manipulate the database fields to perform price calculations, such as calculating a subtotal for each item purchased and generating a grand total from the subtotals in a cart. Furthermore, the Web store must do this for every customer independently using a technique to maintain the state of where each customer is in his or her shopping process.

Before we discuss how the script maintains this "state," a short discussion of client/server technology is in order. When you type a URL into the location window of your favorite browser and hit **Enter**, you are becoming a client to some server from which you are requesting a service. Typically, you will be asking the server to send you a document formatted with HyperText Markup Language (HTML). In the case of CGI, such as a Web store, you ask the server to execute a program and return the results of the processing. Unfortunately, that is all there is to the Web. There is no continuous discussion, dialog, or connection. There is only a simple one-time query and response each time a document or CGI script is requested.

One of the facts of life of client/server architecture is that each request sent from a client and processed by a server is considered a new and unique one. That is, there is only a series of unrelated queries and responses. The server maintains no link with its clients. Instead, the server simply, blindly, and automatically waits for a query, answers the query, and settles back down to wait for the next query to arrive. You may ask it for a second document by clicking another hyperlink or a **Submit** button, but the server will treat you as the unknown stranger that you are. It will not "remember" anything about you or your past interactions with it.

So, how do you create a complex relationship between a customer and a vendor using a Web script? For example, in order for each client to maintain a unique set of shopping cart items, the application must keep track of each client and each clients virtual cart. *Maintaining state*, as this is called, is difficult because HTTP, as we have mentioned, is a "connectionless" protocol. Every time a Web browser requests the attention of your server, it is considered a new request, unrelated to any other requests fulfilled by the server. Because each request is considered independently of others, the server has no way to keep track of what clients have added to their carts in the past.

NOTE It is possible for the browser software to be made responsible for remembering this information using technology like Netscape Cookies. However, using cookies is not the best solution for an online store that hopes to serve customers using a wide assortment of browsers that may not adhere to Netscape's proprietary cookie standard. Furthermore, even the customers who do use Netscape may have the cookies feature turned off for security reasons.

To solve this problem, the application becomes a self-referential script. It continuously calls itself for every request made by the client. However, when it calls itself, it passes to itself information about how to process the new request and information specific to the history of the relationship with the current client. In the case of the clients shopping cart items, the script will pass to itself the location of the clients cart on the server. This cart file will keep track of the items previously purchased. By providing the location in each call, the script continues to keep track of each client and cart.

The Web store does all this while still performing all the usual CGI functions, including reading and parsing incoming form data, checking that form data against bad input, emailing orders, and communicating with the browser via HTTP.

How This Book Is Structured

As you can see, the Web store application has a lot on its plate. The rest of this book will delve into the complex methodology used to solve these problems and provide a manageable framework for you to install and customize the routines for your own unique needs.

The book is divided into three sections.

Part One focuses on the process of downloading, customizing, and running the Web store application. Contained in 10 chapters, Part One goes through several common types of installations, discussing the many facets of customization from configuring your GUI to handling specific order logic ranging from discounts to shipping costs to zip code calculations. This part concludes with a discussion of methods of log analysis and secure shopping with which you can streamline and enhance the functionality and security of your store.

Part Two takes a more in depth look at the scripts that make up the application themselves. This part looks at the actual code of the application, stripping each routine down to its bare algorithms to explain the deep logic behind the store. This application is very powerful because, due to its modularity, you can change not only the look and feel quite a bit, but also the logic and capabilities. After all, you may find down the road that there are features you would like to add that are unique to your own installation or inventory that are not necessarily appropriate for, or coded within, the generic store. These chapters should give you a firm grasp of how to add or remove from the programming of the Web store's core capabilities.

Finally, two appendices close the book. Appendix A discusses the format and usage of the CD-ROM and Appendix B reviews some of the basic tenets of Perl CGI.

Who This Book Is For

This book was primarily written for Web/CGI programmers who wish to set up online stores and programmers who are interested in examining a real-world CGI application that uses nearly every available feature in the CGI/Perl programmer arsenal. Secondly, content providers who are interested in expanding their services beyond simple HTML pages will benefit from the book as a primer on how to set up an online store.

All levels of programmers can benefit from this book. For example, the beginning CGI developer can use the book as a straightforward, example-based way of learning CGI while obtaining information on how to set up a useful real-world script. The script is explained simply enough that we hope it will be accessible to all, and we have taken great pains to isolate the basic installation and usage issues into their own part so that nonprogrammers do not need to spend much time deciphering the code if all they want to do is run the scripts.

Additionally, this book is for advanced CGI developers who are looking for a good, well-documented script that they can sink their teeth into to learn more about how a large, complex CGI application fits together. The discussion in Part Two about the details of the code behind the Web store application will help advanced developers to actually go in and customize the source code to the needs of their more demanding customers.

PART ONE

SETTING UP
THE SHOPPING CART

CHAPTER ONE

GETTING, INSTALLING, AND RUNNING THE APPLICATION

Downloading the Script

Although the script is distributed with the CD-ROM accompanying this book, it is recommended that you point your Web browser to "Selena Sol's Script Archive" to get the latest version of this script. The Script Archive is located at the following URL: http://www.eff.org/~erict/Scripts/.

From the Scripts Archive front page, follow the hyperlinks for "Web Store" to the detailed page dedicated to this script. There you will find several working demonstrations representing different configuration options as well as the scripts for review and download. Feel free to click on the hyperlink **Download the scripts as a single TAR file** in order to transfer the archived scripts to your local machine. For Windows NT Server users, there will be a zipped distribution of the scripts that are configured to run on a variety of Windows NT Web Servers.

Alternatively, you may grab the application off the accompanying CD ROM by following the instructions in Appendix A.

Unpacking the Application

For UNIX Web Servers, the Web Store application is distributed in the form of a single TAR file. **TAR** is a UNIX command that allows you to create a single archive file containing many files. Such archiving allows you to maintain directory relationships and facilitates transferring complex programs with many separate but integrated parts which must have their relationships preserved. TAR has a motley of options that allow you to do archiving and de-archiving in many ways. However, for the purpose of unpacking this application from its TAR file, the commands will be fairly simple.

The Windows NT version of the Web Store will be distributed as a ZIP file. Setting up the Web Store on Windows NT or Windows 95 Web servers will be discussed in a separate section of this chapter.

N O T E

Once you have downloaded the TAR file, transfer it to an executable directory on your Web server and unpack it using the TAR program. On UNIX systems, you may type the following at the command (for this command to work, you must be in the same directory as the TAR file itself resides):

```
tar xvfp web_store.tar
```

If you are using a UNIX server, do not unpack the scripts on a Windows or Mac OS machine and ftp them to the server. Instead, transfer the TAR file to the UNIX machine using binary mode and unpack it there. Otherwise, you may introduce bad characters into the files because Windows and MAC machines typically handle line breaks differently than UNIX machine, inserting **\r\n** for new lines instead of just **\n**.

N O T E

TAR will go through the archive file and separate each of the individual directories and files, expanding them into their appropriate places beneath the current directory. The **xvfp** letters in the TAR command above are parameters that tell the program to extract the files and directories out of the **.tar** file. Specifically, **x** tells TAR to extract the files. **v** tells TAR to output information about the status of its extraction while it is performing the work, **f** informs TAR to use the **.tar** filename as the source of the files to be extracted, and **p** notes that the original permissions should be maintained. The reason the **f** parameter has to be used is that TAR, by default, archives files and directories to a tape drive. TAR is actually short for "[T]ape [AR]chive". Figure 1.1 shows the output of the above command.

```
eff.org:~/.webdocs/Scripts/Source/Web_store$ tar xvfp web_store.tar
x Web_store/Html/Products/Numbers.html, 4257 bytes, 9 tape blocks
x Web_store/Html/Products/Vowels.html, 7234 bytes, 15 tape blocks
x Web_store/Html/Products/Consonants.html, 1709 bytes, 4 tape blocks
x Web_store/Html/Products/Letters.html, 276 bytes, 1 tape blocks
x Web_store/Html/Products/Words.html, 1757 bytes, 4 tape blocks
x Web_store/Html/Products/Memes.html, 2385 bytes, 5 tape blocks
x Web_store/Html/Products/Letters.html.db, 273 bytes, 1 tape blocks
x Web_store/Html/Options/option.html, 472 bytes, 1 tape blocks
x Web_store/Html/home.html, 520 bytes, 2 tape blocks
x Web_store/Html/outlet_frontpage.html, 2376 bytes, 5 tape blocks
x Web_store/Html/outlet_order_form.html, 3483 bytes, 7 tape blocks
x Web_store/Html/toc.html, 885 bytes, 2 tape blocks
x Web_store/Html/frames_frontpage.html, 402 bytes, 1 tape blocks
x Web_store/Html/frontpage.html, 1993 bytes, 4 tape blocks
x Web_store/Html/outlet_frontpage_db.html, 2617 bytes, 6 tape blocks
x Web_store/Html/Images/letters.gif, 537 bytes, 2 tape blocks
x Web_store/Html/Images/memes.gif, 554 bytes, 2 tape blocks
x Web_store/Html/Images/numbers.gif, 721 bytes, 2 tape blocks
x Web_store/Html/Images/symbols.gif, 681 bytes, 2 tape blocks
x Web_store/Html/Images/web_store_front.gif, 4740 bytes, 10 tape blocks
x Web_store/Html/Images/words.gif, 580 bytes, 2 tape blocks
x Web_store/Html/Images/white_space.gif, 54 bytes, 1 tape blocks
x Web_store/Html/Images/eight.gif, 308 bytes, 1 tape blocks
x Web_store/Html/Images/five.gif, 244 bytes, 1 tape blocks
x Web_store/Html/Images/four.gif, 210 bytes, 1 tape blocks
x Web_store/Html/Images/nine.gif, 310 bytes, 1 tape blocks
x Web_store/Html/Images/one.gif, 134 bytes, 1 tape blocks
x Web_store/Html/Images/seven.gif, 242 bytes, 1 tape blocks
x Web_store/Html/Images/six.gif, 316 bytes, 1 tape blocks
```

Figure 1.1   Unpacking the Web store using TAR.

NOTE   If you are using a non-UNIX operating system and Web server, you may download a TAR/UNTAR program by pointing your Web browser to http://www.shareware.com. We suggest using "untar" as your keyword when you search their inventory. In addition, many popular Windows Zip utility programs such as WinZip have inherent functionality that allows them to unpack tar files.

Setting Permissions

Unpacking the files is only one part of the equation of installing the Web Store application and getting it to actually execute. Frequently, the Web server needs to be given special permission to execute your scripts and have the scripts perform their job with the appropriate "rights."

The cardinal rule for setting up Web server software is that the server should be given only minimal capabilities. This definitely rules out the Web server running as the ROOT user (Super-user on UNIX). More often than not, it means that the Web server is run as a user that has no rights to do anything significant—a user "nobody." By default, "nobody" usually does not have permission to read any files in directories that you create. However, when you download scripts, you need to create an environment so that the scripts can be read and executed by the Web server software. In other words, "nobody" has to be able to access the files.

In UNIX, the command for performing this task is **chmod**. The directory structure of the Web store root directory is a good example of how you should use the **chmod** command.

For this example, we will assume that you are sharing a server on an Internet service provider, which is typically the most restrictive situation in terms of your security options, and that all your CGI scripts are located in the default directory called Web_store. The example also assumes that we are in the directory above the one where the CGI scripts actually reside when we execute the chmod command. Finally, this example assumes that the Web server is running as the user "nobody" and does not belong to your user i.d.'s security group. Note that if the Web server is indeed part of your group, you will be able to restrict permissions on the files so that the world cannot do anything with the files, but anyone in your security group can do the minimal operations needed for the script to operate.

There are four different sets of permissions that need to be granted in order for the user "nobody" to have the permissions needed to execute this CGI script. First, the Web_store directory itself must be both readable and executable by the world. The directory is readable because we need to read the entries in the directory, and it is executable so that the Web server can go into the directory and open the files in it. This is done using the following command:

```
chmod 755 Web_store
```

The 755 number tells chmod to make the Web_store directory readable, writable, and executable by the owner of the directory (you) while making it only readable and executable by the world and the group you are in.

How did we come up with the number? Files in UNIX have three types of permissions: User (the owner of the file), Group (the security group you are in), and OTHER (for the world to see). Each digit in the number above corresponds to one of these categories. The first digit is User, the second digit is group, and the final digit is other. Thus in the example above, 7 = USER, 5 = GROUP, and OTHER = 5.

The actual value of the digit determines the permissions granted to that area. Permissions consist of three numbers: 4 for Read, 2 for Write, and 1 for Execute access. By adding these numbers together, you form the permissions that make up one digit. For example, 4 + 2 + 1 = 7, which grants read, write, and execute permissions; 4 + 1 = 5, which grants only read and execute permissions. Thus, 755 grants 7 (read, write, execute) to the owner of the file, and 5 (read and execute) to the group the file is in and to the world. Table 1.1 can be used as a quick reference

Table 1.1   Common Permissions Settings for CGI Applications

Permission			Command
User	**Group**	**World**	
rwx	rwx	rwx	chmod 777 filename
rwx	rwx	r-x	chmod 775 filename
rwx	r-x	r-x	chmod 755 filename
rw-	rw-	rw-	chmod 666 filename
rw-	rw-	r- -	chmod 664 filename
rw-	r- -	r- -	chmod 644 filename

r = Readable; w = writable; x = executable; – = no permission

The files within the Web_store directory need to be readable and executable since the Web server will be running the CGI scripts in it. To set those permissions, we use the following command:

```
chmod 755 Web_store/*.*
```

This command operates in the same way as the one above, except that it changes all the files (*.* pattern matches everything) inside the Web_store directory to be readable and executable by everyone. These scripts themselves should not be writable!

Nor should the Web_store directory be writable, since that would allow other users on the system place scripts there. The Admin_files directory is another issue. However, since it contains log files which the Web server must write to, the Admin_files directory must be made writable so that the script can write to the directory. In addition, the files generated in that directory should also be readable in case the Web Store script needs to access them. To change the directory so that it is writable as well as having read and execute access, use the following command:

```
chmod 777 Web_store/Admin_files
```

This will change the Admin_files directory under the Web_store directory to be readable, writable, and executable by the world.

WARNING

You may be tempted to simply use chmod 777 on all the files and directories since that assures the Web server can do anything with the files. However, it is strongly advised that you do not leave the files in this state. It is considered a major security risk to leave your scripts open to changes by the Web server instead of being read-only. Anyone on the server could use another rogue CGI script to write over your scripts and make them do something completely different. There is still a risk involved in making the Admin_files and User_carts directory writable, but at least if someone is going to be messing with your area, they will only destroy a bit of data and not your main programs. It is OK to set the scripts to 777 if you are troubleshooting a problem and want to rule out permissions entirely, but do not leave the scripts like this.

On another security note, if you are really concerned with the security of your data, do not use a shared server where other people can write CGI scripts using the same Web server configuration. It is much better to use your own server software or purchase space on a virtual server that may be shared, but is set up in such a way that each user's scripts are shielded from each other.

NOTE Not setting your permissions correctly is the chief cause installation failure. Take the time to get this right. The Web store setup checking script described in Chapter 2 can aid you in this endeavor.

Finally, most other files should be simply readable to the Web server. For example, consider the files in the Library subdirectory. Since the script never needs write access to these files, it is best guard them by the strictest permissions possible, making them writable only by you. This will protect those files against malicious hackers or accidental modifications by others in your group (see Figure 1.2).

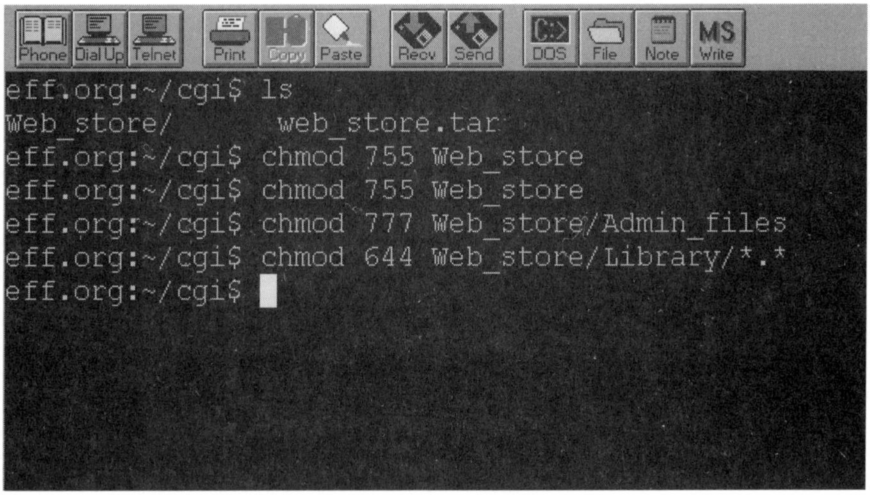

```
eff.org:~/cgi$ ls
Web_store/        web_store.tar
eff.org:~/cgi$ chmod 755 Web_store
eff.org:~/cgi$ chmod 755 Web_store
eff.org:~/cgi$ chmod 777 Web_store/Admin_files
eff.org:~/cgi$ chmod 644 Web_store/Library/*.*
eff.org:~/cgi$
```

Figure 1.2   Setting permissions.

To set permissions for these files, use the following syntax:

```
chmod 644 Web_store/Library/*
```

The actual permissions required for the subdirectories and files used by this application are listed in the next section.

Understanding Web Store Files and Directories

The TAR file expands into a root directory called *Web_store* that contains several subdirectories and several files. Figure 1.3 depicts the directory structure as well as the permissions that must be applied to the files and sub-directories used by the application.

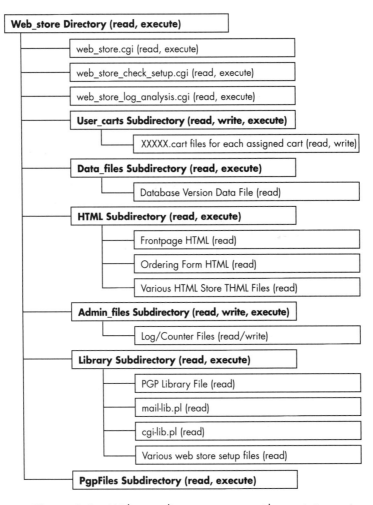

Figure 1.3   Web store directory structure with permission settings.

Web_store is the application's root directory. The Web server must have read and execute privileges for this directory.

The **Admin_files** subdirectory is used to hold various files that the Web server must have permission to read and write to. Within the directory are several logs used to keep track of store usage as well as the counter file. Each of these files must be readable by and writable to the Web server. The subdirectory itself must be readable, writable, and executable by the Web server.

access.log contains information about customers who access the store frontpage. It will contain the values of any environment variables known to your server as well as the date of access in pipe-delimited (|) database rows separated by the newline character.

counter.file is used to generate unique i.d. numbers for every item in customers' carts. Each item that the customer orders must be uniquely identifiable if the script is to modify or delete it.

error.log contains information about errors that have occurred during use of the script. Each pipe-delimited row of the log file contains information about what error has occurred, the line number of the error and any environment variables known by the Web server. Each row is separated by a newline character.

order.log contains a log of all the orders that have been processed by web_store.cgi. Each individual order is separated by a line of dashes (- -).

The **Data_files** subdirectory contains the data file used to generate the product pages in a database-based store or to check against in an HTML-based store with database validation. The directory itself must be readable and executable by the Web server. The data file within it must be readable:

data.file is the file that contains all the store products. Essentially, this is a simple, flat-file, ASCII, pipe-delimited database. It is crucial that you define the structure of the database in the setup file as each column must be defined in several index variables and arrays. The data file and the index variables will be discussed in greater detail in Chapter 2 and Chapter 4.

The **Html** subdirectory holds various HTML documents used by both the HTML-based and database-based versions of web_store.cgi to provide navigation-like functions such as the front page, order form, and list of product pages.

However, in the case of the HTML-based store, it is responsible for containing all of the product pages as well as the navigational pages. The directory and its subdirectories must be readable and executable by the Web server, and the files within the directories must be readable.

Images is a subdirectory containing images used by the default example store in the Web Store distribution.

N O T E   If you are running this script on a server that does not allow you to reference images within the CGI directory, you may have to move this directory elsewhere in order to actually see the images. If you are getting broken images but all else works correctly, this is likely the cause. It is important to note that if you do move this directory, all links hardcoded in the example HTML pages as well as those in data.file must be changed to reflect the new location.

Options is a subdirectory containing any option files that you create. Option files are used in the database-based version of the store when you want many items to have the same option HTML code, but you do not want to write that code in every single database row. Option files will be discussed in greater detail in Chapter 4. This directory must be readable and executable and every option file must be readable.

Products   This subdirectory contains predesigned HTML pages that the store may be asked to display during shopping. There are two types of pages stored here. First, product pages are stored here. *Product pages* are simply HTML forms written with a specific format (using special tags discussed in Chapter 3) that allow customers to buy specific store items (see Figure 1.4). These pages are used for HTML-based stores which cannot generate product pages dynamically from a data file.

Secondly, this subdirectory contains *list of product* pages, which are simply HTML pages that contain hyperlinks to product pages (see Figure 1.5). These lists of product pages are used for both the HTML and database versions of the store. The coding of both product pages and list of product pages will be discussed later.

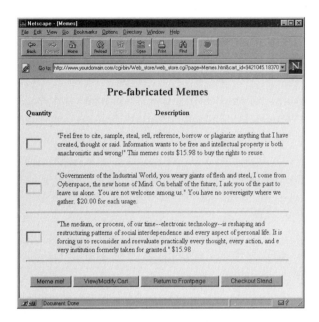

Figure 1.4 Memes.html—An example product page.

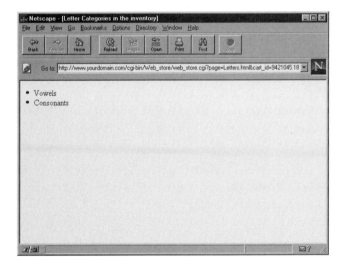

Figure 1.5 Letters.html—An example list of products page.

Letters.html (HTML-based store-specific) and **Letters.html.db** (Database-based store-specific) are examples of a list of product pages, and **Memes.html** is an example of a product page. Other product pages include **Vowels.html**, **Consonants.html**, **Words.html**, and **Numbers.html**.

frames_frontpage.html, **home.html**, **toc.html** and **frontpage.html** are all used in the Frames example of the store. **frames_frontpage.html** defines three frames that point to the other three. These will be discussed more thoroughly in Chapter 6.

outlet_frontpage.html, **outlet_frontpage_query.html** and **outlet_frontpage_db.html** are the frontpage examples for the Html-based store, Query-driven store, and the database-based stores, respectively.

outlet_order_form.html and **outlet_order_form_with_shipping.html** are two examples of how you might create your own order form. **outlet_order_form.html** is a basic example. **outlet_order_form_with_shipping.html** contains the HTML necessary to calculate sample shipping logic.

The **Library** subdirectory is used to hold the associated library files used by this application. The directory itself must be readable and executable by the Web server. The files within it must be readable.

cgi-lib.pl is used to read and parse form data as well as providing a convenient way to exit with explanation in case of a problem in opening a file.

mail-lib.pl is used to send unencrypted email to the store administrator.

pgp-lib.pl is used to send encrypted email to the store administrator.

web_store.setup.* are the six sample setup files distributed by default. These setup files exemplify several methods for defining the interface to the store. The differences among these setup files, and the actual meaning of setup variables will be discussed in Chapter 2, which goes into the details of creating the generic **web_store.setup** .

web_store.setup.db is the basic database-based store with a non–table-based product display. (In use, the setup file creates product displays that mirror the HTML-based store). **web_store.setup.db.table** displays products tabularly; Less visually effective but very efficient, it is used in the distribution to demonstrate query-based searching. Chapter 4 gives the changes needed to make the **web_store.setup.db** operate off of a database. Chapter 5 gives the changes needed to transform the regular database store into a query-driven store.

web_store.setup.frames gives an example of a frames-based store. By default, it uses the nontabular database-based logic for display of products. However, it could just as easily use the tabular-database or HTML logic. Chapter 6 goes into the details of how the frames-based store works.

web_store.setup.frames.javascript takes frames one step further by integrating a JavaScript routine to calculate order totals before customers add items to their carts. **web_store.setup.frames.vbscript** does the same thing, but in VBScript. Chapter 7 illustrates how JavaScript and VBScript were integrated with the Web store.

web_store.setup.html shows an example of using an HTML-based Web store interface. Chapter 3 outlines how the HTML Web store is configured.

web_store_db_lib.pl is a library of subroutines used to search the database.

web_store_html_lib.pl is a library of subroutines used to generate most of the customizable HTML. If you want to change the look and feel of your store, you will probably modify the code in this library. The specifics of the library will be discussed later.

web_store_html_search.pl defines the search routines for the HTML-based store that cannot search a database for keywords but must read through product pages individually searching for hits.

web_store_order_lib.pl defines the routines necessary to process orders.

Pgpfiles is the subdirectory used to store files necessary for processing orders using PGP encryption. The directory itself must be readable and executable by the Web server and files within it must be readable.

PGP is a third-party encryption tool written by Phil Zimmerman for the purpose of encrypting and decrypting files. You have to know how to use PGP in order to use this feature of the cart. By default, we turn off PGP encryption. Basically, you need to obtain PGP, generate a public and private key for your Web Store and then store the public key configuration files inside this directory. The details of this process are discussed in Chapter 9.

The **User_carts** subdirectory is used to store the actual shopping carts used by clients browsing your store. Initially, this subdirectory will be empty. As customers enter your store, the script will automatically fill the directory with new carts and prune the directory of old carts. The directory must be readable, writable, and executable by the Web server; the cart files created within it must be readable and writable. The script will generally create and delete carts on its own.

web_store.cgi is the main script that generates the GUI for the online store. It must be readable and executable by the Web server.

web_store_check_setup.cgi is a script you can use to help with installation. This script will go through and check the permissions and path values you have defined in your setup file and report any problems it finds. The Web server must be able to read and execute this file.

web_store_log_analysis.cgi is a script used to browse your log files. It offers a simple keyword-search box and asks which log file you would like to review. It must be readable and executable by the Web server.

Installing on Windows 95/NT Web Servers

Installing CGI scripts on a Windows NT– or a Windows 95–based Web server is generally more of a challenge than installing them on a UNIX server. This is because, although UNIX servers have standardized the way they handle CGI scripts, 32-bit Windows servers have not. They all have slightly different behaviors when interpreting CGI. To top it off, there is a CGI standard specifically made for Windows and called *WinCGI*. In this section, we will focus on tips and techniques that will help you run the Web store on some of the more popular Windows NT Web servers.

 The various changes discussed below have already been implemented and are distributed on the CD-ROM in order to allow you to have an easier time of making your scripts work on Windows NT or Windows 95 Web servers. Appendix A N O T E covers the CD-ROM distribution in detail.

General Tasks for All NT Servers

The main concern for all NT-based Web servers is to make sure that anything that seems to be UNIX specific either has an equivalent feature on NT or can be substituted by another utility. This generally involves obtaining Perl for NT and make sure that any UNIX specific features on the Web Store are translated into their Windows NT equivalents.

The first step is to obtain Perl for Windows NT/Windows 95. This can be done by doing a simple Web search on **perl** and **nt**. While there are several Perl ports for NT, we currently recommend using the port from Hip Communications. It is Perl 5–compatible and appears to be the port most compatible with UNIX-based Perl at the moment. Installing Perl is easy. Simply unzip it into a directory on your NT server and run the **install.bat** program that exists in the new Perl subdirectory that you have created.

Next, **mail-lib.pl** needs to be replaced with **smtpmail-lib.pl**. In addition, changes need to be done to the **smtpmail-lib.pl** file to make it recognize that it is running on NT. This is discussed in detail at the end of Chapter 8 in the section that discusses configuring **mail-lib.pl**. **Mail-lib.pl** is the only UNIX-specific library in the entire Web store. Similarly, you may need to modify **pgp-lib.pl**. The only reason this library may not work on NT is if the interface to the DOS version of PGP is different from the interface to the UNIX version of PGP. Every other library and program should work as-is on Windows NT.

Tasks Required to Make the Web Store Run on Netscape Commerce Server for NT

The only thing that must be done in addition to the tasks above for Netscape Commerce Server version 1.x (and Netscape Communications Server v1.x) is that the script must be encapsulated inside a Batch file. The v1.x Netscape servers were unable to recognize CGI scripts directly. Thus, you need to wrap the **web_store.cgi** script inside a batch file to make it run. Then, all references to **web_store.cgi** need to be changed to **web_store.bat** in the various HTML files as well as the setup file. In the setup file, there are two url variables that need to be changed to reflect the new batch file name: **$sc_main_script_url** and **$sc_order_script_url**.

The contents of the batch file is easy. The first line consists of **@echo off** so that the DOS-related information does not print out to the Web browser and the second line actually calls the script using Perl.

NOTE

In order for this to work, Perl must be installed so that it is in the path of the machine you are running it on. If it is not in the path of the machine you are running it on, you will need to alter the batch file definition so that Perl is referenced with an absolute path to its location.

```
@echo off
perl web_store.cgi
```

WARNING

Running scripts as encapsulated batch files can open up a can of security worms. To obtain a full appreciation of the problems that may arise, you should read the CGI programming security FAQ located at the following URL: http://www-genome.wi.mit.edu/WWW/faqs/www-security-faq.html.

Tasks Required to Make the Web Store Run on Netscape Enterprise/FastTrack Server for NT

The Netscape Enterprise or FastTrack server has the capability of recognizing and running scripts with the extension of **.cgi** if you have previously associated the Perl executable with **.cgi** extensions in your file manager or Windows explorer. Thus, you do not need to encapsulate the scripts inside a batch file. The bad news is that at the time of this writing, the default behavior of the new Netscape servers is to run the scripts as if they are operating relative to where Perl is located.

This is bad because all the setup script variables are generally configured so that they are expected to be relative paths from the directory where **web_store.cgi** resides. However, your **perl.exe** executable is usually in a totally different subdirectory such as **c:\perl5** or **d:\perl5**. There are two solutions to this problem. First, you could set all the paths in the setup file to be absolute paths instead of relative to the current working directory. However, then, you also have to modify the **web_store.cgi** file so that when the setup file is "required," it is required with the absolute path as well.

An alternative, and probably easier, approach is to add a line to **web_store.cgi** script instead of altering all the setup file options. For this example, we will assume the the the real path where **web_store.cgi** is located on your server is **d:\netscape\server\cgi-bin\Web_store**. Before the line that contains the words **&require_supporting_libraries**, insert the following:

```
chdir(d:\netscape\server\cgi-bin\Web_store);
```

Adding this line will make the Web server reference the web script in the correct subdirectory for the duration of the running of that script. Remember, you must use two backslashes for every backslash in a normal MS-DOS path because backslashes need to be escaped in Perl.

Tasks Required to Make the Web Store Run on the WebSite Server for NT

As of this writing, WebSite has a problem almost identical to that of the Netscape Enterprise/FastTrack servers. Whenever a script is run on the WebSite server, it runs as if it is relative to the current working directory of the WebSite server executable itself. You can fix this problem in the same way we fixed the problem with Netscape Enterprise/FastTrack server.

NOTE   In order for **web_store.cgi** to run on a WebSite server, you need to associate the **.cgi** extension with the **perl.exe** executable just as you do with Netscape Enterprise/FastTrack server.

Tasks Required to Make the Web Store Run on Internet Information Server (IIS) For NT

Microsoft Internet Information Server version 1.0 and 2.0 both have a problem similar to that of the Netscape Enterprise/FastTrack and WebSite Web servers. Of course, just as these two Web servers have their own twist on the problem, IIS has its own peculiarity. Whenever you set up a directory alias on IIS that points to a real subdirectory on the NT server, any scripts that run in subdirectories underneath the original alias will act as if their current working directory is actually the root where the alias started. Thus, if the alias Scripts is configured to look at **d:\inetsrv\scripts**, and you try to run **web_store.cgi** inside a Web_store subdirectory under the d:directory, the script will act as if it is running inside d:cripts. There are two ways around this problem.

First, you can solve it the same way the WebSite and the Netscape Enterprise/FastTrack server problems were solved and use the **chdir** command inside the **web_store.cgi script**. However, IIS offers you an alternative way to solve the problem. You can simply make a new alias! That is, if you want the script to act as though it is running in its own subdirectory, then all you have to do is set up an alias that points directly to the subdirectory where **web_store.cgi** is located and then call **web_store.cgi** using the new alias.

N O T E

In order for **.cgi** extension scripts to run at all on IIS v1.0 and v2.0, you need to set up an association with the **.cgi** extension and the **perl.exe** executable. However, IIS does not recognize the normal NT-wide associations set up in File manager or Windows explorer. You will need to set up these associations manually in the registry. The instructions for doing this are included with the on-line help for IIS. Basically, you need to run **regedt32.exe** and then open the **HKEY_LOCAL_MACHINESControlSetregistry** entry. Then, from the edit menu, select **Add Value** of type **REG_SZ**. Enter the filename extension **.cgi**. Then, in the string editor, type the full path to the **perl.exe** interpreter. Finally, close down the registry editor and restart the IIS server.

Finding Perl

On UNIX, all the CGI scripts written in Perl have a line in them that expects Perl to be located in a particular directory. In addition, some CGI applications may expect external programs such as sendmail to be located in a certain location on the server. For example, the **mail-lib.pl** that is distributed with the UNIX version of the Web store expects Sendmail to be located in the **/usr/lib** directory by default.

The Web store script also has a header line telling the Web server where Perl is located. Most of the time, the references to these locations will be correct since the majority of servers are set up in a standard way. However, you may run across a situation where the programs that the scripts use are not where the script was configured to think they are. Thus, one of the last steps in setting up the Web store to actually run is to figure out where these files are located so that the scripts can be changed to reflect the new file locations on your local server.

The classic example of a reference to an absolute path on a CGI script is the first line of the Perl code:

```
#!/usr/local/bin/perl
```

This line instructs the server to execute the following script through the Perl interpreter and indicates where to find the Perl interpreter. The Perl interpreter is a program that reads your script and translates it into a form that your server can execute. In the example above, the server will know that it can find the Perl interpreter in the directory **/usr/local/bin**.

While many servers may contain Perl in **/usr/local/bin**, there may be others that have installed them in other areas, such as **/usr/bin** or **/opt/bin**. If the location of Perl is not in **/usr/local/bin**, the first bit of customizing you will have to do is to find out where your local Perl interpreter is and change this line to reference the correct location. There are several ways of finding files on your system and not all of them work on every server, so be prepared to experiment with the following techniques.

The first command to try is **which**. At the command prompt of your UNIX server, you would type **which perl** and receive back the following reply:

```
$ which perl
/bin/perl
```

In other words, Perl is located in **/bin** on this system. Thus, you will need to change the first line of your script to

```
#!/bin/perl
```

If that does not work, you might also try the **whereis** command. This command could give you the following output:

```
$ whereis perl
perl: /usr/bin/perl /usr/local/bin/perl /usr/local/bin/perl4.036
/usr/local/bin/perl5.002
```

This gives us a little more information than the **which** command. It gives us information about all the Perl interpreters contained in the system. In other words, there are several versions of Perl installed on this server including 4.036 and 5.002! Since there are several versions, you could choose whichever one you wish to reference in the CGI script.

If those two commands failed, the next step would be to try **whence**. **Whence** is a command which is more specific to the Korn Shell, so you should first change to the Korn Shell if you can. To do this, simply type **ksh** at the command line of your UNIX system. Now, you should be free to use **whence** and get output that looks similar to the following:

```
$ ksh
$ whence perl
/usr/local/bin/perl
```

If all else fails, you might try the **find** command, but that is really pulling out all the guns when a simple email to your systems administrator might suffice. The syntax for find would be

```
find / -name perl
```

Running the Script

This script should be executed by pointing your browser to **web_store.cgi**. For example, you might use a URL such as:

```
http://www.yourdomain.com/cgi-bin/Web_store/web_store.cgi
```

The log analyzer can be accessed with the following URL:

```
http://www.yourdomain.com/cgi-bin/Web_store/web_store_log_analysis.cgi
```

The installation helper script can be executed with the following URL:

```
http://www.yourdomain.com/cgi-bin/Web_store/web_store_check_setup.cgi
```

As a final word of advice, *never* point a customer directly to an HTML document under the Web store. In order for the customer carts to be created and remembered by the application, **web_store.cgi** must filter *all* HTML pages before they are sent to the customer. Thus, you will never point to anything but **web_store.cgi** for every link having anything to do with the store. The moment users link to anything but **web_store.cgi**, they will lose their carts.

NOTE Some companies that have customized earlier versions of this script created a buffer page between the store and any outside site. This buffer page would contain a warning that explained to the client that if they followed this link they would be losing their cart and that if they wished to return to shopping, they should copy down their cart_id number in the form of a URL back to the script. Thus, anytime a link appeared within the store to an outside location, the actual URL would point to the buffer page, which would contain a second level link plus the warning.

If you are experiencing a situation in which customers are either losing their cart contents or having their cart contents merged with the cart contents of other customers, it means that you are probably providing a link to something other than **web_store.cgi**, or you have added a link without the proper state variables contained in the URL string. If you must add links within product pages to other locations within your store, always follow the format exemplified below. This hyperlink reference is taken from the list of product page **Letters.html**:

```
<A HREF = "web_store.cgi?page=Vowels.html&&cart_id=">
Vowels</A>
```

Notice that the **page** and **cart_id** state variables must be added to the call to the Web store script so that filtering can occur. This concept is discussed in greater depth in Chapter 2 and Chapter 3.

Using the Web Store

Once you have begun running the Web store script, a discussion of how to navigate through the Web store is in order. Basically, there are three main areas of the store to be concerned about: browsing the catalog of items and purchasing the ones you want, viewing and managing your cart contents, and finally, actually sending in the order.

Browsing the Online Catalog

When you first start viewing the Web Store, a frontpage is presented. This front page typically has a menu of general categories of items to view plus a minimum of a keyword search engine to allow you to find the specific items you want more quickly. Figure 1.6 contains a sample front page from the HTML Web store.

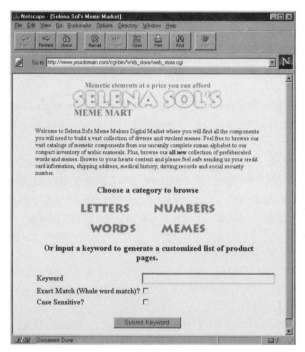

Figure 1.6   Frontpage from the HTML Web store.

The menu of general categories is typically called a list of products page because there is a list of product categories to choose from. If you click on a particular product hyperlink, then the Web Store will take you to an actual product page that contains the products related to the selected category. Alternatively, you can do a keyword search and pull up a list of pages of products that correspond to your keyword search. Figure 1.7 shows a sample product page. Notice that there are text input fields next to each product. You can enter the quantity of the item that you want to purchase in these text boxes. Then, all you have to do is click on the **Add Items To My Cart** button to actually place them in your cart. The **View/Modify Cart** button lets you manage your cart contents, while the **Checkout Stand** button will bring you to the ordering form.

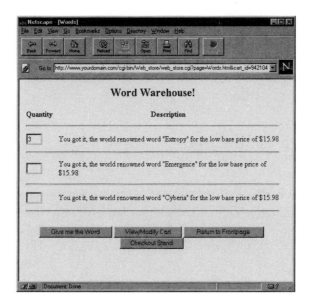

Figure 1.7   Sample product page.

Managing Your Cart Contents

If you click on the **View/Modify Cart** button, you will be brought to a screen that displays your cart contents and gives you options for changing quantities of items you have placed in the cart or removing them entirely. In addition, there are buttons that allow you to continue shopping and take you back where you were, or go to the checkout stand to order the items that you placed in the cart. Figure 1.8 shows an example of the cart page.

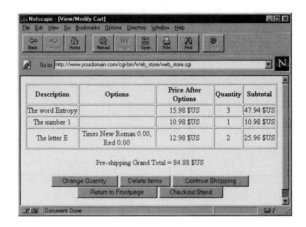

Figure 1.8   The View/Modify Cart page.

Sending in the Order

If you click on the **Checkout Stand** button, you will be brought to the order form. The order form displays your cart again, along with subtotals and any calculations that can be performed without such information about you as discounts based on high-volume purchasing. The order form has standard fields on it which ask for your name, mailing address, phone number, method of payment, and more. A sample order form is shown in Figure 1.9.

Once you submit the order form, the cart is again displayed to you along with any calculations that need to be performed. If have entered your state and shipping type (for example, UPS or FedEx), your sales tax and shipping costs can be calculated. The order is sent transparently to the store owner for processing and your trip through the store is finished. A sample Order Processed screen appears in Figure 1.10.

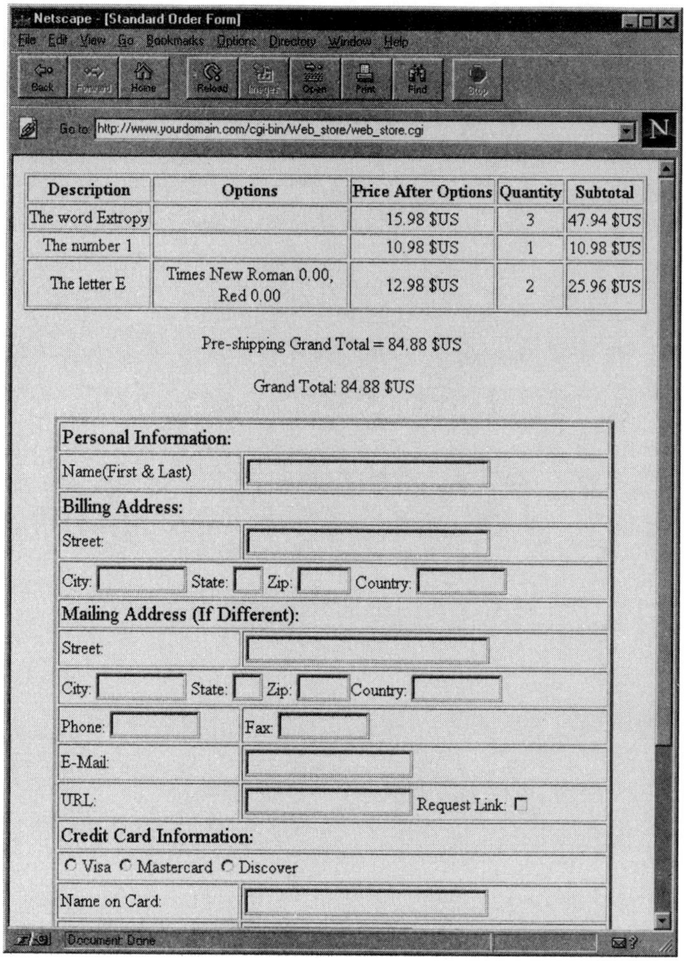

Description	Options	Price After Options	Quantity	Subtotal
The word Extropy		15.98 $US	3	47.94 $US
The number 1		10.98 $US	1	10.98 $US
The letter E	Times New Roman 0.00, Red 0.00	12.98 $US	2	25.96 $US

Pre-shipping Grand Total = 84.88 $US

Grand Total: 84.88 $US

Personal Information:

Name(First & Last)

Billing Address:

Street:

City: State: Zip: Country:

Mailing Address (If Different):

Street:

City: State: Zip: Country:

Phone: Fax:

E-Mail:

URL: Request Link:

Credit Card Information:

Visa Mastercard Discover

Name on Card:

Figure 1.9 Standard order form.

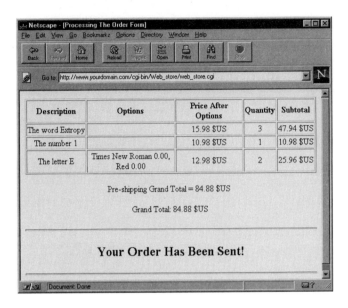

Figure 1.10   Standard order processed page.

Summary

Now that you have been able to successfully run and navigate through the Web Store, you are ready to start setting it up to cover your needs. Chapter 2 will cover the general Setup options. Subsequently, the remaining chapters in Part I will cover the specifics behind setting up different types of Web stores and configuring specific areas such as security and order processing.

CHAPTER TWO

WEB STORE SETUP

Understanding the Setup File

In the Library directory, there are six sample setup files, which you can use to explore the possible store interfaces which may be defined. The six sample setup files are named:

1. web_store.setup.html
2. web_store.setup.db
3. web_store.setup.db.table
4. web_store.setup.frames
5. web_store.setup.frames.javascript
6. web_store.setup.frames.vbscript

These files go over the six most common paradigms used for stores that we have seen in the past, but you can certainly be a lot more creative than we have been. We offer these merely as demonstrations of the flexibility of this script.

1. The HTML store uses predefined HTML product pages to create the interface for the client. The administrator of this type of store has quite a bit of artistic leeway in how product pages are created but must follow a basic format in assigning values to the <INPUT> tag Name arguments. These arguments are discussed in Chapter 3.

2. The Database version of the store grabs the data to be displayed from a pipe-delimited flatfile ASCII text database. It then uses a format string to format the data for display in the browser window. You still have a great deal of artistic leeway in how data is presented but every product must be displayed in the format defined by the format variable. This is unlike the HTML store, which may have separate formats for each product on a page or between separate products pages. In the default setup file for the database store, we defined the format variable so that it will display products in the same way that the HTML store does. However, unlike the HTML store, product pages need not be created in advance because they will be generated on the fly by the script when the database file is queried for the product information.

3. The Query-based table display store is a secondary setup of the Database-based store. In this store, products are simply displayed with a table of database rows accessed by keyword search routines. The look is very generic, but this format may save space and time for customers merely interested in getting a quick list of items in a large store. More interestingly, we use this example to demonstrate the powerful searching tools available when using a database back end. The default front page of this store offers keyword as well as high and low price-range searching.

4. The Frames store is another template that we have provided as a sample. The frames version in the example uses a database method of creating the product pages. However, we could have also used the HTML store method of displaying pages inside the frames. The script presents the store as a frames-based site, including a main display frame, a table of contents frame, and a return to frontpage frame.

5. The JavaScript store is really an extension of option 4, but it allows the customer to do calculations on the product display screen using Netscape's JavaScript language inside the Netscape Web browser. This is the setup file hardcoded into **web_store.cgi** by default.

6. The VBScript store is also an extension of option 4, but allows the user to do calculations on the product display screen using Microsoft's VBScript language in Internet Explorer.

Which of the six setup files are actually used depends on what value you set for the setup file in **web_store.cgi**. At line 86 of **web_store.cgi**, you will see the following line:

```
&require_supporting_libraries (__FILE__, __LINE__,
    "./Library/web_store.setup.frames.javascript");
```

This line tells the script to load up **web_store.setup.frames.javascript**. If you change this to **web_store.setup.html** or **web_store.setup.db,** you will use the alternative setups instead. Eventually, you can settle on just one setup file and delete the others. They are not necessary, but are included as examples.

If you are using a Windows NT or Windows 95 server, you may need to do additional modifications to the Web store to make it run. These changes are discussed in Chapter 1.

NOTE

For the most part, these six setup files are the same. Most of the variables defined in them will be consistent for all the interfaces. Thus, in this chapter we will go over all the variables at one time, pointing out differences when they occur. The specific ways the store can be configured will be covered in more detail in the chapters that follow this one.

All variables defined in the setup file are prefixed with **sc_** to denote that they are global shopping cart variables.

NOTE

Global File Location Variables

Every setup file begins by defining the locations of supporting files that are needed throughout the life of the application. These paths can either be relative to the present working directory of **web_store.cgi** or can be hard-coded as absolute paths. In our default setup, we set paths relative to **web_store.cgi** so that when we define a path as **./Library/file.name** we are referring to a file called **file.name** in a directory called **Library**, which is a subdirectory of the directory containing **web_store.cgi**.

NOTE

If you are using a virtual server, be very careful with paths. What "you" see as your path when you log into your account may not be what the "Web server" sees when it executes **web_store.cgi**. The best thing to do is contact your Internet Service Provider (ISP) and ask them for a detailed explanation of how directories are mapped relative to your account and the Web server's account. In addition, many Windows NT servers do not run the script with the current working directory where the script resides. Possible solutions to these problems are discussed in Chapter 1 regarding the configuration of Windows NT/Windows 95–based Web servers.

In actual use, there is rarely any reason to change these variables from the values that are given in the default distribution. For most servers, the values should work just fine if you keep filenames and relative locations the same as in the distribution.

The only reasons you may want to change them is if you want to rename the files in question to be consistent with local filename standards, you are not allowed to use sub-directories in your ISP's **cgi-bin** directory, or you are on a virtual server with path mapping and the relative paths actually map the wrong locations. For example, your documents may be located in **/home/smithj/www/cgi-bin**. But a "virtual" Web server may see documents located in **/www/cgi-bin** since the server has been configured in such a way as to encapsulate what it sees so that the Web server sees only directories contained in your home directory. References like **./Library** will seem right to you, and will work if you run the scripts from the command line with your own user account, but they will be meaningless to the Web server, which may see a different relative path.

ISPs often do this because it enhances security to make sure that the Web server you are using cannot touch the files created by any other Web server instance on a shared machine.

If you are using a virtual Web server, you will want to get instructions from your ISP on how to use it for running CGI scripts. Remember, there are many different ways that a Web server can be set up. At some point it makes the most sense simply to ask your service provider how scripts should be configured at your site instead of experimenting with all the options and hoping something will work. The moral of this story is that if you want to change these path and filename location variables, feel free—but be careful.

- **$sc_cgi_lib_path** is the location of **cgi-lib.pl,** which is used to read and parse incoming form data.

- **$sc_mail_lib_path** is the location of **mail-lib.pl,** which is used to mail nonencrypted email.

- **$sc_html_search_routines_library_path** is the location of **web_store_html_search.pl**, which is used in case of a keyword search request by the customer using an HTML-based Web store.

- **$sc_html_setup_file_path** is the location of **web_store_html_lib.pl** in which subroutines for printing out much of the Web stores HTML are defined.

- **$sc_db_lib_path** is the location of **web_store_db_lib.pl**, which contains the database search routines

- **$sc_order_lib_path** is the location of **web_store_order_lib.pl**, which contains the routines that are used to process orders.

- **$sc_pgp_lib_path** is the location of **pgp-lib.pl**, which has a routine to automatically encrypt final cart orders for sending in email or logging to a file. You must have previously installed PGP on your Web server and configured it for use. Setting up and using PGP with the Web store will be discussed further in Chapter 9.

- **$sc_user_carts_directory_path** is the location of the subdirectory used to store the customers' shopping carts.

- **$sc_data_file_path** is the location of the ASCII text file database of items. This variable is necessary only if the store uses a database to generate product pages or if the store administrator wishes to check all orders derived from HTML-based product pages against a back-end database file. The reason you might want to do this is because, in theory, someone could hack the data between the product page and the order form and thus manipulate such fields as price. If you did not have a watchful eye over each order filled, someone might be able to sneak some hefty discounts right under your nose. This is discussed in more detail in Chapter 8, regarding order processing.

- **$sc_options_directory_path** is the location of the subdirectory that contains options files. These files are used to store the HTML code for options that may accompany items in a store. This variable is needed only if you are using a database-based store. If you are using an HTML-based interface, you will hard code the options HTML directly into the product pages themselves.

- **$sc_html_product_directory_path** is the location of the subdirectory containing the HTML product pages and/or other HTML pages that aid in store navigation. Such aid is needed for both the HTML and database-based stores because list of product pages (without products but with lists of links that point to products) are used by both the HTML stores and the Database stores.

- **$sc_html_order_form_path** is the location of the HTML order form, which the customer will use to enter their shipping information.

- **$sc_store_front_path** is the location of the HTML front page for your store.

- **$sc_counter_file_path** is the location of the counter file that you will use to keep track of unique database row numbers for every item in the customers cart.

- **$sc_error_log_path** is the location of the flat-file error-log data file.

- **$sc_access_log_path** is the location of the flat-file access-log data file.

- **$sc_main_script_url** is the URL of **web_store.cgi**. This can either be relative or absolute. Remember, this is a URL used by the Web browser. It is not a real directory path on your server.

- **$sc_order_script_url** is the URL of the script that processes orders. If you are using a secure server setup, you may need to store this in a secure directory other than the one the rest of the script is contained in. This can also be either relative or absolute.

Database Definition Variables

These fields are used for the routines using the database-based version of the cart. They are also used for the HTML store if database verification of the products being ordered is turned on. Primarily, they define the format of your database so that the Web store script knows the location of each field of data. The most obvious need is for the script to know the field corresponding to an

in order to make price calculations on items that have been added to customers' carts. The variables are:

- **%db** is an associative array that contains a mapping of your own customer-defined fields to the index number of the fields as they appear in the flat-file database. For example:

```
$db{"product_id"}  = 0;
$db{"product"}     = 1;
$db{"price"}       = 2;
$db{"name"}        = 3;
$db{"image_url"}   = 4;
$db{"description"} = 5;
$db{"options"}     = 6;
```

The code given above shows that **product_id** is the first field in the database. Remember, fields start counting at *zero!* An example of the database row corresponding to the above setup might be as follows:

```
001|Product 1|1.00|1|<IMG SRC = "1.gif">|Number
1|%%OPTION%%opt.html
```

- **@sc_db_display_fields** is an array containing descriptive headers for fields in the database we wish to display to users when they do a query search. Notice that these headers need not include every field defined in **%db**. You may display only some of the information contained in the database row if you so desire. The array takes advantage of the indexes defined in **%db** and, in addition, each descriptive element in this array corresponds to the index numbers in **@sc_db_index_for_display**.

- **@sc_db_index_for_display** is an array containing the index numbers of the database fields that correspond to the **display_fields** array. To access those index numbers, we just utilize the **%db** associative array. There must be one index number in this array for every descriptive element in **@sc_db_display_fields**.

- **@sc_db_index_for_defining_item_id** is an array containing the database fields that correspond to the fields from the database that you wish to associate with a customers cart when they select that item for purchase.

These will be used to determine which fields will make up each item row in the customers cart. If you do not put a database field in this array, it won't be put in the cart nor will be available for display when customers view their cart contents. However, it is essential that the price and options database fields become incorporated into the cart because these are used for cart subtotal calculations.

- **$sc_db_index_of_price** is an index to the field in the database that contains the price. This is used by the Web store to decide how to calculate and display money. In the example above, this value would be 2. Remember that even if you do not display price, its location must still be defined here.

- **@sc_db_query_criteria** is an array containing the criteria that can be used to search on the database with. This is a powerful search mechanism. The array contains pipe-delimited fields inside each list item. These fields are discussed in detail in Chapter 5. The fields are the following:

1. *Form variable name* This is the variable name which you want to associate with the Name parameter of any form field you use to gather customer data. For example, if you have the following text box for getting a keyword:

```
<INPUT TYPE = text NAME = keywords>
```

then the form variable **Name** would be **keywords**.

2. *Index into the database that this criteria applies to* This list corresponds to the **%db** associative array in the same way that **@db_index_for_display** does. Thus, if you want the Description and Name fields to be searched by keyword, the form_data Name would be **keywords** as above and the index into the database would be "3,5".

3. *Operator for comparison* This field is used by the script to determine what logical criteria to apply when searching the database. Possible values include: >, <, >= ,<= ,=, and != (not equal). The operators are compared the following way:

```
form_variable OPERATOR database_field_value
```

That is, field 1 described above is the left side of the operator and field 2 is the right side of the operator.

4. *Data type of the field* This field determines how the operator in field 3 gets applied to the data. The data type can be: date, number, or string If the data type is a date, then the operator for comparison is done after the form value and the fields being compared in the database are converted to dates. If the data type is a number, then the operator for comparison is based on numerical Perl if operators (>, <, ==, etc.). If the data type is a string, then the operator for comparison is done based on string Perl if operators (gt, lt, eq, ne, etc.) with one exception. If the datatype is a string and the operator is =, then the search that is performed becomes a more flexible search using the following logic.

First, all the words in the customer-supplied search string are split apart and searched as separate keywords in the text of the fields. By default, the search on "string = string" is a pattern-match search and is not case-sensitive. If you want this special string, "=" combination searching to be case-sensitive and to match on whole words only, you must set up two new form variables: "case_sensitive" and "exact_match."

If "exact_match" is "on" (the value of a checked checkbox) then the combination of string,"=" in the query criteria array will match on whole words only. If "case_sensitive" is "on" then the combination of string,"="in the query criteria array must have matching case values (upper/lower).

This has been a lot of logic all at once. Perhaps a few examples are in order. They will demonstrate the three main cases that you generally want to set up a **query_criteria** array for:.

Case 1
General keyword search through the database.

Set the first field equal to your keywords form variable (keywords). You will need something like the following in your HTML page:

```
<INPUT TYPE = "text" NAME = "keywords"
       SIZE = "40"  MAXLENGTH = "40">
```

Next, set the second field equal to the field numbers of the database file you want to search. Since you are going to do a keyword search through multiple fields in the database, you want to comma-delimit these For example, assume that we use the sample **%db** defined a few pages back. We might use 1,3,5,6 where database fields 4 and 2 are not searched by keyword. After all, why would we want to keyword search on price and image URL?

Finally, set the operator to = and the data type to **string** so that the keyword search is done using pattern matching and is case insensitive. Then **@sc_db_query_criteria** would be equal to:

```
("keywords|1,2,3,4,6|=|string)
```

With this setup, when a customer submitted a keyword like **letter a**, the script would search fields 1, 3, 5, and 6 in that database.

Case 2

Suppose you just want to do a search on a product category and include that search term within URLs in a front page such as the following:

```
web_store.cgi?product=Vowels
```

In Chapter 4 you will see that this is in fact how we develop product pages on the fly for the Database store.

First, set the form variable equal to the above product. Second, set the second field equal to the field in the database corresponding to a product name (eg 1). Then, set the operator to =, and the data type to **string** to do a keyword search that is case insensitive. After these changes, **@sc_db_query_criteria** would be equal to:

```
("product|1|=|string")
```

Case 3

Finally, suppose you want to make a frontpage form in which several fields in the database are being searched for different types of keywords (or key numbers). That is, suppose you want to allow the user to search on a price range, plus do a keyword search on the description field. To solve this problem, **@sc_db_query_criteria** would be set equal to

```
("price_low_range|2|<=|number",
"price_high_range|2|>=|number",
"description|5|=|string");
```

Notice that we set up two form variables for allowing the price range searching. This is because we need to allow the customer to enter both the low range and the high range of the price they want to search for (assuming that price is database field number 2). Note, also, that the **price_low_range|2|<=** means that the database row returns a match if and only if the value of the **price_low_range** form field is less than or equal to the value of field 2 in the database row.

Thus if you have a database row with a price of $15.00, then entering the low range as **10.00** in the form field will return a match because 10.00 is less than 15.00, but if you enter a low range of **16.00**, a match would not be returned because 16.00 is not less than or equal to 15.00.

Finally, we set the description form variable to be a keyword (=,string) search on database field 5. The form itself would have these fields as HTML:

```
Lowest Price To Search For:
<INPUT TYPE = "text" NAME=price_low_range VALUE = "">
Highest Price To Search For:
<INPUT TYPE = "text" NAME=price_high_range VALUE = "">
Enter Keywords To Search For In Description:
<INPUT TYPE = "text" NAME=description VALUE = "">
```

NOTE Only criteria that is entered on the form is queried against. If the customer leaves one or more fields blank (or you neglect to place them on the form), then those fields never get queried.

Of the criteria entered on the form, all the criteria must be satisfied for that row before the row will be considered safe to display to the customer.

The same goes for the **string,=** data type, operator combination (special case for keywords). When the string is split into keywords separated by white space, all the keywords must be found in the database field before the program will consider it a valid match.

This logic is there because we want to provide the capability of letting users narrow down the query as they enter more data into the form. This query logic is covered in more detail in Chapter 5.

$sc_db_max_rows_returned is the maximum number of rows you will allow to be displayed to the user as the result of a query. If the query gets above this number, the customer is presented with a message letting them know that they need to narrow their query down.

Cart Definition Variables

These variables define the structure of the customer carts.

The **%cart** associative array is similar to the **%db** associative array except that it is specific to the structure of the customers cart. It is defined via the following steps.

First, the first field is always the quantity of the purchased item. Subsequent fields are the same fields defined in the **@sc_db_index_for_defining_item_id** variable. This is done because whatever is defined in this array, becomes the part of the product defined in the customers cart. The field before the next to last always contains the options that the customer has chosen. The next to last field is always the price after options have been calculated in with the normal price. Finally, the last field is always a computer-generated, unique identifier to distinguish cart line items from each other.

If we use the same **%db** definition from the last section, and define **@sc_db_index_for_defining_item_id** as follows:

```
@sc_db_index_for_defining_item_id =
  ($db{"product_id"} ,
  $db{"product"} ,
  $db{"price"} ,
  $db{"name"} ,
  $db{"image_url"} ,
  $db{options} );Scc 3 bot
```

Then we would set the **%cart** associative array as follows:

```
$cart{"quantity"}          = 0;
$cart{"product_id"}        = 1;
$cart{"product"}           = 2;
$cart{"price"}             = 3;
```

```
$cart{"name"}                = 4;
$cart{"image_url"}           = 5;
$cart{"options"}             = 6;
$cart{"price_after_options"} = 7;
$cart{"unique_cart_line_id"} = 8;
```

- **$sc_cart_index_of_price** is the original database price of the item, which in this example is 3.

- **$sc_cart_index_of_price_after_options** is the price after the customer-selected options have been chosen—which, in the above example, equals 7.

- **$sc_cart_index_of_measured_value** is the index value of whatever field you want to use as a measured value in other calculations (specifically for calculating such things as shipping). For example, you may have a weight field that you wish to total in the cart so that the shipping cost changes with weight. Complex shipping logic is covered in Chapter 8.

- **@sc_cart_display_fields** is an array containing the descriptive names of the headers for displaying the cart fields. This follows the same logic as **@sc_db_display_fields** but is specific to **%cart** instead of **%db**.

- **@sc_cart_index_for_display** is an array containing an index into the cart for every field to be displayed to customers when they are viewing their own carts. These numbers must correspond to the descriptive names in **@sc_cart_display_fields**.

- **$sc_cart_index_of_item_id** is the index to the unique product i.d., which in the example above is equal to 1.

- **$sc_cart_index_of_quantity** is the index to the field of the the customer-submitted quantity for the item they are currently purchasing, which in the example above is 0. Remember, fields start counting at zero in Perl.

Order Form Definition Variables

The nuts and bolts of custom designed order form logic is covered in depth in Chapter 8. However, a brief overview appears here:

- **%sc_order_form_array** is the associative array of form variables, used on the order form to send in an order, such as asking for the user's name, address, and more. It maps a form field name with a descriptive name so that a legible email will be produced later.

- **@sc_order_form_required_fields** is an array containing the form field names (as defined in **%sc_order_form_array**) that are required fields. The order will not be processed without these field names being entered on the form.

- **$sc_order_with_hidden_fields** is "yes" or "no." If you want to submit orders to another server or to a MAILTO: url, then you can use this option to make sure that hidden fields are actually generated with the contents of the cart in them.

The following variables tell the ordering part of the script how to calculate shipping, discount, and sales tax and in what order.

The values are numerical (1, 2, 3, or 0 if we do not want to process anything). First, we determine whether these item (sales tax, shipping, and discount) are even calculated at all at either the display order form or at the point where the order form has been submitted for processing (**process_form**).

Variables that we do not calculate at a given time are given a value of 0 to show that they never enter into the calculation. Otherwise, they are given an order number of 1, 2, or 3 to show in what order they are calculated.

Here are the variables:

```
$sc_calculate_discount_at_display_form
$sc_calculate_discount_at_process_form
$sc_calculate_shipping_at_display_form
$sc_calculate_shipping_at_process_form
$sc_calculate_sales_tax_at_display_form
$sc_calculate_sales_tax_at_process_form
```

And below are a few examples of usage.

Example 1

We want shipping, discount, and sales tax to be calculated off of the original subtotal and then added to the subtotal all at once on the order form:

```
$sc_calculate_discount_at_display_form = 1;
$sc_calculate_shipping_at_display_form = 1;
$sc_calculate_sales_tax_at_display_form = 1;
```

Because they are all set to 1, they are all calculated at the same time and then added to the subtotal.

Example 2

We want the sales tax to get calculated first, added to the subtotal and then the discount and shipping gets calculated on the order form:

```
$sc_calculate_discount_at_display_form = 2;
$sc_calculate_shipping_at_display_form = 2;
$sc_calculate_sales_tax_at_display_form = 1;
```

Because **sales_tax** is 1, it gets calculated before the other values and then added to the subtotal. Then, the discount and shipping (value = 2) are calculated together and added to the subtotal based on the subtotal from above.

If you are calculating something on the order form level, you need to calculate it on the **process_form** level as well; otherwise, the information will not be sent with the order in email.

If a particular field such as shipping is dependent on the user entering a value into the order form, it cannot be calculated on the order form level. This is because the customer has not entered the form field value yet! Thus, you will need to set shipping to 0 at the **display_form** stage but set it to the appropriate value at the **process_form** stage since the customer will have, by then, entered the form value on the order form display.

- **@sc_order_form_shipping_related_fields** is an array containing the names of those form variables on the order form that will be used in calculating shipping. If you are calculating shipping without regard to form values, leave this array empty.

- **@sc_order_form_discount_related_fields** is an array containing the names of those form variables on the order form that will be used in calculating a discount for the customer. If you are calculating a discount without regard to form values, leave this array empty.

- **@sc_shipping_logic** is an array containing the logic for applying the shipping cost to the order. Each criteria is a separate list element. The fields within the criteria are pipe-delimited (|).

The values of the criteria are equal whole values (such as UPS or 5 or 11) or they can be ranges separated by hyphens (1-5, 1-, -5). If a number is left off one end of the hyphen, then the range is open-ended up to the value defined by the hyphen. For example, 5- signifies anything greater than or equal to 5.

The first fields correspond to the fields in the **@sc_order_form_shipping_related_fields** array. If this array is empty, then no fields in **@sc_shipping_logic** will correspond to the shipping.

The next field is the subtotal amount to compare against if you are determining shipping cost based on the total sum of money needed to purchase what is in the cart.

The next field after that is the quantity of items to compare against for determining shipping based on quantity.

The next field after quantity is the measured total of items based on the measured field index determined in the cart setup above.

The final field is the cost of the shipping if the criteria is matched in the above fields. If the value is followed by a % symbol, then the value of the shipping will be a percent of the current subtotal instead of a whole dollar amount.

Lets summarize this logic with a couple of examples. The first example will demonstrate a simple shipping based on quantity. The customer will simply choose items and the quantity of those items will determine the shipping price. Thus, **@sc_order_form_shipping_fields** will be empty because customers will not be able to change the shipping logic based on anything they fill out on the order form:

```
@sc_order_form_shipping_related_fields = ();
```

Next, we define the shipping logic:

```
@sc_shipping_logic = ("|11-||5",
  "|1-10||10");
```

In this example, the related fields are empty, so the logic fields start with the comparison of the subtotal. There is nothing in the logic field for subtotal, so it is not compared in determining shipping.

The next field has **11-**, and this is the quantity comparison field, so the quantity must be eleven or greater. For the second row (**1-10**), the quantity is compared to see if it falls within the range of 1 through 10.

The next field is blank (measured value) and because it is blank, it never enters into the matching check.

The final values (5 and 10) for the elements of the array are the dollar amounts that the shipping would be if the criteria was satisfied on the row. Thus, if the quantity is **1-10**, the shipping is $10.00. If the quantity is greater than or equal to 11, the shipping is $5.00.

In the second example, shipping is dependent upon form variables. The client is able to choose between either UPS or FedEx. The shipping logic depends on which company the client chooses. Since the variable is customer-defined, we need the following form tag in the order form:

```
<SELECT NAME = "22-shipping">
<OPTION>UPS
<OPTION>FEDEX
</SELECT>
```

We will also need to define our setup variables as follows:

```
@sc_order_form_shipping_related_fields =  ("22-shipping");
@sc_shipping_logic =  ("ups|1-10||5",
                       "ups|11-||10%",
                       "fedex|1-10||20",
                       "fedex|11-||30%");
```

Since there is one related form variable (**22-shipping**), the first field of the shipping logic is corresponds to the value of the **22-shipping** form variable. The rest of the fields are assigned in a manner similar to our first example..

If the form value of **22-shipping** is **UPS** and the quantity is greater than or equal to **1** and less than or equal to **10**, then shipping is $5. If the form value of **22-shipping** is **UPS** and the quantity is greater than **11**, then shipping is 10% of the current subtotal for the cart. If the form value of **22-shipping** is **FEDEX** and the quantity is greater than or equal to **1** and less than or equal to **10**, then shipping is $20. If the form value of **22-shipping** is **FEDEX** and the quantity is greater than **11**, then shipping is 30% of the current subtotal for the cart.

- **@sc_discount_logic** is an array containing the logic for applying a discount to the order. The discount is calculated as a dollar amount. Do not make the amounts negative. The Web store subtracts the values in this array from the subtotal when the discount is calculated.
- **$sc_sales_tax** is the value of sales tax. For example, Maryland has 5% sales tax, so this would be **.05** for Maryland residents.

- **$sc_sales_tax_form_variable** is the name of a form variable that will be used on the order form to determine if the sales tax is applicable.

- **@sc_sales_tax_form_value** are the possible (case-insensitive) values that the form variable above should be equal to in order to apply sales tax (such as **md** or **maryland**) .

- **$sc_order_email** is the email address to send orders to. Don't forget to escape any @ signs. Thus:

  you@yourdomain.com

  must be written as:

  you\@yourdomain.com

- **$sc_send_order_to_email** should be set equal to **yes** if you want orders sent to the above email address.

- **$sc_send_order_to_log** should be set equal to **yes** if you want the orders to be recorded in a local log file.

- **$sc_order_log_file** is the path and filename of the logfile where you want orders recorded if the above variable is **yes**.

- **$sc_order_check_db** should be set equal to **yes** if you want to use the database routines to double-check that the customer has not attempted to fool around with the database by entering in values for items based on form manipulation. If this variable is yes, the script double checks to see if the price in the cart is the same as the recorded price in the current database file.

- **$sc_use_pgp** should be set equal to **yes** if you want to use the PGP library to communicate with PGP for encrypting orders. You must have previously installed PGP on your system and set up your public/private key pairs. This is discussed in Chapter 9.

- **$sc_pgp_temp_file_path** is the path where you want the PGP program to generate temporary files. This should be a directory that is writable to the Web server.

Store Option Variables

- **$sc_use_html_product_pages** defines whether or not you want the script to be an HTML or Database store. If you set this to **yes**, the script will generate navigation using predesigned HTML pages in the

Html/Products subdirectory. If you set it to **no**, it will generate product pages dynamically from the d**ata.file** in the **Data_files** subdirectory.

- **$sc_should_i_display_cart_after_purchase** determines where the customer will go when they hit the **add this item to my cart** submit button. If this variable is set to **yes**, the customer will be sent to the cart display page where they can see the current contents of their cart (including the new item). If you set this equal to **no**, the customer will be sent back to whatever product page display they were just at with a note at the top of the page reminding the customer that the item had been added to the cart.

- **$sc_shall_i_let_client_know_item_added** defines whether or not the customer should be specifically told that the items they just ordered were added to the cart. If it is set to **yes** they will be told that items have been purchased. This is useful in the case that **$sc_should_i_display_cart_after_purchase** has been set to **no** because then customers have some feedback after being transported back to the page from which they just ordered (Figure 2.1).

Figure 2.1 Customer feedback after order placement.

- **$sc_item_ordered_message** is the message that the customer receives if you have set **$sc_shall_i_let_client_know_item_added** equal to **yes**.

- **$sc_shall_i_email_if_error** defines whether or not the administrator receives an email whenever an error occurs. If this is set to **yes** the administrator will receive email whenever an error occurs during the processing of the script. If it is set to **no**, the administrator will receive nothing in email but is still free to review the error logs if the variable below is set to **yes**.

- **$sc_shall_i_log_errors** defines whether or not the script should log errors when they occur. If it is set to **yes**, all errors will be logged in the **error.log** file. If it is set to **no**, no logging will occur.

- **$shall_i_log_accesses** defines whether or not the script will log new access to **access.log.** If the variable is set to **yes**, all new accesses will be logged. If it is set to **no**, no accesses will be logged. Be careful with your log files. They may grow quickly so you may want to review them often and, if necessary, rotate them at some regular interval.

HTML Search Variables

These variables are used by HTML-based Web stores for document search requests:

- **$sc_root_web_path** defines the actual location of the HTML product pages that are being searched for keywords. This is not a URL, it is the actual path of the root HTML directory as the server would see it.

- **$sc_server_url** is the URL to the root HTML directory of product pages.

- **@sc_unwanted_files** is the list of all file extensions which should not be searched by the HTML search routines. Thus, if **.cgi** is in the list, the keyword search routine will not search any file with the file extension **.cgi**. Of course, you really should not store anything but HTML product pages under your HTML root directory.

Error Message Variables

- **$sc_page_load_security_warning** is the content of the error message sent to the browser window if someone attempts to view files that do not satisfy the **@acceptable_file_extensions_to_display** test.

- **$sc_randomizer_error_message** is the error message displayed to the browser if the application is not able to find a unique cart i.d. number.

Miscellaneous Variables

- **$sc_admin_email** is the email address to which error notifications are sent.

- **$sc_shall_i_email_if_error** is **yes** if you want to email to **$sc_admin_email** if an error occurred. Do not forget to escape any **@** signs in the **$sc_admin_email** variable. Thus:

  you@yourdomain.com

  must be written as:

  you\yourdomain.com

- **@acceptable_file_extensions_to_display** lists the extensions that you will allow this application to display to the browser window. The goal is to restrict browsers to the absolute minimum files possible so that their ability to hack is limited to files that are publicly available anyway.

- **$sc_money_symbol** is the monetary symbol that you would like to display with prices. Make sure to escape the dollar sign ($) if you wish to use that symbol. Thus:

  ```
  $sc_money_symbol = "";
  ```

  is the correct syntax, *not:*

  ```
  $sc_money_symbol = "$";
  ```

- **$sc_money_symbol_placement** defines whether or not you want the amount to be placed in front or in back of the money symbol. If you set this variable equal to **back,** the monetary symbol will be placed after the number. If you set it to **front,** it will be placed in front. Thus, you might have $12.56 (front) or 12.56 $US (back).

- **$sc_current_century** is the current century. Note that if the year is 1997, you should set this value to **20**. The script will subtract one from this number when it prints out the current year.

- **$sc_number_days_keep_old_carts** defines how long old carts are kept in the **User_carts** subdirectory. The trick to this is that you want to leave carts in the directory long enough for the clients to finish shopping, but not so long that your hard disk usage gets too large. We recommend the compromise of half a day, which is writen as **.5.**

- **$sc_no_frames_button** defines the contents of any buttons you wish to display in nonframes implementations. This is usually the case with a button like **Return to Frontpage,** which loads the store frontpage again. The problem with the Frames version is that Submit buttons may not take a TARGET, so if the customer is able to hit a Return to frontpage button, they will cause the main window to be divided into a subframe with its own table of contents and main window. Thus, if you are running a Frames implementation, this variable should be empty. Otherwise, you may add the Return to frontpage button, which is shown by default.

- **$sc_product_display_title** is the text that should appear between the **<TITLE>** and **</TITLE>** tags on the dynamically generated databasebased product pages.

- **$sc_product_display_header** is the header HTML used to display products in the database implementations. Notice that we use the **%s** characters to substitute for any given product information. The script will substitute product data for each product in place of **%s** when the variable is actually used.

- **$sc_product_display_footer** is the footer for each product
- **$sc_product_display_row** is the %s embedded product row variable.

Using web_store_check_setup.cgi

Using **Web_store_check_setup.cgi** is relatively easy. All you have to do is configure it to use the correct Setup file and then run it from your Web browser. This CGI script is designed to look into how your Setup file is defined and automatically check to see that all the directories and files have the appropriate permissions set to allow the Web server to run the script properly.

The first step is to change the setup file definition. Recall that in order to use a different Setup file in **web_store.cgi**, we had to edit **web_store.cgi** and change the actual setup file that was being referenced. You have to do the same with **web_store_check_setup.cgi**.

Line 34 of this file says the following:

```
$sc_setup_file = "./Library/web_store.setup.frames";
```

Change this variable to reflect the actual setup file you are using.

Then, all you have to do is run the script through your browser. For example, if your Web server is called **www.yourdomain.com**, and your Web store scripts are located under **cgi-bin/Web_store,** then you would call the check setup script with the following URL:

```
http://www.yourdomain.com/cgi-bin/Web_store/web_store_check_setup.cgi
```

Figure 2.2 shows an example of the output you should expect to see from the Setup checker script. The number-one setup problem usually encountered is that the scripts are not seen by the Web server as relative to the directory where the script is actually located. Thus, the first thing that the Web store Setup checking script does is print out the current working directory. The current working directory should be the same physical directory that the script is located in. If it is not, then you will need to configure the setup variables as absolute paths instead of paths relative to what you thought was the current working directory, or you can add a **chdir** command to the **web_store.cgi** script as we described in Chapter 1 under the possible Windows NT server Setup configurations.

If the current working directory is fine, the setup file will be required and then all the setup path/location related variables will be checked to see if the

Web server has permission to do what it needs to do to those directories. For example, the user carts subdirectory is checked to see if it is readable, executable, and writable by the Web server, but the libraries subdirectory is merely checked to see if it is readable and executable. If any permissions seem incorrect, a message will be printed out to let you know that there is a potential problem with running the script.

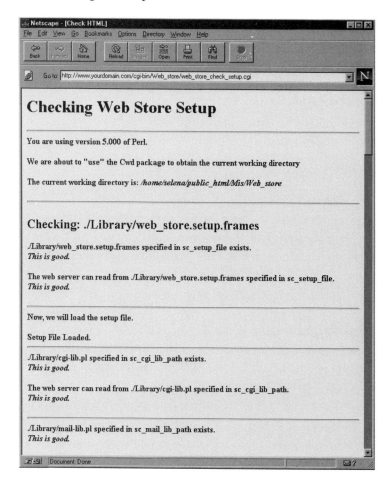

Figure 2.2   Sample output from **web_store_check_setup.cgi**.

Understanding the HTML Library

For the most part, **web_store_html_lib.pl** contains all of the customizable HTML aspects of this application. If you want to change the look and feel of the Web store installation, you will probably have to make changes to this file.

Usually, this is as simple as cutting and pasting some of your template HTML in place of our default code. However, there are a few things that you should know about this file before you start changing it.

Taking Precautionary Measures

First, as always, make a backup of the original file before you start doing anything. Also, when you make changes, do so as a series of small changes. Make many small changes, running the script each time. That way you will not get caught making so many changes that you will not be able to easily recall at which point you made your error.

Using the "qq" Custom Quote Delimiter Feature

This library uses the **qq** Perl feature liberally. That means that you need to be aware of what the delimiter is in every bit of HTML code displayed. For the most part, we use the standard qq! and **qq~** when we are going to display a long bit of HTML code. The qq parameter will change the delimiter of a print string from double quote marks (") to whatever follows the **qq**. This is done to allow double quote marks (which are very common in HTML) to be included in strings without requiring us to escape them everywhere using the backslash (character. Escaping the double-quote characters inside of HTML code makes the HTML look quite messy. Recall that normally we use the double quote marks to delineate the beginning and the ending of a text string to be printed. However, using **qq!** we can replace the double-quotes as delimiters with the ! character.

Thus:

```
print "She said hi";
```

would become

```
print qq!She said "Hi"!;
```

Notice that in the first case, we had to escape the double quote marks in order to use the double quote marks as string delimiters. Since we use a lot of double quote marks in our HTML, it is easier to just change the delimiter to the bang (!) sign or the tilde (~) sign.

However, though the qq method does solve the problem of embedded double quotes, it does not solve the problem of Perl special characters. If you wish to include a dollar sign ($) or an *at* sign (@), for example, you will need to escape them with a backslash (\). Thus, to display:

```
send all $$$ to selena@eff.org
```

you must use backslashes as follows:

```
send all  to selenaeff.org
```

The reason for this is that the dollar and at signs have special meanings to Perl other than to denote price or an email address; specifically, to name scalar variables and list arrays.

If you are getting a **document contains no data** error message, it is a good bet you forgot to escape a Perl special character in this file.

Another thing to keep in mind is that we have included some variables within the default displays. For example, in **product_page_header** discussed later, we use both **$page_title** as well as **$hidden_fields** within the HTML. You probably want to leave these the way they are and write your own template HTML "around" them. If you delete them, make sure to keep a log of the changes you made so that you can retrieve them if you want them later.

Finally, a quick note about library syntax is in order since it will help you understand what is happening.

There are three levels of routines that you will be faced with in the Web store:

```
Individual routines
Application Specific Subroutines
Inter-Application Libraries
```

Individual Routines

Routines are merely pieces of code that perform some sort of action in a specific way. For example, an algorithm that adds two numbers can be expressed as:

```
x + y.
```

However, its use is very specific. To add 31,289 and 23,990, you would use the following Perl code:

```
$sum = 31289 + 23990;
```

This is a pretty simple routine. But it is also pretty specific to just one case. Programs typically consist of many routines like this put together. However, there comes a time when one wants to make the routine generic so that one can call it over and over again in other parts of the program without having to rewrite the routine. This is where application-specific subroutines come in.

Application-specific Subroutines

Routines that are general enough that they are used several times in the same application should usually be placed in a subroutine. A subroutine encapsulates an algorithm so that other parts of the program can refer to it by its subroutine name. Consider the addition routine from above.

What if we needed to add various numbers several times through our program, but did not want to create a separate piece of code for each instance of addition? If the algorithm were four or five lines long, it would be annoying to type the similar lines over and over again. Even worse, if you ended up changing the logic of the algorithm, you would have to hunt down every occurrence of the algorithm and change each one. Maintaining a program like this could become a nightmare, since many errors could arise from forgetting to change one of the lines of code in any of the duplicate routines or from changing one of them incorrectly.

When faced with such a circumstance, a programmer can create a "subroutine" within the application that can be used again and again by other parts of the program. **web_store.cgi** uses subroutines liberally. In fact, 90 percent of the program is actually contained in one subroutine or another.

In order to create and use subroutines in Perl, we need three things: a subroutine reference, a subroutine identifier, and a parameter list of variables to pass to the subroutine.

NOTE Subroutine definitions can be placed anywhere in the script even if the call to that subroutine appears earlier in the program. This is because Perl first goes through the entire script and compiles references to all subroutines before it actually starts running the script. Although the subroutines may be placed anywhere in the program, their definitions are usually placed at the end of the script since it makes the main code easier to find and read.

In order to use a subroutine, the ampersand symbol (&) precedes the name of the routine. This tells Perl to look for the subroutine in the program and call it. For example, **&AddNumbers** would direct Perl to execute the **AddNumbers** subroutine.

However, we will also need to be able to send the subroutine some information. Specifically, we will need to send the subroutine parameters which it will use to customize its output. If we want to get the sum of 2 and 3, for example, we can pass 2 and 3 to the subroutine using the following format:

```
&AddNumbers(2,3);
```

The definition of the subroutine itself is marked off in the program using a **sub** marker and the code belonging to the routine is delimited with curly brackets ({}). The following example shows what the **AddNumbers** subroutine definition might look like:

```
sub AddNumbers
  {
  local($first_number, $second_number) = @_;
  print $first_number + $second_number;
  }
```

Note the third line above. We use the **local** keyword to make sure that the **$first_number** and **$second_number** variables will be considered local to only that subroutine. That is, the subroutine will not affect any other variables that may be called **$first_number** or **$second_number** in other subroutines within the program.

Also, in Perl, **@_** is a special name for the list of parameters that have been passed to the function. **$first_number** is set equal to the first parameter and **$second_number** is set equal to the second parameter in the **@_** list of parameters. If the routine is called by **&AddNumbers(2,3)**, 2 and 3 will be assigned to **$first_number** and **$second_number**, respectively.

NOTE

It is important to use local variables within subroutines so that they do not overwrite variables used by the main script. In complex scripts that use dozens of variables, you may easily forget which variables you are using. Using local variables assures that if you do end up using the same name for a variable, you can keep them separated. Whenever you want to add numbers, you can simply use the subroutine call **&AddNumbers(x,y)** instead of writing out each addition individually. As an added bonus, if you need to change the logic of the addition algorithm, you need only change it in the subroutine.

Finally, a subroutine can return a value to the main script by using the keyword **return** and assigning the value to a variable at the time of the call. Thus, the following code would set **$sum** equal to 5.

```
$sum = &AddNumber(2,3);
sub AddNumber
{
local($left_hand_side, $right_hand_side) = @_;
return ($left_hand_side + $right_hand_side);
}
```

Inter-application Libraries

Good design does not stop with the mere use of subroutines. Often, several different scripts will incorporate the use of similar routines into their design. Or similar or customizable subroutines will be broken out for easy access or modification (as in the case of **web_store_html_lib.pl** which brings all the customizable HTML into one place). In this case, it makes sense to remove the common routines from the programs and place them in a separate file of routines.

This file can then be loaded as a library of subroutines into each program as needed.

For example, most CGI applications will need a form gathering/parsing routine, a template for sending out the HTTP header, and perhaps another subroutine to generate template HTML code such as:

```
<HTML><HEAD><TITLE>My Script Title</TITLE></HEAD>
```

In this case, we use library files and "require" them from the main script. A library file in Perl is simply a text file containing subroutines that are shared in common by several different Perl scripts.

NOTE

In addition to all the normal Perl code for subroutines, a Perl library must end with a **1;** on the last line. This is because the REQUIRE command evaluates the script when it reads in the library routines. The last **1;** makes the script itself evaluate to TRUE. In other words, a return value of 1 in the Perl library means the library was read in successfully by the main Perl script.

In order for these library files to be usable by the script, the permissions must be set on the library file to make it readable, and the script must be in the Perl library path or its location must be explicitly referenced with its directory path location. For example, if we wanted to load Steven Brenner's **cgi-lib.pl** library into our script and **cgi-lib.pl** was located in the same directory as the script calling it or was in a directory included in the **@INC** array, we would use the following:

```
require "cgi-lib.pl";
```

When this is done, every subroutine in **cgi-lib.pl** becomes accessible to the main script as if it were actually written into the script's code. Thus we can simply reference a subroutine contained in **cgi-lib.pl** as we would any other subroutine in the main program.

NOTE

Library files need to be readable by the script that requires them. If your server is running as "Nobody" in reference to Chapter 1 on setting up script permissions, you may need to make the library files readable by the world.

Well, that was a lot of information to swallow at once. But now you are ready to go and play havoc with the HTML in this file that are contained as "subroutines" and are "required" by **web_store.cgi**. Do not forget to make a backup, but feel free to experiment. The store distributed by default is kept bland on purpose. By remaining simple, it makes customizing the interface easier for most people. It is your job to turn the default interface into your own unique store.

If you would like to see how others have customized the interface, check out Selena Sol's Script Archive. There you can explore the section called "Web Store Scripts in Action" located at http://www.edd.org/verict/Scripts/ to look at the dozens of existing real-world implementation of the Web store.

HTML Library Routines

The following is a list of all the subroutines that are defined in the HTML library. Use this as your road map to deciding what routines you need to change in order to alter the cosmetic look-and-feel of your specific Web store:

- **product_page_header** is used to display the shared HTML header used for database-generated product pages. It takes one argument, **$page_title**, which will be used to fill the data between the **<TITLE>** and **</TITLE>**. Typically, this value is determined by **$sc_product_display_title** in **web_store.setup**. The subroutine is called with the following syntax:

  ```
  &product_page_header("Desired Title");
  ```

- **product_page_footer** is used to generate the HTML page footer for database-based product pages. It takes two arguments, **$db_status** and **$total_rows_returned** and is called with the following syntax:

  ```
  &product_page_footer($status,$total_row_count);
  ```

- **html_search_page_footer** is used to generate the HTML footer for HTML-based product pages when the script must perform a keyword search and generate a list of hits. It is called with no arguments with the following syntax:

  ```
  &html_search_page_footer;
  ```

- **standard_page_header** is used to generate a standard HTML header for pages within either the HTML-based or Database-based stores. It takes a single argument and the title of the page to be displayed. Itis called with the following syntax:

```
&standard_page_header("TITLE");
```

- **modify_form_footer** is used to generate the HTML footer code for the "Modify quantity of items in the cart" form page. It takes no arguments and is called with the following syntax:

```
&modify_form_footer;
```

- **delete_form_footer** is used to generate the HTML footer code for the "Delete items from the cart" form page. It takes no arguments and is called with the following syntax:

```
&delete_form_footer;
```

- **cart_footer** is used to generate the HTML footer code for the "View items in the cart" form page. It takes no arguments and is called with the following syntax:

```
&cart_footer;
```

- **bad_order_note** generates an error message for users in case they have not submitted a valid number for a quantity. It takes no arguments and is called with the following syntax:

```
&bad_order_note;
```

- **cart_table_header** is used to generate the header HTML for different views of the cart. It takes one argument, the type of view we are requesting and is called with the following syntax:

```
&cart_table_header(TYPE OF REQUEST);
```

- The job of **display_cart_table** is to display the current contents of the customers cart for several different types of screens that all display the cart in some form or another. The subroutine takes one argument, the reason that the cart is being displayed, and is called with the following syntax:

```
&display_cart_table("reason");
```

There are really only five values that **$reason_to_display_cart** should be equal to:

1. **""** (view/modify cart screen)
2. **"changequantity"** (change quantity form)
3. **"delete"** (delete item form)
4. **"orderform"** (order form)
5. **"process order"** (order form process confirmation)

Notice that this corresponds closely to the list in **cart_table_header** because the goal of this subroutine is to fill in the actual cells of the table created by the **cart_table_header** subroutine.

- **cart_table_footer** is used to display the footer for cart table displays. It takes one argument, the pre shipping grand total and is called with the following syntax:

```
&cart_table_footer(PRICE);
```

- **make_hidden_fields** is used to generate the hidden fields necessary for maintaining state. It takes no arguments and is called with the following syntax:

```
&make_hidden_fields;
```

- **PrintNoHitsBodyHTML** is utilized by the HTML store search routines to produce an error message in case no hits were found based on the customer-defined keywords. It is called with no arguments and the following syntax:

```
&PrintNoHitsBodyHTML;
```

- **PrintBodyHTML** is utilized by the HTML store search routines to produce a list of hits. These hits will be the pages that had the customer-defined keywords within them. The subroutine takes two arguments, the filename as it will appear in the URL link as well as the text that should be visibly hyperlinked. It is called with the following syntax:

```
&PrintBodyHTML("file.name", "Title to be linked");
```

Summary

After finishing this chapter, you should have a general idea of how to set up the Web Store script. The following chapters will cover the specific types of installations that are used on the Internet and how using each of them affects the various configuration options for the Web Store. In addition, other chapters will take certain topics that have been covered lightly here such as ordering logic and explain them with the depth necessary for more advanced Web Store setups.

Chapter Three

Focus on the HTML Store

The HTML Store, which uses pre-designed HTML pages to display products for sale, is one of the most commonly used configurations of the Web store. In fact, over the last year, dozens of companies have chosen to use the HTML interface and have customized a wide array of storefronts. Many of these companies have registered their URL with us and are listed at Selena Sol's Script Archive at the following URL:

```
http://www.eff.org/~erict/Scripts/
```

We recommend that you browse through this list to get ideas as to how you might create your own "storefront" look.

The HTML store is popular because of its versatility and ease of use. The HTML store uses pre-designed HTML pages to create the store environment and as such, makes customizing a wide array of unique pages easy and less intimidating. Figure 3.1 shows a product page: **Vowels.html**.

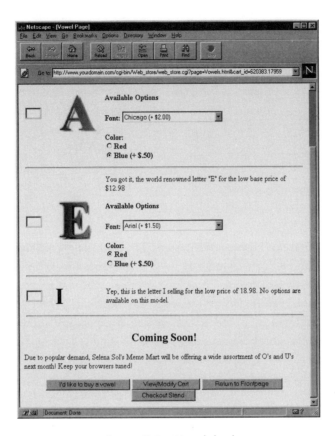

Figure 3.1   Vowels.html.

In fact, its two most cited benefits are the ease with which a CGI novice can customize the store without ever reading the code and the fact that creating the store with HTML pages gives the store designers an infinite amount of flexibility with the presentation of products. After all, the lack of a database back end, and the dependence upon HTML as the medium of programming, make the HTML Store just like doing straight HTML. The little bit of customization that is necessary can be summed up in a few simple tags that, when embedded in your HTML, will create the necessary link between your customers and the application. This chapter will discuss these tags to give you a firm basis for creating your own tagged HTML product pages.

Changes to the Setup File

As with all versions of this script, the first thing you must do is to customize the Setup file. For the most part, the setup file for the HTML store will be like any other implementation. Eighty percent of the setup should remain constant through all versions. However, there will be some differences. In the following section, we will go through **web_store.setup.html** highlighting variables specific to the HTML store and explain their usage. Variables not mentioned should be considered globally important to all versions of the store and will be defined the same way regardless of which implementation you choose. Chapter 2 covers all these general variables.

Global File Location Variables

The first variable of interest in **web_store.setup.html** is **$sc_db_lib_path**. **$sc_db_lib_path** defines the location of **web_store_db_lib.pl** used to perform searches on the data file. Because we will be using HTML product pages, there will be no need to search the data file and no need for that variable. Searching is done with **web_store_html_search.pl**, which will search every HTML product page for customer-submitted keywords and create a dynamic list of hits. However, just because we will not be searching the data file does not mean that the data file is useless for the HTML store. In fact, many HTML stores will utilize the database back end to verify orders received from the product pages as discussed in Chapter 8. If you are using this double-check method, you will still want to define **$sc_data_file_path**. If you do not want to double-check orders against a datafile, you may disregard that variable completely.

Similarly, there is no neeed to be concerned with **$sc_options_directory_path**. This variable defines the locations of the options files used by the Database store to create option-related HTML. Since you will be including all option HTML in the actual product pages themselves, you will not have any need for separate Option files, the Options subdirectory, or the **$sc_options_directory_path** variable.

$sc_html_product_directory_path, however, is crucial. As mentioned earlier, this variable defines the location of the directory in which you put your product pages as well as your list of product pages.

A *list of products* page is a page that contains hyperlinks to pages containing products called *product pages*. These are mainly used for store navigation and the categorization of similar types of products.

N O T E

The application must know the location of this directory if it is to filter requested product pages.

When a customer clicks on a button or hyperlink for a product, the script should receive a **$page** variable as form data. This **$page** variable will correspond to a specific HTML document that the script should filter and display in the browser window.

For example, in **Letters.html**, which is our example of a list of products page located in the distribution Products subdirectory, you will find a link to the Vowels product page with the following syntax:

```
<A HREF =
"web_store.cgi?page=Vowels.html&cart_id="">Vowels</A>
```

Figure 3.2 shows **Letters.html** as it appears on the Web.

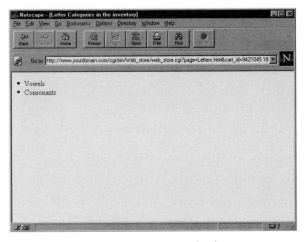

Figure 3.2   Letters.html.

Notice that in the above URL, we have passed the variable **page** with the value of **Vowels.html** to the script. We will discuss the **cart_id=** tag later. However, in order to actually find the page **Vowels.html**, the script must know the location of the file on your server. **$sc_html_product_directory_path** provides it with that information. Thus, if you set this variable equal to **/usr/local/httpd/cgi-bin/Web_store/Html/Products/**, the script will expect to find the file **Vowels.html** using the following location **/usr/local/httpd/cgi-bin/Web_store/Html/Products/Vowels.html**.

You may also define subdirectories in your hyperlink calls if you decide to partition your HTML product pages. Thus, the following hyperlink would access **e.html** in the **/usr/local/httpd/cgi-bin/Web_store/Html/Products/Letters/Vowels/Lower_case/** subdirectory:

```
<A HREF = "web_store.cgi?page=Letters/Vowels/Lower_case/
e.html&cart_id= ">Vowels</A>
```

Understanding the Tags for Maintaining State

Now that we have started discussing the concept of a list of products page and introduced the strange **cart_id=** tag, we should take a moment to explain state maintenance tags in more detail. The trick about list of product pages like **Letters.html** as well as product pages like **Vowels.html** for that matter, is that they are tagged so that the script can automatically insert state information when it filters them. pAs we said in the previous chapter, all HTML pages must be filtered through **web_store.cgi** if the customer's state information is to be maintained. For list of product pages, there are two bits of state information that must be passed: (1) the product page from the list that the customer wants to see, and (2) the location of the customer's unique shopping cart.

In fact, every internal-store hyperlink (most commonly used in list of product pages) must communicate that information. The problem is that when you write the list of product pages in HTML, there is no way for you to know in advance what the cart i.d. will be. In fact, many different customers, all with different cart ids will be navigating through the same page. There is no way to hardcode that information into your HTML. But you can provide a tag which the script will recognize and dynamically exchange for the current value it has for the customer's cart.

This task is handled in the **display_page** subroutine in **web_store.cgi**. The three magic lines are as follows:

```
s/cart_id=/cart_id=$cart_id/g;
s/%%cart_id%%/$cart_id/g;
s/%%page%%/$form_data{'page'}/g;
```

These three lines assure that every HTML page passed to **web_store.cgi** will be filtered for these two state variables. Let's consider the line in **Letters.html**.

```
<A HREF = "web_store.cgi?page=Vowels.html&cart_id=">Vowels</A>
```

In this line, we see that we left the URL encoded hyperlink undone. Specifically, we did not set a value for **cart_id**. We simply left it dangling. However, the script is prepared for that and is actually looking for the **cart_id** flag.

As the script filters the file, preparing it to send to the Web browser, it checks to see if the flag exists. If it does, the script substitutes the incomplete phrase **cart_id=** with **cart_id=[THE ACTUAL CART VALUE]**.

So what are the other two lines with the %% flags? Well these are used to filter hidden form tags instead of hyperlinks. After all, there are two ways to submit information to a script: by URL encoded hyperlink or by hitting a Submit button on a form. If a submit button is used, state information must be passed as hidden form fields. This is most common for product pages on which customers can hit the submit button to purchase an item. Thus, we need a tag which the script will use to filter hidden <INPUT> tag fields. A quick glance at the hidden fields in **Vowels.html** provides an example of how you should prepare the flag:

```
<INPUT TYPE = "hidden" NAME = "cart_id"
VALUE = "%%cart_id%%">
<INPUT TYPE = "hidden" NAME = "page"
 VALUE = "%%page%%">
```

These two lines will be "filtered" by **web_store.cgi** which will insert the actual value of **cart_id** and page.

In summary, it is essential that all product pages have the **%%** hidden form tag flags and that all hyperlinks have the **cart_id=** flags.

Bypassing Database Definition Variables by Encoding your Product Pages

Because we are not using a database, the entire group of database definition variables in the Setup file becomes unnecessary unless you are using the database check functions. This is not to say that we will not need to define a specific format for our products. In fact, you will need to follow a very specific format for defining the fields that make up this information in your HTML product pages. **Vowels.html** is an excellent example of a product page.

Each product page begins with a standard header. In the **Vowels.html** example, we use a simple borderless table to position our products. Of course, you can change this to reflect the specifics of your own site—that is the beauty of the HTML store.

NOTE

Be absolutely sure that the form call in every page points to **web_store.cgi**. Every page that the customer sees must be processed by **web_store.cgi**

```
<HTML>
<HEAD>
<TITLE>Vowel Page</TITLE>
</HEAD>
<BODY BGCOLOR = "FFFFFF" TEXT = "000000">
<FORM METHOD = "post" ACTION = "html_web_store.cgi">
<H2><CENTER>Vowel Mart!</CENTER></H2>
<TABLE>

<TR>
<TH>Quantity</TH>
<TH></TH>
<TH>Description</TH>
</TR>

<TR>
<TD COLSPAN = "3"><HR></TD>
</TR>
<TR>
```

The syntax defining a product appears next.

```
<TR>
<TD ALIGN = "center"><INPUT TYPE = "text"
NAME = "item-0010|Vowels|15.98|The letter A|~lt~IMG SRC =
~qq~/~erict/Scripts/Web_store/Html/Images/a.jpg~qq~ ALIGN =
~qq~left~qq~~gt~" SIZE = "3" MAXLENGTH = "4"></TD>

<TD ALIGN = "center"><IMG SRC =
"/~erict/Scripts/Web_store/Html/Images/a.jpg" ALIGN =
"left"></TD>
<TD>You got it,the world renowned letter "A" for the plow base price
of $15.98<BR><P>
```

You can customize this to display in any way you would like so long as you follow a few rules. Specifically, every purchasable item *must* have a text field entry box representing a quantity and the INPUT tag must follow the following basic format:

```
<INPUT TYPE = "text"
        NAME = "item-WWW|XXX|YYY|ZZZ"
        SIZE = "3" MAXLENGTH = "4">
```

where **WWW** is a **UNIQUE** product identification (like an ISBN number) and **XXX**, **YYY**, and **ZZZ** are bits of information that you want displayed in the customer's cart view. p<NOTE>Each item has a **TEXT** input field associated with it. This text field is three characters long and provides a maximum of four characters by default. Since this corresponds to the quantity that the customer might want to order, it is set to allow only orders less than 9999 quantity. You can change this if you want. pThe definition of this **NAME** value will correspond exactly to the logic of **@sc_db_index_for_defining_item_id**. In fact, that variable is used to dynamically generate the same code for the database store that you must personally do on HTML pages.

Defining an Item

The process of writing your own **NAME** value is not difficult, but it must be painstakingly accurate. First, and most importantly, notice that the **NAME** argument of the **INPUT** field is item-0010|Vowels|15.98|The letter A|~lt~IMG SRC=~qq~Html/Images/a.jpg~qq~ ALIGN=~qq~left~qq~~gt~".

This is where you will define what information gets added to the customer's shopping cart. There are three points to note about the **NAME** string. pFirst, the **NAME** string corresponds to the **%cart** just as **@sc_db_index_for_defining_item_id** did in the Setup file discussed in Chapter 2. You are simply hardcoding that array for each item.

Second, notice that the tag **item-** has been appended to the product i.d. We do this in order to differentiate items from other incoming form data when the customer submits an order. The **item-** tag will be stripped off by the script when it adds the row to the cart, but it *must* be there in your HTML code so that the script will know that this field represents an item.

Finally, notice the **<IMG SRC>** reference. It has several special tags which we use to represent characters that may cause trouble within your HTML code (specifically, characters used in the HTML code standard itself). There are three in particular. **~qq~** represents a double quote mark ("), **~gt~** represents a greater than symbol (>) and **~lt~** denotes a less than symbol (<). The script knows how to translate these when it uses them to display the customer's cart but you must encode them here so that they will not confuse the **<INPUT>** tag in which they are embedded.

Cart Definition Variables

Now that we have gone through all the trouble of hardcoding our product information into all our HTML pages, it is time to make it pay off. The Cart Definition variables will be used to index the product information coming in to the script in the form of text field **NAME** form data. Let's go through the cart definition for the Vowels page discussed previously.

Given the definition of the letter *A* for sale on the **Vowels.html** page, we can tell that the format of **%cart** must be

```
$cart{"quantity"}                 = 0;
$cart{"product_id"}        = 1;
$cart{"category"}         = 2;
$cart{"price"}                 = 3;
$cart{"description"}       = 4;
$cart{"image_location"}           = 5;
$cart{"options"}                  = 6;
$cart{"price_after_options"}      = 7;
```

As was discussed in Chapter 2, fields 1 through 5 are the same as defined in the **NAME** argument of the quantity text box which defines what gets passed to the cart for each item.

All other variables will depend upon utilizing these array elements.

Order Form Definition Variables

These variables will basically be the same for all versions of the Web store regardless of whether they take their information from product pages or a data file because they will all have the same order-processing interface. In terms of the HTML store though, there will be one important variable, **$sc_order_check_db**. If you set this variable to **yes**, the script will use the database routines to double-check that the customer has not attempted to fool around with the cart values by entering fake values on their own custom designed HTML pages or by creating their own URL encoded string. For example, what do you think would happen if some customer typed in the following URL string?

```
http://www.yourdomain.com/cgi-
bin/Web_store/web_store.cgi?page=Words.html&add_to_cart_
button=IHACKEDYOU&cart_id=8427734.9651&item-
1000|Words|14.98|Extropy=5
```

Well, to put it bluntly, they would have just received a discount. If you check the Meme product page, you will see that the Extropy Meme is 15.98, not 14.98. Unfortunately, if you are not careful, you may miss such a sneak attack and the hacker could get away with a discount. Thus, it is advisable for high-traffic stores, for you to create a database backend for your HTML product pages so that all values can be checked against a database that is safely on your server. When the customer attempts to order, if there are any discrepancies, the script will alert you and the customer. As a side note, this could also help in case you make typos in your product pages because the script will recognize accidental as well as intentional discrepancies.

This is not meant to frighten you away from using the HTML store. The versatility of the HTML interface gives you quite a bit of power with creative sites that the Database store cannot give. It is simply a warning for you to take care when processing orders and to suggest that you implement the database checking routines as soon as possible. The extra work will pay off in terms of a good night's sleep.

Store Option Variables

Of course the most basic variable definition for the HTML store is **$sc_use_html_product_pages**. The only way to use product pages is to set this variable to **yes**. If it is set to **no**, the script will look for a data file from which to dynamically generate product pages.

HTML Search Variables

One of the powerful tools of the HTML Web store is the built-in search engine. The search engine takes a list of whitespace separated keywords and searches every product page for pages that contain all of those words. The keywords are entered in a standard FORM text box defined with the following code:

```
<INPUT TYPE = "text" NAME = "keywords">
```

NOTE

Unlike the Database-based search engine included with this script that can search by dates, keyword, or number, the HTML-based search can only search by keyword, since the nonstandardized HTML format does not allow the more complicated searching.

Figure 3.3 shows the HTML frontpage with the search input box included on the bottom.

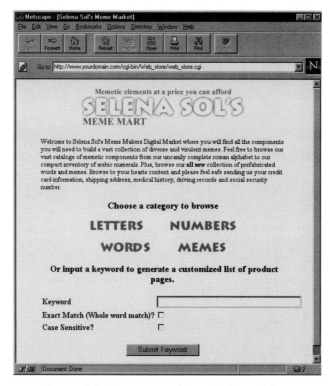

Figure 3.3 Frontpage with Keyword Search box.

The customer can enter as many keywords as he or she wishes and the script will generate a list of pages that satisfied all the keywords entered.

The HTML keyword search uses the "and" methodology so that every keyword must be found on a page for that page to be displayed as a hit.

NOTE

Figure 3.4 shows a dynamically generated "list of hits" page that includes hyperlinks to every page that satisfied the customer's search criteria.

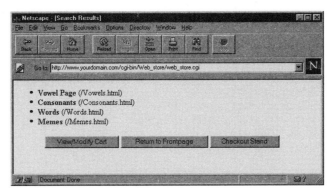

Figure 3.4 List of Hits page.

$sc_root_web_path is the location of the root directory containing all the HTML product pages. In the distribution, this is "./Html/Products/".

@sc_unwanted_files is the list of all the file types which you do not want to be searched when submitting a search term for keyword match. This subject will be discussed more thoroughly in Chapter 13.

Error Message Variables and Miscellaneous Variables

These variables are global for all versions of the Web store and have already been discussed in sufficient detail in Chapter 2.

Understanding Options

Before you begin coding your product pages, there is one last thing to discuss: options. *Options* are unique characteristics that can be applied to a generic product. For example, a basic T-shirt might come in black, blue, or green or small, medium or large. We need a way to communicate to the script what an option is, which item it belongs to, what effect it will have on the base price of that item, and the value set by the customer.

The first part in this process is to make sure that we associate options with items for sale. We do this by using the NAME argument of the form tag which defines each option. Below is an example of using a select menu for options.

```
<P><B>Available Options<B><P>
Font: <SELECT NAME = "option|1|0001">
<OPTION VALUE = "Times New Roman|0.00">Times New Roman (No
charge)
<OPTION VALUE = "Arial|1.50">Arial (+ $1.50)
<OPTION VALUE = "Chicago|2.00">Chicago (+ $2.00)
</SELECT>
<P>
```

In this case, the name syntax breaks down as follows:

1.   *Option flag* This flag tells the script that the incoming data is an option, not an item Thus the first field in a pipe-delimited option **NAME** value will *always* be **option**, just as item **NAME** tags **ALWAYS** begin with **item-**

2.   *Unique sequence number of the option* Each item for sale may have several options associated with it. It is essential that they each gets its own number. If item #0001 had all its options called "option|0001," it would be impossible to parse them separately. So we will name them uniquely, as in "option|1|0001" for color, "option|2|000" for size, or "option|3|0001" for brand name.

3.   *The i.d. of the item that the option is associated with* Notice that this i.d. is the same as what was used in the **NAME** argument for the quantity text box in a product field box. This is deliberate and essential. Options must be associated with the items they modify. Figure 3.5 shows how options might be integrated into a product page.

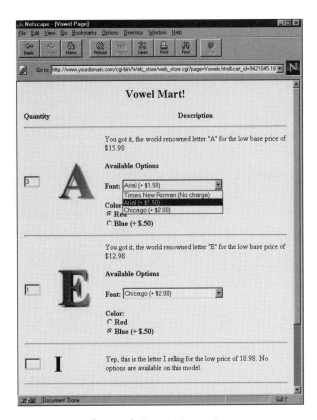

Figure 3.5   Using options.

Finally, notice that options also contain VALUES which are two field pipe delimited lists containing an option description and an option price. The option description will be used for display in the customer's cart and the price will be used to modify the base price of an item.

The following is an example of using a radio button to create an option. It uses the same naming conventions as the **<SELECT>** tag but included here for variety.

```
Color: <BR>
<INPUT TYPE = "radio" NAME = "option|2|0001"p        VALUE = "Red|0.00"
CHECKED>Red<BR>
<INPUT TYPE = "radio" NAME = "option|2|0001"
        VALUE = "Blue|.50">Blue (+ .50)
```

In other words, product number 0001 has two possible options. Font type is option 1 and color is option 2. The customer may choose from three font types. If she chooses "Arial," $1.50 will be added to the base price of the item. She can also order "red" or "blue." If she chooses "red," nothing will be added to the base price of the item.

If this option modified the "letter A" discussed above, and a customer ordered three of them, all red with Arial font, the cart row would appear as follows:

```
3|0010|Vowels|15.98|The letter A|<IMG SRC =
"/~erict/Scripts/Web_store/Html/Images/a.jpg" ALIGN =p"left">|Arial
1.50, Red 0.00|17.48|358
```

Simple Item Definition

Options are not mandatory, of course. In fact, we have also provided an example of an item with no options in case you don't care about options and just want an example without them. This is obviously much simpler since all you need to worry about is the one NAME argument of each item for sale. In **Vowels.html** we have prepared the letter *I* as an example without options.

Finally, the entire code of both **Vowels.html** and **Letters.html** are included for a complete reference:

Vowels.html

```
<HTML>
<HEAD>
<TITLE>Vowels Page</TITLE>
</HEAD>
<BODY BGCOLOR = "FFFFFF" TEXT = "000000">
<FORM METHOD = "post" ACTION = "web_store.cgi">
<INPUT TYPE = "hidden" NAME = "cart_id"p      VALUE = "%%cart_id%%">
<INPUT TYPE = "hidden" NAME = "page"p      VALUE = "%%page%%">
```

```
<TABLE BORDER = "0">
<TR>
<TH>Quantity</TH>
<TH></TH>
<TH>Description</TH>
</TR>

<TR>
<TD COLSPAN = "3"><HR></TD>
</TR>
<TR>p<TD ALIGN = "center"><INPUT TYPE = "text"
NAME = "item-0010|Vowels|15.98|The letter A|~lt~IMG SRC =
~qq~/~erict/Scripts/Web_store/Html/Images/a.jpg~qq~ ALIGN =
~qq~left~qq~~gt~"
SIZE = "3" MAXLENGTH = "4"></TD>

<TD ALIGN = "center"><IMG SRC =
"/~erict/Scripts/Web_store/Html/Images/a.jpg" ALIGN =
"left"></TD>

<TD>You got it,the world renowned letter "A" for the low
base price of$15.98<BR><P>
<B>Available Options<B>
<P>
Font:p<SELECT NAME = "option|1|0010">
<OPTION VALUE = "Times New Roman|0.00">Times New Roman (No charge)
<OPTION VALUE = "Arial|1.50">Arial (+ $1.50)
<OPTION VALUE = "Chicago|2.00">Chicago (+ $2.00)
</SELECT>

<P>
Color:p<BR>
<INPUT TYPE = "radio" NAME = "option|2|0010"
        VALUE = "Red|0.00" CHECKED>Red<BR>
<INPUT TYPE = "radio" NAME = "option|2|0010"
        VALUE = "Blue|.50">Blue (+ $.50)
</TD>

</TR>
</TR>
<TR>p<TD COLSPAN = "3"><HR></TD>
</TR>
<TR>p<TD ALIGN = "center"><INPUT TYPE = "text"
NAME = "item-0011|Vowels|12.98|The letter E|~lt~IMG SRC =
~qq~/~erict/Scripts/Web_store/Html/Images/e.jpg~qq~ ALIGN =
~qq~left~qq~~gt~" SIZE = "3" MAXLENGTH = "4"></TD>
```

```
<TD ALIGN = "center"><IMG SRC =
"/~erict/Scripts/Web_store/Html/Images/e.jpg" ALIGN =
"left"></TD>

<TD>You got it, the world renowned letter "E" for the
low base price of $12.98<BR><P>
<B>Available Options<B>
<P>
Font:p<SELECT NAME = "option|1|0011">
<OPTION VALUE = "Times New Roman|0.00">Times New Roman (No charge)
<OPTION VALUE = "Arial|1.50">Arial (+ $1.50)
<OPTION VALUE = "Chicago|2.00">Chicago (+ $2.00)
</SELECT>

<P>
Color:p<BR>
<INPUT TYPE = "radio" NAME = "option|2|0011"
       VALUE = "Red|0.00" CHECKED>Red<BR>
<INPUT TYPE = "radio" NAME = "option|2|0011"
       VALUE = "Blue|.50">Blue (+ $.50)
</TD>

</TR>
<TR>p<TD COLSPAN = "3"><HR></TD>
</TR>
<TR>p<TD ALIGN = "center"><INPUT TYPE = "text" NAME = "item-
0012|Vowels|18.98|The letter I|~lt~CENTER~gt~~lt~FONT SIZE =
~qq~+4~qq~~gt~I~lt~/FONT~gt~~lt~/CENTER~gt~"
SIZE = "3" MAXLENGTH = "4"></TD>

<TD ALIGN = "center"><CENTER><FONT SIZE =
"+4">I</FONT></CENTER></TD>

<TD>Yep, this is the letter I selling for the low price
 of 18.98. No options are available on this model.
<BR></TD>

</TR>
<TR>p<TD COLSPAN = "3"><HR></TD>
</TR>

</TABLE>
<P>
```

```
<CENTER>
<INPUT TYPE = "submit" NAME = "add_to_cart_button"
      VALUE = "Add Items to my Cart">
<INPUT TYPE = "submit" NAME = "modify_cart_button"p        VALUE =
"View/Modify Cart">
<INPUT TYPE = "submit"p        NAME = "return_to_frontpage_button"
      VALUE = "Return to Frontpage">
<INPUT TYPE = "submit" NAME = "order_form_button"p        VALUE =
"Checkout Stand">
</FORM>
</CENTER>
</BODY>
</HTML>
Letters.html
<HTML>
<HEAD>
<TITLE>Letter Categories in the inventory</TITLE>
</HEAD>
<BODY BGCOLOR = "FFFFFF" TEXT = "000000">

<LI><A HREF =
"web_store.cgi?page=Vowels.html&cart_id=">Vowels</A>
<LI><A HREF =
"web_store.cgi?page=Consonants.html&cart_id=">Consonants</A>

</BODY>
</HTML>
```

Summary

To utilize the HTML-based interface, you must satisfy several requirements. First, you must change the following variables in the setup file:

```
$sc_data_file_path
$sc_html_product_directory_path
$sc_order_check_db
$sc_use_html_product_pages
$sc_root_web_path
$sc_unwanted_files
```

Second, any list of product pages that you create for navigation must be hard-coded with the **page** and **cart_id=** flags for filtering.

Finally, you must create product pages with text field boxes with hard-coded **NAME** values according to the data you want transferred to the cart. Options must also be prepared where appropriate.

CHAPTER FOUR

FOCUS ON THE

DATABASE STORE

The Database store generates product pages dynamically from an ASCII text file (flatfile) that contains a pipe-delimited database. The Database store has several important advantages over the HTML store. First and foremost, using a database means that the store administrator need not code any HTML. This can save a lot of time and energy for stores with extensive inventories of hundreds or even thousands of items (see Figure 4.1). Because the Web store is designed to generate HTML pages dynamically from the database, the store administrator need only prepare the database (often a preexisting database reformatted to be delimited by the pipe (|) symbol). There is no need to code an HTML page for every product category. And as we will see in Chapter 5, the database back end facilitates more complex search algorithms.

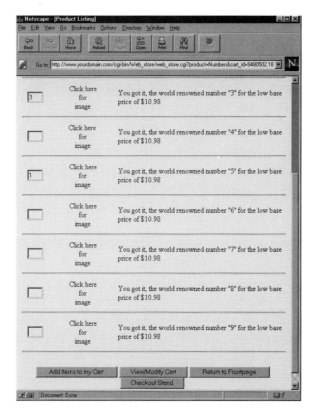

Figure 4.1 The Database product page.

The second benefit is the ability to lessen dependence on HTML code that can be manipulated by the sly customer. Instead, cart contents are generated and checked from your local database and not from hidden elements in the HTML. There is continual error checking at all points in the shopping process to make sure that prices of items in the cart match prices in the database.

Finally, through the use of the format strings in the Setup file and coded URLs in the data file, you can devise quite complicated and creative displays for products. Even though every product must be presented in a standard format, that format can be quite complex or graphic-intensive, even mimicking some of the more standardized HTML store displays.

As with the HTML store, many companies have opted for the Database version in the past. These versions can all be found in the second half of the

Scripts in Action list at http://www.eff.org/~erict/Scripts/web_store.html. If you are interested in seeing how others have utilized the Database back end, we recommend taking a few minutes to browse through the examples there.

Customizing the Setup File

As with all versions of this script, the first thing you must do is to customize the Setup file. For the most part, the setup file for the Database store will be like any other implementation. Eighty percent of the setup should remain constant throughout all the versions. However, there will be some differences. In the following section, we will go through **web_store.setup.db** and highlight variables specific to the Database store and explain their usage. Variables not mentioned should be considered globally important to all versions of the store and will be defined the same way regardless of which implementation you choose. They are also discussed in Chapter 2.

Global File Location Variables

The first variable of interest in **web_store.setup.db**, which is an example setup file in the distribution, is **$sc_html_search_routines_library_path**. **$sc_html_search_routines_library_path** defines the location of **web_store_html_search.pl** which is used to perform searches in the Products subdirectory of the HTML directory. Because we will be searching the data file directly, there will be no need to search the product pages in the Products subdirectory and no need for that variable. However, we will still have to define **$sc_html_product_directory_path,** because we will store list of product pages in that directory.

Since we will be searching the data file in order to generate product pages, **$sc_data_file_path** must be defined and pointed at the location of the data file and **$sc_db_lib_path** must be defined and set equal to the location of **web_store_db_lib.pl**.

$sc_options_directory_path defines the locations of the Options files used by the Database store to create option-related HTML. This must be set relative to the script or absolutely based upon the server's directory structure. The options files themselves will be discussed later in this chapter.

$sc_store_front_path must point to a frontpage specific to a Database implementation. Because hyperlink references differ slightly in the Database and HTML implementations, you may not use the same front page for both. When composing hyperlinks, we will use the **product** keyword when pointing to product pages instead of the **page** keyword. The **page** keyword will be reserved for pointing to list of product pages, which are simply HTML pages that contain hyperlinks to product pages.

An example of a hyperlink to a list of products page can be seen in **outlet_frontpage.db.html** in the hyperlink referencing, **Letters.html**.

Figure 4.2 shows **Letters.html** as it appears on the Web:

```
<A HREF = "web_store.cgi?page=Letters.html.db&cart_id=">
```

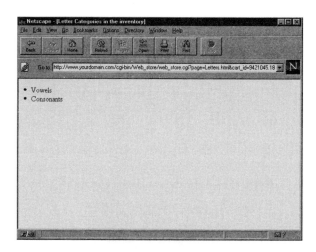

Figure 4.2 Letters.html

Notice that in the above URL, we have passed to the script the variable **page** with the value of **Letters.html**. (We will discuss the **cart_id=** tag later). **Letters.html** is an example of a list of products page, which is simply a subcategory with links to two product pages, **Vowels** and **Consonants**. Because we do not want to generate that page from the database, we tell the script to go to the **Html/Products** subdirectory and grab **Letters.html** for display.

$sc_html_product_directory_path provides it with the information it needs to find **Letters.html**. Thus, if you set this variable equal to:

```
/usr/local/httpd/cgi-bin/Web_store/Html/Products/
```

the script will expect to find the file using the following location:

```
/usr/local/httpd/cgi-bin/Web_store/Html/Products/Letters.html
```

You may also define subdirectories in your hyperlink calls if you decide to partition your HTML product pages. Thus, the following hyperlink would access **Lower_case.html** in the subdirectory:

```
/usr/local/httpd/cgi-bin/Web_store/Html/Products/Letters/Vowels/
<A HREF =
"web_store.cgi?page=Letters/Vowels/Lower_case.html&cart_id=">Vowels</A
>
```

Unlike the HTML store, however, the Database store cannot use the **page** variable to display product pages because no HTML product pages actually exist. The Web store must be responsible for generating product pages on the fly based upon which products the customer wants to see.

This chore is handled by using the product keyword in the hyperlinks leading to product pages. Consider the following hyperlink to the "Numbers" Page:

```
<A HREF = "web_store.cgi?product=Numbers&cart_id=">
```

Notice that we use the keyword **product** to specify those items in the data file we want displayed for the customer. The value associated with the product's keyword will correspond to a field in the database that you will use to group products that should be displayed on the same product page. Thus, every item with a Products field equal to **Numbers** will be displayed when one clicks on the above link.

There will be more details on how to set up your products fields and how the script knows which field to search when we discuss the Database definition variables in the Setup file, but it is important to drive home the fact that the **page** variable is used only for list of products pages and that the **products** keyword is used to point to product pages.

Understanding Tags for Maintaining State

Now that we have opened the list of products discussion and introduced the strange **cart_id=** tag, we need to take a moment to explain state maintenance tags in more detail. The trick about list of product pages such as **Letters.html** is that they are tagged so that **web_store.cgi** can automatically insert state information when it filters them.

As we said in Chapter 2, all HTML pages must be filtered through **web_store.cgi** if the customer's state information is to be maintained. When using list of product pages, there are two items of state information that must be passed: (1) the product page from the list that the customer wants to see and (2) the location of the customer's unique shopping cart.

In fact, every internal-store hyperlink (most commonly used in list of product pages) must communicate that information. The problem is that when you write the list of product pages in HTML, there is no way for you to know in advance what the cart i.d. will be. In fact, many different customers, all with different cart i.d.s will be navigating through the same page. There is no way to hard code that information into your HTML. But you can provide a tag which the script will recognize and dynamically exchange for the current value it has for the customer's cart.

This line is handled in the **display_page** subroutine in **web_store.cgi**:

```
s/cart_id=/cart_id=$cart_id/g;
```

This line assures that every HTML page passed to **web-store.cgi** will be filtered for these two state variables. Let's consider the line in **outlet_front page.db.html** discussed above:

```
<A HREF = "web_store.cgi?page=Letters.html.db&cart_id=">
```

In this file, we see that we left the URL encoded hyperlink incomplete. Specifically, we did not set a value for **cart_id**. We simply left it dangling. However, the script is prepared for that and is actually looking for the **cart_id=** flag.

As it is going through the file, preparing it to send to the Web browser, it checks to see if it finds that flag. If it does, it substitutes the incomplete phrase **cart_id=** with **cart_id=[THE ACTUAL CART VALUE]** using the regular expression. Thus, every hyperlink within the store *must* have the cart_id= flag.

Defining Products with the Database Definition Variables and the Datafile

When the customer clicks on a link for a product page such as **Numbers,** the script must search through the data file and dynamically generate a products page with the appropriate items and the HTML <FORM> code necessary for the customer to order those products. In essence, the script must dynamically generate the HTML product pages discussed in Chapter 3.

However, because the script generates the Name values for all the product input fields, the Database store administrator need not go through the process of coding all the Name attributes for products. That is, no HTML product pages need be created. Instead, she must prepare a data file and describe each field in the setup file so that the script can do it by itself.

Let us first look at the data file. A data file, again, is a simple flatfile ASCII file which has pipe delimited fields and newline separated rows. Below is an example:

```
ID|Category|Price|Description|Image
1|Vowel|10.98|A|~lt~IMG SRC = ~qq~Images/a.gif~qq~~gt~
2|Vowel|10.98|E|~lt~IMG SRC = ~qq~Images/e.gif~qq~~gt~
3|Cons|11.98|T|~lt~IMG SRC = ~qq~Images/t.gif~qq~~gt~
4|Number|13.98|1|~lt~IMG SRC = ~qq~Images/1.gif~qq~~gt~
```

There are a few important things to note about a data file.

First, every data file is a set of standardized items with separate fields in a predictable order. Notice that in every item above, the price is the third field. The standardization of fields is essential. If you misplace fields, the script will not know how to display your items when it generates product pages. Thus, even blank fields must be defined. For example, if there was no description associated with the number 1 above, you would still have a row that looked like the following:

```
4|Number|13.98|||~lt~IMG SRC = ~qq~Images/1.gif~qq~~gt~
```

The field would still be in the data row, it would just be blank.

Second, several special tags must be used to represent characters which may cause trouble within your HTML code (specifically characters used in the HTML code itself). There are three in particular:

~qq~ represents a double quote mark ("), **~gt~** represents a *greater than* symbol (>), and **~lt~** denotes a *less than* symbol (<). The script knows how to translate these when it uses them to display the customer's cart but you must encode them here so that they will not confuse the <INPUT> tag in which they are embedded. After all, how would the browser interpret the following **NAME** value?

```
<INPUT TYPE = "text" NAME = "<IMG SRC = "Images/1.gif">">
```

The extra quote marks and the greater than and less than symbols would be too confusing for the Web browser to interpret!

Third, every row (item) is separated by a newline character. Thus, you may not include a newline character within the data. However, this should not be a problem since newline characters translate to a space in HTML. If you wished to include a line break, you would use the <BR> tag.

Fourth, each item must be uniquely identifiable with some form of product i.d. field. We must do this so that the script will have some absolute way of differentiating items that it must display (specifically, how to apply options).

Finally, no pipe characters are allowed within the data because the pipe is used as a field delimiter. If you included a pipe character in your data, it would cause the script to incorrectly display your item.

Once we have created our data file, we must describe it for the script in the setup file. That way the script will know how to define each product in the HTML it must dynamically generate.

%**db** is an associative array that contains a mapping of your own customer defined fields to the index number of the fields as they appear in the flatfile database.

For example, in our sample data file above, we would create the following associative array:

```
$db{"product_id"} = 0;
$db{"product"}   = 1;
$db{"price"}    = 2;
$db{"name"}     = 3;
$db{"image_url"} = 4;
```

 Remember, fields start counting at 0.

NOTE

@**sc_db_display_fields** is an array containing the descriptive headers for the fields in the database we wish to display to the user when they do a query search. Notice that these headers need not include every field defined in %**database**. You may display only some of the information contained in the database row if you so desire. The array takes advantage of the indexes defined in %**database** and each descriptive element in this array corresponds to the index numbers in @**sc_db_index_for_display**. @**sc_db_index_for_display** is an array containing the index numbers of the **db** fields that correspond to the **display_fields** array. To access those index numbers, we just utilize the %**darabase** associative array. There must be one index number in this array for every descriptive element in @**sc_db_display_fields**.

@**sc_db_index_for_defining_item_id** is an array containing the **database** fields that correspond to the fields from the database that you wish to associate with a customer's cart when he or she selects that item for purchase. These field values will be used to determine the fields that make up each item row in the customer's cart. If you do not put a database field in this array, it won't be put in the cart and will not be available for display when customers view their carts. It is mandatory that the Price and Options database fields become incorporated into the cart as these are used for cart subtotal calculations.

$sc_db_index_of_price is an index to the field in the database that contains the price. This setupvariable is used by the Web store to decide how to calculate and display money. In the example above, this value would be 2. Remember that even if you do not display price, it must be defined here so that the script will be able to do subtotaling.

@sc_db_query_criteria is an array containing the criteria that can be used to search on the database. This is a powerful search mechanism. Though searching is discussed in greater detail in Chapter 5, we will touch on it here as it relates to developing product pages on the fly. The array contains pipe-delimited fields inside each list item. The fields are the following:

1. *Form variable name* This is the variable name which you want to associate with the products to display. For example, if you have the following hyperlink for getting a product page:

   ```
   <A HREF = "web_store.cgi?product=Numbers&cart_id=">
   ```

   then the form variable name would be **product**.

2. *Index into the database that this criteria applies to* This list corresponds to the **%db** associative array in the same way that **@db_index_for_display** does. Thus, if you want the product field to be searched by keyword, the hyperlink variable would be **product** as above and the index into the database would be **1** according to our sample **%db** associative array.

3. *operator for comparison* This field is used by the script to determine what logical criteria to apply when searching the database. Possible values include >, <, >=, <=, =, != (not equal),

   and the operator is compared the following way:

   ```
   form_variable OPERATOR database_field_value
   ```

That is, item 1 above is the left-hand side of the operator and item 2 above is the right-hand side of the operator. Typically, we'll use "=" for generating product pages since we will be searching by keywords.

4. *data type of the field* This field determines how the operator in (3) gets applied to the data. Typically we will use the string comparison.

Perhaps some examples are in order. Typically, you just want to do a search on a product category and include that search term within URLs in a frontpage such as the following:

```
web_store.cgi?product=Vowels.
```

To do so, we must set the form variable equal to the above (**product**), set the second field equal to the field in the database corresponding to a product name (for example, 1), set operator =, data type **string** to do a keyword search that is case insensitive. Thus, **@sc_db_query_criteria** would be equal to:

```
("product|1|=|string")
```

$sc_db_max_rows_returned is the maximum number of rows you will allow to be displayed to the user as the result of a query. If the query gets above this number, customers are presented with a message letting them know that they need to narrow their query.

Cart Definition Variables

Now that we have gone to the trouble of defining our data file, it is time to make it pay off. The Cart Definition variables will be used to index the product information coming in to the script in the form of text field Name form data. Let's go through the cart definition for the sample data file proposed previously.

Given the structure of the data file and the value of:

```
@sc_db_index_for_defining_item_id
```

%cart must be

```
$cart{"quantity"}            = 0;
$cart{"product_id"}          = 1;
$cart{"category"}       = 2;
$cart{"price"}               = 3;
$cart{"image_location"}           = 4;
$cart{"options"}             = 5;
$cart{"price_after_options"}       = 6;
```

All other variables will depend upon utilizing these array elements.

Order Form Definition Variables

These variables will basically be the same for all versions of the Web store regardless of whether they take their information from product pages or a data file because they will all have the same order processing interface.

Store Option Variables

Of course the most basic variable definition for the Database store is **$sc_use_html_product_pages**. The only way to dynamically generate product pages is to set this variable to **no**. If it is set to **yes**, the script will look liek the predesigned HTML product pages in the **Html/Products** subdirectory.

HTML Search Variables

Because we will use the search routines in the Database search library, we will not need to worry about any of these variables. They are all specific to the HTML store.

Error Message Variables

These variables are global for all versions of the Web store and have already been discussed in sufficient detail.

Miscellaneous Variables

$sc_product_display_title is the title that you would like to appear on your product pages. Unfortunately, one of the limitations of the Database store is the inability to custom design titles.

$sc_product_display_header is the header HTML used to display products in the database based implementation. Notice that we use **%s** to substitute for any given product information. The script will substitute product data for each product in place of the **%s** when the variable is actually used.

<NOTE> There must be a **%s** for every item in **@sc_db_index_for_display** because those elements will be what gets substituted for each **%s** in the order they are defined in the array.

$sc_product_display_footer is the footer for each product

$sc_product_display_row is the **%s** embedded product row variable.

Understanding Options

Options are unique characteristics that can be applied to a product. For example, a basic T-shirt might come in black, blue, or green or small, medium, or large. Options modify a generic product. We need a way to communicate to the script what an option is, which item it belongs to, what effect it will have on the base price of that item, and the value set by the customer. Figure 4.3 depicts a product page with options:

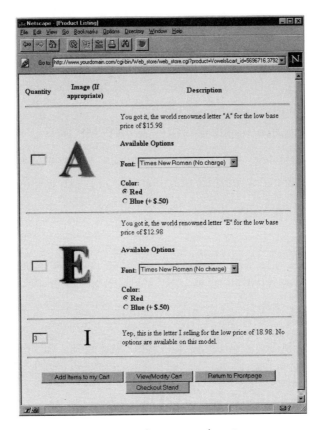

Figure 4.3 Product page with options.

The first part in this process is to make sure that we associate options with items for sale in the data file. To do so, we will use a special database field with a specific format. Here is an example row from the distributed version of the data file.

```
0010|Vowels|15.98|The letter A|~lt~IMG SRC = ~qq~Html/Images/a.jpg~qq~
ALIGN = ~qq~left~qq~~gt~|You got it, the world renowned letter
"A"|%%OPTION%%option.html
```

Notice that the fifth field reads **%%OPTION%%option.html**. The special way that options are denoted in the database is by using the format **%%OPTION%%filename** in the data file. This string includes two important pieces of information.

First, the string begins with **%%OPTION%%**. This is a flag that lets the script know that it needs to deal with this database field as if the field were an option. When the script sees the flag, the string will then look to the string following the flag to see which file the string should load. Thus, in this example, the script would load the file **option.html** for display.

Why go through all the trouble? Basically, we need to create a system that will handle large chunks of similar HTML code within the database. Options on product pages are likely to be repeated fairly often. For example, every item in a database might have an option like tape, CD, or LP. By creating one **option.html** file, we could easily put all the code into one shared location and not worry about typing it in for every single database entry.

The option file is opened and read and every line of the option file is appended to the product when it is displayed and the file is closed again.

However, options files themselves have another important flag, the **%%PRODUCT_ID%%** flag. Because options must be associated with the items they modify and because you do not know in advance what those items will be, you must let the script make this connection at run time. The connection is achieved by the flag. The current product i.d. number will be substituted by the script for the **%%PRODUCT_ID%%** flag, which is a mandatory tag contained in all options files.

With the exception of this **%%PRODUCT_ID%%** flag, the option definitions follow those in the HTML store. First you must associate options with the items they modify. We make this connection by using the NAME argument of the form tag that defines each option. Below is an example of using a Select menu for options.

```
<P><B>Available Options<B><P>
Font: <SELECT NAME = "option|1|0001">
<OPTION VALUE = "Times New Roman|0.00">Times New Roman (No
charge)
<OPTION VALUE = "Arial|1.50">Arial (+ $1.50)
<OPTION VALUE = "Chicago|2.00">Chicago (+ $2.00)
</SELECT>
<P>
```

In this case, the NAME syntax breaks down as follows:

1. *Option flag* This flag tells the script that the incoming data is an option, not an item. Thus, the first field in a pipe-delimited option Name value will *always* be **option** just as item Name tags *always* begin with **item-**.

2. *Unique sequence number of the option* Each item for sale may have several options associated with it. It is essential that each gets its own number. If item #0001 had all its options called **option|0001**, it would be impossible to parse them separately. So we will name them uniquely such as **option|1|0001** for color, **option|2|0001** for size, or **option|3|0001** for brand name.

3. *I.D. of the item that the option is associated with* Notice that this i.d. is the same as what was used in the Name argument for the quantity text box in a product field box. This is deliberate and essential. Options must be associated with the items they modify. This is where we must use the **%%PRODUCT_ID%%** flag.

Finally, notice that options also contain Values, which are two field pipe-delimited lists containing an option description and an option price. The option description will be used for display in the user's cart and the price option will be used to modify the base price of an item.

The following is an example of using a radio button to create an option. It uses the same naming conventions as the <SELECT> tag but is included here for variety:

```
Color: <BR>
<INPUT TYPE = "radio" NAME = "option|2|0001"
    VALUE = "Red|0.00" CHECKED>Red<BR>
<INPUT TYPE = "radio" NAME = "option|2|0001"
    VALUE = "Blue|.50">Blue (+ .50)
```

In other words, product number **0001** has two possible options. Font type is option number 1 and color is option number 2. The customer may choose from three font types. If she chooses Arial, $1.50 will be added to the base price of the item. She can also order red or blue. If she chooses red, nothing will be added to the base price of the item.

If this option modified the letter *A* discussed above, and a customer ordered three *As*, all red with Arial font, the cart row would appear as follows:

```
3|1|Vowels|10.98|A|~lt~IMG SRC = ~qq~Html/Images/a.jpg~qq~ ALIGN =
~qq~left~qq~~gt~|Arial 1.50, Red 0.00|12.48|1
```

Below, for you to review, is the code for the sample **option.html** file:

```
<P>
<B>Available Options<B>
<P>

Font:
<SELECT NAME = "option|1|%%PRODUCT_ID%%">
<OPTION VALUE = "Times New Roman|0.00">Times New Roman (No charge)
<OPTION VALUE = "Arial|1.50">Arial (+ $1.50)
<OPTION VALUE = "Chicago|2.00">Chicago (+ $2.00)
</SELECT>

<P>

Color:
<BR>
<INPUT TYPE = "radio" NAME = "option|2|%%PRODUCT_ID%%"
    VALUE = "Red|0.00" CHECKED>Red<BR>
<INPUT TYPE = "radio" NAME = "option|2|%%PRODUCT_ID%%"
    VALUE = "Blue|.50">Blue (+ $.50)
```

Summary

To utilize the Database-based interface, you must satisfy several requirements. First, you must modify the following variables in the Setup file as discussed above:

```
$sc_html_product_directory_path
$sc_data_file_path
$sc_db_lib_path
$sc_options_directory_path
$sc_store_front_path
```

```
@sc_db_display_fields
@sc_db_index_for_display
@sc_db_index_for_defining_an_item
$sc_db_index_of_price
@sc_db_query_criteria
$sc_db_max_rows_returned
$sc_use_html_product_pages
$sc_product_display_title
$sc_product_display_header
$sc_product_display_footer
$sc_product_display_row
```

Second, any list of product pages that you create for navigation must be hard-coded with the **page** and **cart_id=** flags for filtering.

Third, you must create an ASCII text file (flat file) database that includes pipe-delimited database rows separated by the newline charcter. The fields of this database must correspond to the **db_index** variables defined above.

Finally, options files must be created for any options that you wish to use to modify products in your database. The options must be prepared for filtering with the **%%PRODUCT_ID%%** flag and must be included as specially flagged fields in the data file.

CHAPTER FIVE

FOCUS ON THE QUERY-DRIVEN DATABASE STORE

While the HTML version of the store and the product/category-driven store work well for small inventories, both start to break down once a large catalog of items is involved. For example, if you have a catalog of 2500 separate products, maintaining HTML pages for all those products in the HTML-based store can be a nightmare. You could use the database store and let the users select the product category that they wish to see, but then you have to present the user with a lot of categories in order to make any of the lists reasonably short for viewing. Even if 2500 items were broken up into twenty categories, the user would still have to browse through an average of 125 items per category. Thus the natural evolution of Web stores with many items to display is the full Query-driven store, where the user can enter multiple search terms in order to narrow the amount of data retrieved.

The Query-driven store is almost identical to the Database store discussed in the previous chapter. However, in the previous chapter, the query interface was minimal. A Query-driven store allows the user to query on many different fields in many different ways.

Two changes must be done to the Database store configuration to make the Query-driven store possible. First, the frontpage query form must have more search terms added as <INPUT> and <SELECT> tags. Second, the Setup file must be configured to map the new search terms on the front page with the fields in the database. An example of a full query-driven search form appears in Figure 5.1.

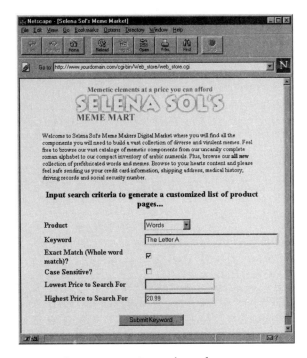

Figure 5.1   Query-driven frontpage.

Changes to the Setup File

The changes to the setup file are nearly identical to the changes discussed in Chapter 4 (The standard Database Store). However, with the query driven database store, you must pay more attention to the database query related variables. The setup file **web_store.setup.db.table** contains an example template of a query-driven store. In addition to providing a query interface, this setup file contains minor cosmetic changes designed to make the resulting product list display as a table. A description of the variables that differ in the Query-driven Web store are described below.

Database-Related Changes to the Setup File

@sc_db_query_criteria is an array containing the criteria that defines the logic used to search the database. Each element in this array is a pipe-delimited set of fields. The fields correspond to the possible query search terms. Sample code that defines this variable is shown below from **web_store.setup.db.table.**

```
@sc_db_query_criteria =
("query_price_low_range|2|<=|number",
 "query_price_high_range|2|>=|number",
 "product|1|=|string",
 "keywords|1,2,3,4,5|=|string");
```

The first field of each element in the array is the form variable name that this search term should match against. Remember, search terms are entered by the user on the frontpage form. Thus you will need to come up with a form field name that is used as a particular search term. For example:

```
<INPUT TYPE=text NAME=query_price_low_range>
```

would be a sample form input field corresponding to the first element in the **@sc_db_query_criteria** array shown above.

The second field contains a comma-delimited list of the indexes in the database row that correspond to the database fields the criteria applies to. For instance, in the example above, the values **1,2,3,4,5** would signify that the second, third, fourth, fifth, and sixth fields from the database will be compared against the **keywords** form variable.

NOTE

Remember, fields in PERL start counting at zero. The first field is really field number 0. Thus the second field is referred to as field number 1. The third field is referred to as field number 2. The fourth field is referred to as field number 3. The fifth field is referred to as field number 4 and finally, the sixth field is referred to as field number 5.

In the Setup file, the **%db** associative array can be used to determine which indexes apply to which database field numbers. This use of **%db** was discussed previously in Chapter 2 and Chapter 4.

The third field contains the operator that will be used to compare the form field to the database fields. Possible operators include greater than (>), greater than or equal to (>=), less than (<), less than or equal to (<=), equals (=), or not equals (!=). The operators are applied with the form variable on the left-hand side and the database fields on the right hand side. If there is more than one database field specified, then the operator will be applied once to each database field.

For example, if the form variable name was **expiration_date** and the database index for the expiration date was 3, then the equals operator would be applied just as the pseudocode example below shows.

```
if ([EXPIRATION DATE]=[FIELD #3 IN DATABASE)
{
  [WE FOUND A MATCH]
}
```

Finally, the fourth field is the data type of the fields we are comparing. The values for the data type can be date, number, or string—a most important point. For example, if you mistakenly specified a numeric value as a string, and the user types in a number—**30**, for example—while the value in the database is actually **30.00**, a string comparison will reveal that the string **30** is definitely not equal to the string **30.00**. But if you had compared these two strings as numbers, then they would actually match correctly. The number **30** is equal to the number **30.00**. Figure 5.2 graphically illustrates the structure of elements in the query criteria array.

The data type, therefore, can be thought of as affecting how the comparison operators perform their job. If the data type is a number, then the form field and database fields are compared as straight numbers. If the data type is a string, then the fields are compared as strings. If the data types are dates, then they are converted to a date format to know whether one date actually occurs before, after, or is equivalent to another date.

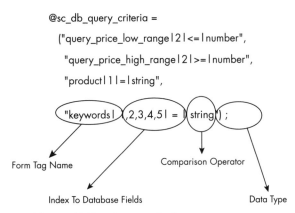

Figure 5.2   Query criteria array structure.

There is one exception to the way operators work. If the data type is a string and the operator is equal (=), then two extra form variables alter the way the string equality is performed: **exact_match** and **case_sensitive.**

By default, string equality matching is *fuzzy.* That is, the match is performed in a case-insensitive manner and the keywords that are typed into the form variable have the ability to satisfy *partial-word matches*—if the keyword matches part of a word in the database, then the match is considered successful.

During string equality matches, the words that are typed as form input are separated by white space (including spaces, tabs, and carriage returns). The Web store script actually considers each word separately and searches on them individually. All the words typed into the form variable must match the database fields in order to consider the match to be successful.

The string equality comparison is case insensitive only if the form variable, **case_sensitive**, is equal to **on**. This generally happens if you have an <INPUT> form variable of TYPE **checkbox** and NAME equal to **case_sensitive** that has been checked on. You can also force case sensitive searches by including a hidden field on the form with a name of **case_sensitive** and the value of on. An example of the HTML code for this tag appears below:

```
<INPUT TYE=checkbox NAME=case_sensitive>
```

Furthermore. the string equality comparison matches only whole words to whole words if the form variable **exact_match** is equal to **on**. Like **case_sensi-**

tive, you will usually place this form variable on the form as an <INPUT> tag of type checkbox such as the following HTML code:

```
<INPUT TYPE=checkbox NAME=exact_match>
```

Finally, it is important to note that the query criteria is additive with regards to narrowing down what the user sees. For example, if there are two separate elements that are being queried on, then a record in the database must successfully satisfy both selection criteria before being considered a totally successful match. In other words, the elements follow the and rule. The first element and any other elements must match together.

Also, only form fields that have values are compared against the query criteria. For example, even if the query criteria has an element that matches the Price field of the database, if the user has not entered a price to match against, then the price will not be considered part of the query. This makes sense because generally we want to give the user the ability to pick and choose what combination of fields on the form will enter into the query results. Furthermore, as the user fills in more and more fields, the query will become additively more and more restrictive.

In summary, the first field is the form variable **NAME**, the second field contains the index to the database fields being compared, the third field is the comparison operator to use, and the fourth field is the data type. In addition, when the query is actually performed on the database, only fields that have been entered by the user enter into the query results. As the user fills in more query fields on the query form, the query becomes more restrictive because more criteria has been entered by the user. The section below goes into the details of possible ways to configure the **@sc_db_query_criteria** variable to suit the most common cases.

Cosmetic Changes to the Setup File

The variables that display the resulting product pages were altered in **web_store.setup.db.table** to display the results of the query using an HTML table view. The three affected variables are **$sc_product_display_header**, **$sc_product_display_footer**, and **$sc_product_display_row**.

$sc_product_display_header is the header of the table The code that configures this variable in the Setup file appears below:

```
$sc_product_display_header = qq!
  <TABLE BORDER = "1">
  <TR>
  <TH>Quantity</TH>
  <TH>%s</TH>
  <TH>%s</TH>
  </TR>!;
```

The table border is set to **1** so that a table border is created. Next, the first table row is defined with **Quantity** plus two other table headers defined as **%s**. The **%s** formats will eventually match the values from **$sc_db_display_fields** (Image (if appropriate), Description).

$sc_product_display_footer is very simple. All it does is close the table. The code for **$sc_product_display_footer** follows:

```
$sc_product_display_footer = qq!
  </TABLE>!;
```

Finally, **$sc_product_display_row** contains information about every row from the database that will be displayed. The code for $sc_product_display_row is defined as follows:

```
$sc_product_display_row = qq~
<TR>
<TD ALIGN = "center"><INPUT TYPE = "text"
            NAME = "item-%s"
            SIZE = "3" MAXLENGTH = "4"></TD>
<TD ALIGN = "center">%s</TD>
<TD>%s<BR>%s</TD>
</TR>~SCC 3 BOT
```

The table column has an input tag generated with the name of **item-** plus **%s**. The first **%s** format string of any database query is always a pipe-delimited list of values that uniquely identify the item and which will define the fields of the item that will go into the cart. This pipe-delimited list is defined by the Setup variable **@sc_db_index_for_defining_item_id**. The variable above has two more table columns. The first has one database field displayed in it (one **%s**), and the second has two database fields displayed in it (two **%s**) in the format string. The setup variable **@sc_db_index_for_display** tells the Web store script which database fields map against the **%s** when the row is being displayed. In this case, the three fields are **image_url**, **description**, and **options**.

That is all you have to do to make sure that the product pages are viewed as simple, plain HTML tables.

Creating the Queries

This section covers the basic queries that most Web stores are configured to handle. The first queries that are covered are the general keyword search on the whole database row and the product category search, since they are the most common database query terms. The subsequent cases covered will show how to deal with data types and the different types of comparisons that can arise when dealing with different data types.

The following query cases assume that the database is set up as described below, using the **%db** associative array discussed in Chapter 4.

```
$db{"product_id"}          = 0;
$db{"product"}             = 1;
$db{"expiration_date" }    = 2;
$db{"price"}               = 3;
$db{"name"}                = 4;
$db{"image_url"}           = 5;
$db{"description"}         = 6;
$db{"options"}             = 7;
```

Query on a General Keyword

The first step of any query that you wish to set up is the configuration of query-related form variables. In this case, because we want to do a keyword search, there are three form variables to consider. First, you need to allow users to enter their keywords to search on. Second, you should give users the option to make the search case-sensitive, and third, you should also give users the option to make the search match whole words only. The following HTML contains a sample definition for these form variables:

```
<INPUT TYPE = "text" NAME = "keywords"
      SIZE = "40"  MAXLENGTH = "40">
<P>
<INPUT TYPE=checkbox NAME="exact_match">
Exact Match Search (Whole Words Only)
<P>
<INPUT TYPE=checkbox NAME="case_sensitive">
Case Sensitive Search
<HR>
```

The next step is to set up the **@sc_db_query_criteria** so that there is one element of the array that corresponds to the keyword query. Recall that you only need one element for matching against the **keywords** form variable. The other two form variables are not actually compared they merely modify how string searches are performed by **web_store.cgi**. Thus, the first field which corresponds to the form variable name will be **keywords**.

The next field must contain a comma-delimited list of all the database fields that a general keyword search should be performed on. Since this is a general keyword search, you will want to match against all the text fields in the database. Thus, this field value should be **0,1,2,3,4,6**. In this example, field number 5 is left out because it is an image URL that should not be searched because an image is a picture, not text. Remember, fields in Perl start counting at 0.

Finally, the operator is set to equal (=) and the data type is set to **string** for doing string-based keyword searches. The resulting **@sc_db_query_criteria** code appears below:

```
@sc_db_query_criteria
     = ("keywords|0,1,2,3,4,6|=|string)
```

Query on a Single Product Category

Another popular search can be done to let the user choose a specific category of the database to browse. In this case, although only one form variable will be used, there are many different ways to present the choice of several different categories to the user.

One possibility is that you may wish to present the user with a static list of HTML hypertext references to a page representing each product category. This would be represented with the following HTML in the front page and is discussed in Chapter 4:

```
<A HREF=web_store.cgi?cart_id=&product=Vowels>
Vowels</A><BR>
<A HREF=web_store.cgi?cart_id=&product=Letters>
Letters</A><BR>
<A HREF=web_store.cgi?cart_id=&product=Numbers>
Numbers</A>
```

Another possibility is that the user may want to select from a drop-down menu of items as part of a **<SELECT>** tag. This option is presented below:

```
<SELECT NAME=product>
<OPTION VALUE=Vowels>Vowels
<OPTION VALUE=Letters>Letters
<OPTION VALUE=Numbers>Numbers
</SELECT>
```

If neither of these methods will be used, it can suffice to have a standard text **<INPUT>** tag to allow the user to enter a product name just like the keyword search that was discussed above.

Once the HTML form has been coded using the above tags, the **@sc_db_query_criteria** is easy to construct. The form variable name is product. There is only one database field that corresponds to the product category. In our example, the database index of the product category is **1**. Finally, just like the keyword search, the data type is **string** and the comparison operator is equals (=). The code below shows a sample of what **@sc_db_query_criteria** will look like:

```
@sc_db_query_criteria
    = (product|1|=|string);
```

Query on an Exact Value

Querying on one specific value, such as the price of the product, is similar to the previous query on the product category. First, you need to create a form input tag in order to allow the user to enter a price. This tag is demonstrated below:

```
<INPUT TYPE = "text" NAME = "product_price"
      SIZE = "10"  MAXLENGTH = "10">
```

Next, the **@sc_db_query_criteria** element for matching the **product_price** is created. The first field in the query criteria element is **product_price**. The second field is **3** because that is the index number of the price field in this database. The third field is equals (=) and the fourth field is **number**, since this query involves a numeric comparison. The code for the **@sc_db_query_criteria** follows:

```
@sc_db_query_criteria
    = (product_price|3|=|number);
```

Query on Price Range

Querying on a price range is a little more complex than checking for one exact value match. Since a range is being compared, this actually involves two separate queries criteria elements. The first checks for the low end of the range, and the second checks for the high end of the range. Thus for checking a price range, you would need to have two form variables as shown below:

```
Lowest Price To Search For:
<INPUT TYPE = "text" NAME = "query_price_low_range"
      SIZE = "10"  MAXLENGTH = "10">
Highest Price To Search For:
<INPUT TYPE = "text" NAME = "query_price_high_range"
      SIZE = "10"  MAXLENGTH = "10">
```

For each of these form variables, there needs to be a separate element in the query criteria array—one for comparing the low range and another for comparing the high range. The sample **@sc_db_query_criteria** is presented below.

```
@sc_db_query_criteria
    = ("query_price_low_range|3|<=|number",
       "query_price_high_range|3|>=|number");
```

For the first element, the first field is **query_price_low_range** and the second field is **3** to match the price. The comparison operator is **<=** and the data type is **number**. Basically, this corresponds to the statement that the value entered into the **query_price_low_range** form field must be less than or equal to whatever price is in the record for the product in order to produce a successful match. For example, if the user has entered **10.00** into the low range field, then a product with a price of **5.00** will not match successfully but a product with a price of **15.00** would match successfully. This is correct behavior because the user wanted to make sure that the lowest price that matched was **10.00**.

For the second element, the first field is **query_price_high_range,** and the second field is **3** to match the price. The comparison operator is **>=** and the data type is **number**. This corresponds to the statement that whatever the user has entered into the **query_price_high_range** form field should be greater than or equal to the price for the record in the database in order to produce a successful match.

Query on Date Range

Producing a query on the date range follows the same basic logic as producing a query on a price range except that the data type will be **date** instead of **number**. An example of a query date range search would be to allow the user to search on the low and high range of an expiration date. Sample HTML to produce the form variables is described as follows:

```
Lowest Expiration Date To Search For:
<INPUT TYPE = "text" NAME = "query_exp_date_low_range"
      SIZE = "10"  MAXLENGTH = "10"> <BR>
Highest Expiration Date To Search For:
<INPUT TYPE = "text" NAME = "query_exp_date_high_range"
      SIZE = "10"  MAXLENGTH = "10"> <BR>
```

The **@sc_db_query_criteria** would be assigned using the code below:

```
@sc_db_query_criteria
    = ("query_exp_date_low_range|2|<=|date",
    "query_exp_date_high_range|2|>=|date");
```

The first field of each element corresponds to the form variables **query_exp_date_low_range** and **query_exp_high_range**. The second field is **2**, which corresponds to the expiration date. Finally, the comparisons are done based on the **<=** and **>=** operators with a data type of **date**. One example, is that the user could fill in **12/15/96** as the low range for the expiration date. If the database has a record that has an expiration date of **12/1/96**, then this will not produce a successful match because **12/15/96** is not less than or equal to **12/1/96**. However, if the expiration date for a record in the database is **12/17/96**, then this will produce a successful match because **12/15/96** is less than **12/17/96**.

NOTE

The date query mechanism built into the Web store relies on the fact that dates must be in the format MM/DD/YY where MM is the month, DD is the day, and YY is the year. The Web store also supports four-digit years as well.

Query on Multiple Text (String) Fields

Querying on many string fields is different from the keyword search because instead of querying all the fields at once, the user is allowed to enter specific keywords to match individual fields. The form is more complex as well because there must be multiple <INPUT> tags corresponding to each database field that is being searched. The HTML below contains sample input tags for allowing the user to search separately on **product_category**, **product_name**, and **product_description**. Also included are field to allow the user to select whether or not the matches in these fields are exact or case sensitive:

```
Product Category:
<INPUT TYPE = "text" NAME = "product_category"
      SIZE = "20"  MAXLENGTH = "20"> <BR>
Product Name:
<INPUT TYPE = "text" NAME = "product_name"
      SIZE = "20"  MAXLENGTH = "20">  <BR>
Product Description:
<INPUT TYPE = "text" NAME = "product_description"
      SIZE = "20"  MAXLENGTH = "20">
<P>
<INPUT TYPE=checkbox NAME="exact_match">
Exact Match Search (Whole Words Only)
<P>
<INPUT TYPE=checkbox NAME="case_sensitive">
Case Sensitive Search
<HR>
```

The **@sc_db_query_criteria** array must have a separate element for each data-base field being searched. The sample code for assigning **@sc_db_query_criteria** appears below:

```
@sc_db_query_criteria
    = ("product_category|1|=|string",
    "product_name|4|=|string",
    "product_description|6|=|string");
```

Query for Multiple Fields of Different Types

In the final example of query criteria, all the elements of querying are brought together. This example will include a date range, price range, and a multiple-field keyword search. The HTML form must include the capability to allow the user to enter all this criteria. Sample HTML appears below:

```
Product Category:
<INPUT TYPE = "text" NAME = "product_category"
        SIZE = "20"  MAXLENGTH = "20"> <BR>
Product Name:
<INPUT TYPE = "text" NAME = "product_name"
        SIZE = "20"  MAXLENGTH = "20">  <BR>
Product Description:
<INPUT TYPE = "text" NAME = "product_description"
        SIZE = "20"  MAXLENGTH = "20">
<P>
<INPUT TYPE=checkbox NAME="exact_match">
Exact Match Search (Whole Words Only)
<P>
<INPUT TYPE=checkbox NAME="case_sensitive">
Case Sensitive Search<P>
Lowest Expiration Date To Search For:
<INPUT TYPE = "text" NAME = "query_exp_date_low_range"
        SIZE = "10"  MAXLENGTH = "10"> <BR>
Highest Expiration Date To Search For:
<INPUT TYPE = "text" NAME = "query_exp_date_high_range"
        SIZE = "10"  MAXLENGTH = "10"> <BR>
Lowest Price To Search For:
<INPUT TYPE = "text" NAME = "query_price_low_range"
        SIZE = "10"  MAXLENGTH = "10">
```

```
Highest Price To Search For:
<INPUT TYPE = "text" NAME = "query_price_high_range"
       SIZE = "10"  MAXLENGTH = "10">
```

Finally, an **@sc_db_query_criteria** array must be constructed to allow all these form variables to be matched. This job is easy because it involves setting up all the elements discussed previously. The final **@sc_db_query_criteria** array code appears below:

```
@sc_db_query_criteria
= ("product_category|1|=|string",
   "product_name|4|=|string",
   "product_description|6|=|string",
   "query_exp_date_low_range|2|<=|date",
   "query_exp_date_high_range|2|>=|date",
   "query_price_low_range|3|<=|number",
   "query_price_high_range|3|>=|number");
```

Summary

In conclusion, the examples above show that **@sc_db_query_criteria** is a highly flexible variable that allows for a variety of querying to take place on an ASCII text database file. This query mechanism is not available with the HTML version of the Web store. By merely adjusting the form variables and the array, many different ways of viewing the data can be presented to the user—from simple product category matches to full-blown queries based on the data type of each database field. In addition, we introduced how adjusting the **$sc_product_display_row**–related variables in the Setup file allows you to change the look and feel of the Database store so that the products are viewed in a tabular format.

CHAPTER SIX

FOCUS ON

THE FRAMES INTERFACE

In the ever-expanding, high-paced world of Web development, companies are forced continually to modify and upgrade their Web sites in order to take advantage of every new technological bell and whistle made available by browser manufacturers. The Web has become an MTV medium in which presentation becomes nearly as important as content. A site with yesterday's technology, especially an online store, risks becoming a deleted bookmark. For better or worse, the Web demands perpetual activity on the part of the companies that populate it.

One of the more recent technological advancements to have hit the is that of Frames. Frames allow you to not just utilize the presentation of your information within the browser window, but they also allow you to change the nature of the browser window itself. Frames give you the ability to break the base window into separate cells (or frames) as if each were its own browser. Each frame has its own history list and can be manipulated independently of every other frame, or it can be used to change the contents of other frames.

As with any HTML tag, Frames can be a very useful method of helping your customers get to the information they want as quickly as possible. However, when used poorly, Frames can also be atrocious and can actually make browsing your site awkward. We recommend that before you modify your site to include Frames, you make a careful study of what works and what does not. After all, the more powerful our tools, the easier for us to misuse them. A large list of Web store implementations can be found at the following URL:

```
http://www.eff.org/~erict/Scripts/web_store.html
```

Many of the stores on the list take advantage of Frames. We recommend you browse through the list before you settle upon your own design.

However, once you have decided that Frames will enhance your own catalog, making Frames work with the Web store is a fairly simple process. This chapter will discuss what changes you will need to make to your scripts in order to adopt a Frames interface.

What Are Frames?

Though it is not within the scope of this book to present a detailed discussion of the HTML necessary to build complex Frames-based Web sites, we will take a moment to introduce the main tags which we use in our examples.

 One good resource on Frames is O'Reilly's, "HTML: The Definitive Guide" written by Musciano and Kennedy. There are also many other HTML Frames references available.

NOTE

The basic components of a Frames-based site consist of three HTML tags: <FRAMESET>, <FRAME>, and <NOFRAME>.

<FRAMESET> defines the collection of Frames that will describe the browser window. The <FRAMESET> tag takes two attributes, **ROWS** and **COLS,** which define how many rows and columns you will break the base window into and how much of the available screen each frame will take up. Thus, the following tag would create two equal-sized rows of frames, each with three equal-sized frame cells:

```
<FRAMESET ROWS = "50%, 50%"
          COLS = "33%, 33%, 33%">
```

What actually goes within a frame cell is defined by the <FRAME> tag. The <FRAME> tag takes several attributes including **MARGINHEIGHT, MARGINWIDTH, NAME, NORESIZE, SCROLLING,** and **SRC**. However, for the purposes of the Frames implementations which we use, the **SRC** and **NAME** attributes will be enough.

The **SRC** attribute defines the location of the object that will be loaded into the frame cell while the **NAME** attribute defines what the frame cell will be referred to within the entire frame document.

For example, consider the following <FRAME> tag

```
<FRAME SRC = "frontpage.html" NAME = "main">
```

In this example, the frame cell will display within it the contents of the document **frontpage.html**. Further, it may be referred to as **main** by other objects in the window. Thus, the following hyperlink when clicked would cause **Vowels.html** to be loaded in the Frame defined above (replacing **frontpage.html**).

```
<A HREF = "Vowels.html" TARGET = "main">
```

Thus, by using the **TARGET** parameter, we are able to affect the contents of any named frame.

Finally, the <NOFRAMES> and its corresponding </NOFRAMES> tags are used to define a default HTML page for browsers that do not support Frames technology. Thus, you might include the following section in any site based on Frames:

```
<NOFRAMES>
We are sorry, but this site takes advantage of Frames.  Why not con-
sider upgrading your browser to Netscape 3.0
</NOFRAMES>
```

Setting up the Web Store to Use Frames

As stated earlier, using a Frames-based Web store is pretty simple. In fact, you need only change a few aspects of the interface. Almost every other setup factor will depend on whether you use a Database or HTML back end. But your choice of back end you use makes no difference in the Frames interface. The Frames interface can handle either choice.

In fact, there are really only two things that you need to do in order to transform your Web store into a Frames-based Web store. First, you must make sure to create all the elements the frames that you wish to display. Second, you must make sure not to fall prey to endlessly recursive front pages.

Let us first deal with preparing the elements of the frames displays. In the sample Frames store we provide in the distribution as **web_store.setup.frames** (notice that we use a Database store back end by default), the interface is divided into three frames. Figure 6.1 shows the results of **frames_frontpage.html** on the Web:

```
<HTML>
<HEAD>
<TITLE>Selena Sol's Meme Mart</TITLE>
</HEAD>
<FRAMESET COLS = "111, 80%">
<FRAMESET ROWS = "90, 60%">
<FRAME SRC = "web_store.cgi?page=../home.html&cart_id="
        SCROLLING = "no">
<FRAME SRC = "web_store.cgi?page=../toc.html&cart_id="
        SCROLLING = "auto">
</FRAMESET>
<FRAME NAME = "main"
        SRC = "web_store.cgi?page=../outlet_frontpage_db.
            html&cart_id=">
</FRAMESET>
```

As you can see, **frames_frontpage.html** defines the frames-based interface as having two navigational frames and one display frame.

The first navigational frame simply loads a static HTML document referencing the front page with the following code:

```
<CENTER>
<A HREF = "web_store.cgi?cart_id=&page=../outlet_frontpage_db.html"
    TARGET = "main">
<IMG SRC = "Html/Images/animated_circuit.gif"
        BORDER = "0"></A>
<BR>Meme Mart Home
</CENTER>
```

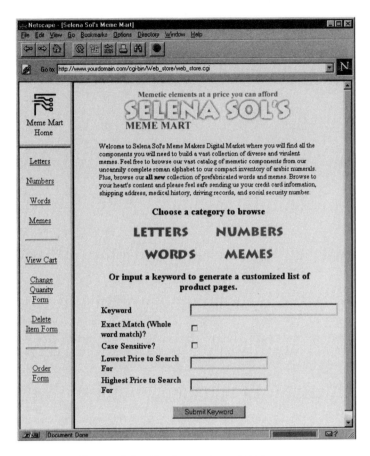

Figure 6.1   The Frames-based Web store.

The link, when clicked, instructs the Web browser to use **web_store.cgi** to load **outlet_frontpage.db.html** into the main window.

The second navigational window is the primary navigational frame which provides links for every place in the store with the following code:

```
<CENTER>
<A HREF = "web_store.cgi?page=Letters.html.db&cart_id="
   TARGET = "main">Letters</A>
<P>
<A HREF = "web_store.cgi?product=Numbers&cart_id="
   TARGET = "main">Numbers</A>
```

```
<P>
<A HREF = "web_store.cgi?product=Words&cart_id="
   TARGET = "main">Words</A>
<P>
<A HREF = "web_store.cgi?product=Memes&cart_id="
   TARGET = "main">Memes</A>
<P><HR><P>
<A HREF = "web_store.cgi?modify_cart_button=yes&cart_id="
   TARGET = "main">View Cart</A>
<P>
<A HREF = "web_store.cgi?change_quantity_button=yes&cart_id="
   TARGET = "main">Change Quanity Form</A>
<P>
<A HREF = "web_store.cgi?delete_item_button=yes&cart_id="
   TARGET = "main">Delete Item Form</A>
<P><HR><P>
<A HREF = "web_store.cgi?order_form_button=yes&cart_id="
   TARGET = "main">Order Form</A>
</CENTER>
```

This is basically the familiar list of products page discussed in Chapter 3 and Chapter 4, with the bonus of a set of cart manipulation links. The navigational frame becomes a site map allowing customers to jump anywhere in the site regardless of where they are located.

Finally, the browser includes a "main" frame into which all subsequent store pages are loaded. Initially, **outlet_frontpage_db.html** is loaded into the frame.

One crucial thing to note about the use of frames is that every frame is filtered through **web_store.cgi**. As you will recall from previous chapters, it is essential that no HTML page be introduced to the customer without its first being filtered through the script. As always, every link includes the **cart_id=** flag which the script will recognize and replace with the actual unique cart i.d. of the customer when it loads **frames_frontpage.html**.

The second issue to deal with when creating a Frames interface is the variable **$sc_no_frames_button** defined in the Setup file. **$sc_no_frames_button** must be set to nothing if frames are to work. The reason for this is that frames have the nasty possibility of creating endlessly recursive front pages. That is, consider what would happen if you had the **Return to Frontpage** button in the "main" window. If the customer clicked on it, the **frames_frontpage.html** file would be loaded inside the main frame. Thus, the main frame would be subdivided into the three basic frames. Figure 6.2 depicts this unfortunate situation.

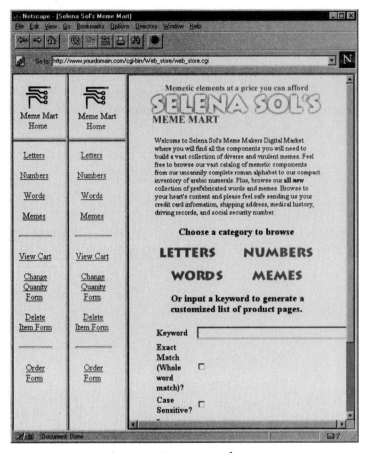

Figure 6.2 Recursive frames.

This could go on indefinitely until the browser fails. Thus, we have isolated out the Return to Frontpage button into a setup variable. If you set this variable equal to nothing, then you will not get a button in your main window and will only be able to reload the front page from the top left frame which will reference **outlet_frontpage.html** instead of **frames_frontpage.html**.

Summary

In summary, to utilize a Frames-based interface, you must do two things. First, you must create the HTML pages that will fill the frames divided within the browser window. Plus, each of these HTML pages must be filtered through **web_store.cgi** before it is displayed in the frame however.

Finally, in the Setup file you must set **$sc_no_frames_button** equal to nothing so that you will not create recursive frames within your browser window.

CHAPTER SEVEN

FOCUS ON JAVASCRIPT

AND VBSCRIPT EXTENSIONS

Among the more creative and interesting ways to enhance the Web store is through advanced HTML tags. Today, among the most advanced of these tags are those that make your HTML come alive inside your browser. JavaScript and VBScript are both scripting languages whose programs actually reside inside the HTML document.

This situation differs from both CGI/PERL scripts as well as the new Java language. CGI/PERL scripts run on the server, whereas JavaScript and VBScript scripts run inside your browser. That is, although the JavaScript and VBScript code exists inside the HTML document, the code does not actually run until it is downloaded into the user's Web browser that is responsible for the execution of the code. CGI/PERL scripts, on the other hand, run on the Web server and simply send HTML back to the browser. Once the HTML has been sent to the user, the CGI/PERL script has finished processing. In contrast, JavaScript and VBScript embedded in HTML documents, however, actually start running after the whole document has been transferred to the user's browser. Furthermore, they continue to run as long as the user keeps displaying the HTML document with the JavaScript or VBScript code.

Although they run in the browser, Java applets are actually individual programs that are downloaded with the HTML document but are nonetheless separate compiled entities apart from the HTML document. JavaScript and VBScript, on the other hand, are extensions of the HTML document itself. They are compiled on the user's browser. Java applets are precompiled before they are even downloaded to the user's browser.

Because the Web store is so flexible in allowing you to change the HTML look and feel of the store, you can change the HTML in many different ways. A natural extension is that you can add JavaScript and VBScript enhancements to your store by adding the appropriate code to the HTML output of the Web store. The majority of the enhancements used to spice up an online store usually involve graphical tricks with a scripting language. For example, a programmer might make a frames menu that makes the menu item images change color and shape as the user's pointer moves over them. You can see such an enhancement at: http://www.americal.com/.

In this chapter, the use of JavaScript and VBScript are illustrated to demonstrate more practical ways to enhance your store besides simple cosmetic changes. As a demonstration, we will add a utility that allows customers to automatically calculate in real time the potential cost of adding items to their carts, including the calculation of option costs. For the sake of completeness, both JavaScript and VBScript versions of this calculation are presented here with comments detailing how they were programmed. Figure 7.1 shows an example of a screen where this calculation would be performed. Notice, at the bottom of the cart screen, there is now a new button to calculate the subtotal for what the user enters, as well as a text box in which that subtotal is displayed.

How to Use JavaScript and VBScript

Using JavaScript and VBScript is not that difficult. There are two key points to remember. First, you can create subroutines to perform various operations on the HTML form. Second, these subroutines must be triggered somehow. These triggers are generally termed *events*. It is beyond the scope of this book to go into the details of how to make your own programs in the various scripting languages. However, the paragraphs below should give you enough background to follow along with the discussion. If you want a more detailed discussion of JavaScript or VBScript, there are many books available.

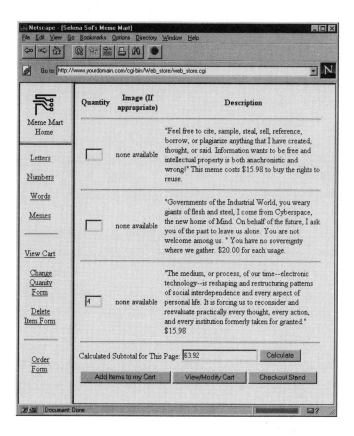

Figure 7.1   Example of JavaScript subtotal calculation screen.

Events

An *event* is simply something that happens on the form or a particular object on the form. For example, a common event that many people code for is the "clicked" event on a button. Whenever a button is clicked, the clicked event fires and the subroutine that is linked to that event performs its duty. There are many other events such as the act of the form loading and unloading, the act of form submission, the act of moving the mouse on top of a control, and more.

In the scripts below, we create a button called *subtotal* and a text box called *subtotal* that is initially empty. There is no magic to this. These creations consist of straight HTML form tags. The magic occurs in the button tags where we explicitly state that when the button is clicked, it will call our JavaScript or

VBScript subroutine. This HTML code will be presented below inside the **$sc_product_display_footer** in the setup file. Recall from Chapter 2 that **$sc_product_display_footer** allows us to specify how the database search results footer is displayed to the user. In this case, we simply add some extra HTML information to allow the user to calculate subtotals on the fly before actually submitting the form itself.

Subroutines

The second part of the JavaScript/VBScript extension is that we need to code the subroutine that will handle each event. We could code the subroutine directly in the footer as well, but typically it is considered better style to program the subroutines in the top part of an HTML document. This is a design decision that is generally made so that if the user hits the **Cancel** button on the HTML form so that it never entirely finishes downloading, then at least the subroutine will be completely downloaded before the button is displayed that would normally trigger that subroutine. It would not make sense for us to have the button definition appear before the subroutine definition and risk the user being able to cancel the HTML form download before the subroutine was complete. Thus, we define the JavaScript and VBScript routines inside the **$sc_product_display_header** of the setup file.

It is important to note that the sample code for the JavaScript and VBScript versions of the setup file are contained in the files **web_store.setup.frames.javascript** and **web_store.setup.frames.vbscript,** respectively.

JavaScript Changes to the Setup File

The core of the JavaScript changes are in the **$sc_product_display_header** setup variable. This contains the calculateSubtotal JavaScript subroutine definition. The product display header is not double-quote delimited. Instead, **qq~** is used below to change the quote-delimiter to the tilde (~) symbol. The first line of the script is:

```
<SCRIPT LANGUAGE="JavaScript">
```

This starts off the tag that lets the browser know to start interpreting the rest of what it reads as JavaScript until it reaches the script closure tag (</SCRIPT>).

NOTE Remember that although the routines are written as VBScript or JavaScript, the actual definition of the setup variables is Perl. Thus, the Perl constructs **qq~** and **qq!** are used to redefine the quote delimiters for the variable definitions in the **web_store.setup.frames.javascript** and **web_store.setup .frames.vbscript** files.

NOTE Between the <SCRIPT> and </SCRIPT> tags are **<!--** and **-->** HTML comment tags. This is a standard JavaScript/VBScript practice. All JavaScript/VBScript code is typically placed between HTML comment tags just in case a browser that does not know how to interpret the <SCRIPT> tags is encountered.

```
$sc_product_display_header = qq~
<SCRIPT LANGUAGE="JavaScript">
<!--
```

The **calculateSubtotal** subroutine is defined as a function and the variables **subtotal**, **price**, and **quantity** are initialized to **0.**:

```
function calculateSubtotal() {
  subtotal = 0;
  price = 0;
  quantity = 0;
```

The entire routine is designed to check all the <INPUT> tags on the form and see if any of the quantity-related text fields have been filled in by the customer. If they have, then the routine checks the price of the item and the value that the user typed in and then multiplies the two together. In addition, the option-related <INPUT> tags are parsed to see if the user has selected any options which affect the price.

In JavaScript, the <INPUT>, <SELECT>, and other elements of a form comprise an array of elements inside of the form object. Specifically, the routine checks through all the elements in the first form (form[0]) of the current HTML document. The length property of an array gives you the number of elements in the array.

In JavaScript, arrays are referenced starting at zero just as in Perl. This is why the for loop is going to go through elements numbered 0 through the size of the array minus 1.

NOTE

```
for (i=0;i < document.forms[0].elements.length ; i++) {
```

If the form element starts with **item-** and the value is greater than 0, then the form field is a quantity field and the user has entered something into it. Since the **item-** is followed by a pipe-delimited list of information about the item, the routine parses it in order to get the price of the item so that the price can be multiplied by the quantity to get the subtotal for that line item.

In order for this routine to work, the price must be the third element in the **item-** definition. This is defined by the setup file variable **@sc_db_index_for_defining_item_id**. In addition, the itemid must be the first element of the **item-** item definition. This **itemid** will be used further below to figure out the option costs.

NOTE

```
if ((document.forms[0].elements[i].name.substring(0,5)
== "item-") &&
    (document.forms[0].elements[i].value > 0)) {
        quantity = document.forms[0].elements[i].value;
        itemname = document.forms[0].elements[i].name;
        itemid =
itemname.substring(5,itemname.indexOf("|"));
        itemname =
itemname.substring(itemname.indexOf("|")+1);
        itemname =
itemname.substring(itemname.indexOf("|")+1);
price  =
        itemname.substring(0,itemname.indexOf("|"));
```

substring and **indexOf** are JavaScript subroutines that allow us to parse strings. The **indexOf** subroutine returns the location in a string where a particular character occurs. In the code above, the character that is being searched for is a pipe (|). The **substring** subroutine takes a string, a starting value, and an optional length and returns just that substring. For example, the substring with a starting value of 2 and a length of 3 for the word *hello* would be *ell*.

NOTE

Now that the script has an item i.d., it must parse through all the elements of the form in order to look for option tags related to that item. If a tag whose name begins with "option" is found, then the **optionid** is stripped out of the definition and compared with the **itemid**.

Recall that an option tag basically has a name that begins with the word *option* and is followed by a pipe, the number of the option, another pipe, and then the item i.d. that the option refers to. The value of the option tag is the name of the option followed by a pipe and then the price of that option value:

```
for(j=0;j<document.forms[0].elements.length;j++){
        optionname =
 document.forms[0].elements[j].name;
        if (optionname.substring(0,6) == "option") {
           optionid = optionname.substring(
                            optionname.indexOf("|")+1);
optionid = optionid.substring(
           optionid.indexOf("|")+1);
```

If they match, the routine knows that it has found an option for the current item that is being examined:

```
           if (optionid == itemid) {
```

First, the routine takes a look at the value of the option. If the option has a value, then the routine determines whether it is looking at a radio button or a checkbox. If the option has no direct value, then the routine make the determination that it is looking at an element formed from a <SELECT> tag. In the case of the select tag, the routine has to look up the index of the selected element in order to determine the cost. In the case of the radio button or checkbox, the routine can simply parse the rest of the option to get the price of the option and the value of whether the option is "on" or not:

```
optionvalue =
document.forms[0].elements[j].value;
            // If there is no direct value, we are
  // looking at a <SELECT> tag
            optionprice = "0.00";
            if (optionvalue.indexOf("|") < 1) {
               index = document.forms[0].elements[j].
selectedIndex;
               optionvalue =
```

```
document.forms[0].elements[j].
options[index].value;
              optionprice =
optionvalue.substring(optionvalue.
indexOf("|")+1);
              } else { // It is a radio button
                if (document.forms[0].elements[j].checked== true) {
                  optionprice =
                    optionvalue.substring(optionvalue.indexOf("|")+1);
}
                }
```

Now that the price of the option has been gathered, it is added to the current **price** variable to get the total price of the item that the user is purchasing. The **parseFloat** function is used to convert the **price** and **optionprice** strings to floating point variables for the purposes of numeric addition.

NOTE In JavaScript, variables are polymorphic. They can be both strings and numbers. However, if they are strings, they need to be coerced back into numbers through the roundabout way of calling the **parseFloat** function before adding them together. Otherwise, they would append to one another like two strings.

```
              price = "" + (parseFloat(price) +
parseFloat(optionprice));
              }
            }
          }
```

The subtotal is calculated by multiplying the final price with options by the quantity and then adding it to the running subtotal:

```
        subtotal += quantity * price;
      }
    }
```

The script converts the subtotal to a string so that it can be reformatted and displayed in a format suitable for money. This means that if it has no decimal point, then **.00** is added to the end of it. If the number has too many decimal places, then they are stripped out so until there is only two left. If there is only one decimal place, then a **0** is added to the end of the string. The following code takes care of this conversion.

NOTE   No rounding is performed in the routine below. Since quantities have to be whole numbers, there will never be more than two decimal places in a resulting price. This differs from calculations done on an order form such as sales tax. Sales tax generally consists of adding a fraction of the subtotal back to itself. This fraction might need rounding. However, on the catalog pages, none of the prices should have more than two decimal places. Multiplying a whole number times a number that has fewer than three decimal places will always result in a number that has at most two decimal places. Thus, no rounding needs to be done.

```
subtotaltext = subtotal + "";
  decimalstart = subtotaltext.indexOf(".");
  if (decimalstart > 0) {
    subtotaltext =
subtotaltext.substring(0,decimalstart+3);
  }
  if (decimalstart < 1) {
subtotaltext = subtotaltext + ".00";
  }
  if(subtotaltext.substring(decimalstart+1).length <2){
    subtotaltext = subtotaltext + "0";
  }
```

The last thing the subroutine does is assign the subtotal to the form element **subtotal** on the form so that the value will appear in this subtotal text box. Then, the function ends and the </SCRIPT> closure tag ends the JavaScript section. The rest of the code is straight HTML code for the table header that defines the look of the product display header:

```
  document.forms[0].subtotal.value = subtotaltext;
}
//-->
</SCRIPT>
  <TABLE BORDER = "0">
  <TR>
  <TH>Quantity</TH>
  <TH>%s</TH>
  <TH>%s</TH>
  </TR>
  <TR>
  <TD COLSPAN = "3"><HR></TD>
</TR>~;
```

Finally, the **$sc_product_display_footer** actually defines the end of the product display table and the form tags that are relevant to the JavaScript function defined above. The calculated subtotal is an <INPUT> tag of type text with the name of **subtotal**. The button that calculates the subtotals is an <INPUT> tag of type button with the name of calculate.

The magic of this button lies in the definition of the **OnClick** event. Here, **OnClick** is defined as calling the **calculateSubtotal()** function which is the function name that was defined above in the **$sc_product_display_header** code:

```
$sc_product_display_footer = qq!
  </TABLE>
  Calculated Subtotal For This Page:
  <INPUT TYPE=TEXT NAME=subtotal VALUE="">
  <INPUT TYPE=BUTTON NAME=calculate VALUE="Calculate"
  OnClick="calculateSubtotal()">
  !;
```

qq! is used to change the default double-quote string delimited to an exclamation point (**!**).

N O T E

VBScript Changes to the Setup File

Just as with the JavaScript version of the store, the core of the VBScript changes are in the **$sc_product_display_header** setup variable. This contains the **calculateSubtotal** VBScript subroutine definition. The product display header is not double-quote delimited. Instead, **qq~** is used below to change the quote-delimiter to the tilde (~) symbol. The first line of the script is:

```
<SCRIPT LANGUAGE="VBScript">
```

This tag lets the browser know to start interpreting the rest of what it reads as JavaScript until it reaches the script closure tag (</SCRIPT>). Note that the "<!—" comment tag is used just as before so that if a browser that cannot interpret VBScript tags encounters the code, then this code will look as if it is just an HTML comment to that browser:

```
$sc_product_display_header = qq~
<SCRIPT LANGUAGE="VBScript">
<!--
```

The **calculateSubtotal** function is defined as a Visual Basic subroutine and the variables **subtotal**, **price**, and **quantity** are initialized to **0**:

```
sub calculateSubtotal()
  subtotal = 0
  price = 0
  quantity = 0
```

The main contents of the subroutine checks through all the <INPUT> tags on the form to see if any of the quantity related text fields have been filled in. If they have, then the routine multiplies the price of the item with the value (quantity) that the user has typed in. In addition, the option related <INPUT> tags are parsed to see if the user has selected any options which affect the price. In VBScript, the <INPUT>, <SELECT>, and other elements of a form comprise an array of elements inside of the form object. Specifically, the script checks through all the elements in the first form (form(0)) of the current HTML document. Recall that this is basically the same logic that we used in the JavaScript version of the code:

```
for i = 0 to (document.forms(0).elements.length - 1)
```

If the form element starts with **item-** and the value is greater than 0, then the routine knows that it has a quantity <INPUT> tag that has had a quantity entered by a user. Since the **item-** is followed by a pipe-delimited list of information about the item, this information gets parsed in order to get the price of the item so that it can be mulitiplied later by the quantity to get the subtotal for the line item. Of course, even if we get the price, the routine still needs to check whether any options have been selected that would affect the final price of the item.

NOTE   In order for this routine to work, the price must be the third element in the **item-** definition. This order of items in the item definition is defined by the setup file variable **@sc_db_index_for_defining_item_id**. In addition, the **itemid** must be the first element of the item definition. This **itemid** will be used further below to figure out the option costs.

```
    if (left(document.forms(0).elements(i).name,5) =
"item-") then
        itemvalue = document.forms(0).elements(i).value
        itemvalueint = 0
        if (IsNumeric(itemvalue)) then
           itemvalueint = cint(itemvalue)
        end if
        if (itemvalueint > 0) then
           quantity = itemvalueint
           itemname = document.forms(0).elements(i).name
           itemid =
mid(itemname,6,Instr(itemname,"|") - 6)
           itemname =
mid(itemname,Instr(itemname,"|") + 1)
           itemname =
mid(itemname,Instr(itemname,"|") + 1)
           price   =
cDbl(left(itemname,Instr(itemname,"|") - 1))
```

NOTE   VBScript has different subroutines to parse strings that differ from those in JavaScript. The VBScript language corresponds to Visual Basic. For example, to get the index for the location of a string within another string, VBScript uses the **instr** subroutine. To return a substring that starts at the left-hand side of a string and then continues to a specified length, the **left** subroutine is used. The **mid** subroutine is used to get the middle of a string. Finally, because VBScript variables are less forgiving than JavaScript if the data type changes, we use conversion functions to convert strings to floats and integers such as the **cint** and **cDbl** subroutines.

Now that the script has an item, it parses through all the elements of the form in order to look for option tags related to that item. If a tag whose name begins with **option** is found, then the **optionid** is stripped out of the definition and compared with the **itemid**:

```
        for j = 0 to
(document.forms(0).elements.length - 1)
           optionname =
document.forms(0).elements(j).name
           if (left(optionname,6) = "option") then
           optionid =
mid(optionname, Instr(optionname,"|") + 1)
optionid =
```

```
mid(optionid, Instr(optionid,"|") + 1)
```

If they match, then the routine knows that it has found an option for the current item being examined:

```
if (itemid = optionid) then
```

On Error Resume Next is a function call in VBScript that is placed here so that if an error is encountered, the script will not stop. The routine will simply keep going on to the next command. This was done so that if the value of an option-related tag was tested for which there was no value, the script would not halt. Instead, if the value is not there, then the script knows that the tag is a <SELECT> tag rather than an <INPUT> tag of type *radio button* or *checkbox*:

```
On Error Resume Next
```

If the value of the option tag is NULL, then the routine knows that the column has to be the result of a <SELECT> tag where it really needs to know the index of what was selected. The above **On Error Resume Next** statement protects the script from crashing with an error if the value is NULL. Normally, NULL values inside of objects in VBScript are treated as run-time errors. If the value of the option is not null, and it has been checked, then the option price is parsed out of the option value. If the value of the option is null, then the script looks for the selected index value in order to parse the price out of the one selected option:

```
optionprice = 0
            if IsNull(document.forms(0).elements(j).value)) then
                index =
document.forms(0).elements(j).
selectedIndex
                optionvalue =
document.forms(0).elements(j).
options(index).value
                optionprice =
cDbl(mid(optionvalue,Instr(
optionvalue,"|")+ 1))
            else
                if (document.forms(0).elements(j).checked = 1) then
```

```
                    optionvalue =
document.forms(0).elements(j).value
                    optionprice =
cDbl(mid(optionvalue,Instr(
optionvalue,"|")+ 1))
                end if
            end if
```

Since the routine has the new **optionprice**, the **optionprice** is added to the price. The FOR loop is executed again to see if there are any other options that need to be figured into the price. Since the routine has been maintaining the types of the variables (numeric stays numeric, strings stay strings), the addition of **price** to **optionprice** is fairly trivial. This contrasts with the JavaScript version where the prices are added as numbers, but later are dealt with as strings for reformatting purposes. Typically, VBScript is less forgiving of mixing datatypes than JavaScript, so the routine keeps careful track of what type each variable is from the start:

```
            price = price + optionprice
        end if 'itemid = optionid
    end if
next
```

The subtotal is then calculated by adding the result of multiplying the final price with options by the quantity to the existing subtotal.

```
        subtotal = subtotal + quantity * price
    end if
  end if
next
```

Now that the routine has calculated the subtotal, it needs to be converted to a string. This is done so that it can be reformatted to display as money. This means that we need to take a straight number and make sure it has exactly two decimal to represent the cents in the display of the money. The code below takes care of this reformatting:

```
subtotaltext = cstr(subtotal) + ""
decimalstart = Instr(subtotaltext,".")
```

```
if (decimalstart > 0) then
  subtotaltext = left(subtotaltext,decimalstart+3)
end if
if (decimalstart < 1) then
  subtotaltext = subtotaltext + ".00"
end if
if (len(mid(subtotaltext,decimalstart+1)) < 2) then
  subtotaltext = subtotaltext + "0"
end if
```

The last thing that the subroutine does is to assign the subtotal to the form element **subtotal** on the form. This form element is actually an <INPUT> tag of type text. Then, the function ends and the </SCRIPT> tag closes the VBScript section. The rest of the code is straight HTML code for the table header that defines the look of the product display header:

```
document.forms(0).subtotal.value = subtotaltext
end sub
'-->
</SCRIPT>
  <TABLE BORDER = "0">
  <TR>
  <TH>Quantity</TH>
  <TH>%s</TH>
  <TH>%s</TH>
  </TR>
  <TR>
  <TD COLSPAN = "3"><HR></TD>
  </TR>~;
```

Finally, the **$sc_product_display_footer** defines the end of the product display table and the form tags that are relevant to the VBScript subroutine defined above. The calculated subtotal and button to calculate the subtotal are both <INPUT> tags of type *text* and *button*, respectively. The magic of the calculate button lies in the definition of the **OnClick** event. Here, **OnClick** is defined as calling the **calculateSubtotal** routine that we defined earlier. There is an added tag to let any browser know to call the routine within the context of VBScript instead of JavaScript:

```
$sc_product_display_footer = qq!
  </TABLE>
```

```
Calculated Subtotal For This Page:
<INPUT TYPE=TEXT NAME="subtotal" VALUE="">
<INPUT TYPE=BUTTON NAME="calculate" VALUE="Calculate"
  OnClick="calculateSubtotal" language="VBScript">
  !;
```

qq! is used to change the default double-quote string delimited to an exclamation point (**!**).

NOTE

CHAPTER EIGHT

ORDER PROCESSING SETUP

The final step of any online store is the actual placement of the customer orders. Unfortunately, this is also an area where a great number of changes are made in order to accommodate the individual logic needed by each store front.

For example, the logic for ordering from some online stores is straight-forward. All the store owner wants is a subtotal of all the items and then uses this total to charge the customer. However, other store owners may want more complex logic including the automatic calculation of sales tax, automatic discounts based on volume or quantity purchased, or automatic shipping costs calculated based on whether the customer wants to ship via UPS, U.S. Postal Service, FedEx, or other shipping carriers.

The Web store order processing has been programmed with these various scenarios and more in mind. Through mere changes in the Setup file, you should be able to accommodate any type of order processing logic you need to express. In addition, since ordering frequently involves the processing of credit card information, we will cover server security related to orders in this and the next chapter.

Changes to the Outlet Order Form

The outlet order form is the heart of order processing. In the Setup file (discussed below) there is a variable that specifies which HTML file contains the Web store's order form. This is the form displayed to users when they click the **Checkout**

Stand button while they are shopping. The Web Store script displays the contents of their cart as well as a form on which they can fill in information related to the order they are placing. By default, this file generally called **outlet_order_form.html**.

You may wonder, if this is a static HTML file, how dynamic information such as the user's cart contents can be displayed inside the HTML form. The answer lies in the fact that the **web_store.cgi** script actually filters the outlet order form before displaying it. When **web_store.cgi** finds certain tags, it replaces them with this dynamic information.

The two tags the script looks for are the form tag and the tag that lets the **web_store.cgi** script know where to place the displayed cart contents. The first tag is the FORM tag. If the script finds any line that contains a <FORM string in it (FORM tag), it will replace this with a new <FORM> tag that actually points to the script specified in the Setup file for order processing (**$sc_order_script_url**). Special hidden input-field tags that include information about the user's current cart i.d. are also presented after the replaced <FORM> tag. For example, the following line in the default **outlet_order_form.html** file would be replaced when it is filtered by **web_store.cgi**:

```
<FORM ACTION = "web_store.cgi" METHOD = "post">
```

An example of the code that would replace it appears below.

```
<FORM ACTION="https://www.yourdomain.com/cgi-
bin/Web_store/web_store.cgi" METHOD="post">
<INPUT TYPE = "hidden" NAME = "page"
          VALUE = "[PREVIOUS PAGE]">
<INPUT TYPE = "hidden" NAME = "cart_id"
          VALUE = "[CART ID]">
```

Also, the tag <H2>CART CONTENTS HERE</H2> automatically gets replaced with a display of the user's cart contents. Figure 8.1 displays an example of what the resulting Web store order form would look like.

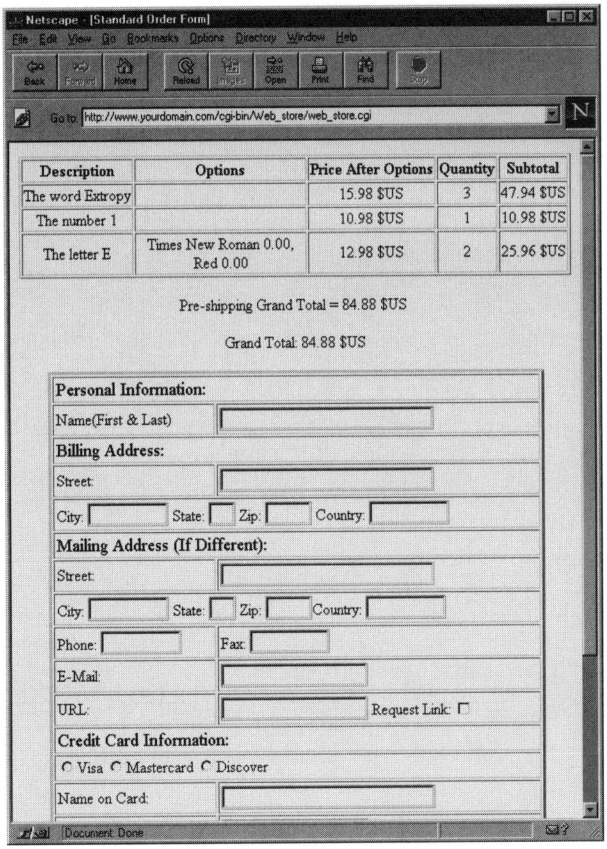

Figure 8.1   Sample order form display.

The rest of the order form contains the actual input elements for users to enter when they wish to make an order. Obviously, users need to enter certain basic information such as first name, last name, address to send the order to, how they intend to pay for the order, and more. In the Setup file discussion below, you will find that there is an array that specifies the names of the <INPUT> tags you can use on the form. These input tags must have two-digit numbers preceding them so that the Web store script can automatically determine the correct order to display the information back to the user once it has been entered in. An example of the HTML that exists in **outlet_order_form.html** appears below:

```
<HTML>
<HEAD>
<TITLE>Standard Order Form</TITLE>
</HEAD>
<BODY BGCOLOR="#ffffff">


<!-- The following will be replaced with
     another form tag plus hidden input fields
-->
<FORM ACTION = "web_store.cgi" METHOD = "post">


<!-- The following will be replace with
     the contents of the users cart
-->
<H2>CART CONTENTS HERE</H2>


<CENTER>
<TABLE WIDTH="90%" BORDER="3" CELLPADDING="2">


<TR>
<TD COLSPAN="2"><FONT SIZE=+1>Personal Information:</FONT></TD>
</TR>
<TR><TD>Name(First &amp; Last)</TD>
<TD><INPUT TYPE="text" NAME="01-name" SIZE="30" MAXLENGTH="30"></TD>
</TR>


<TR>
<TD COLSPAN="2"><FONT SIZE="+1">Billing Address:</FONT></TD>
</TR>


<TR>
<TD>Street:</TD>
<TD><INPUT TYPE="text" NAME="02-b_street_address" SIZE="30"></TD>
</TR>


<TR>
<TD COLSPAN="2">City:
<INPUT TYPE="text" NAME="03-b_city" SIZE="10">
<INPUT TYPE="text" NAME="03-b_city" SIZE="10">
State:
<INPUT TYPE="text" NAME="04-b_state" SIZE="2" MAXLENGTH="8">
Zip:
<INPUT TYPE="text" NAME="05-b_zip" SIZE="5" MAXLENGTH="5">
Country:
```

```
<INPUT TYPE="text" NAME="06-b_country" SIZE="10" MAXLENGTH="20">
</TD>
</TR>


<TR>
<TD COLSPAN="2"><FONT SIZE="+1">Mailing Address (If
Different):</FONT></TD>
</TR>


<TR>
<TD>Street:</TD>
<TD><INPUT TYPE="text" NAME="07-m_street_adress" SIZE="30"></TD>
</TR>


<TR>
<TD COLSPAN="2">
City:
<INPUT TYPE="text" NAME="08-m_city" SIZE="10"> State:
<INPUT TYPE="text" NAME="09-m_state" SIZE="2" MAXLENGTH="8">
Zip:
<INPUT TYPE="text" NAME="10-m_zip" SIZE="5"
MAXLENGTH="5">Country:
<INPUT TYPE="text" NAME="11-m_country" SIZE="10" MAXLENGTH="20">
</TD>
</TR>


<TR>
<TD>
Phone:
<INPUT TYPE="text" NAME="12-phone" SIZE="10" MAXLENGTH="12">
</TD>
<TD>
Fax:
<INPUT TYPE="text" NAME="13-fax" SIZE="10" MAXLENGTH="12">
</TD>
</TR>


<TR>
<TD>
E-Mail:
</TD>
<TD>
<INPUT TYPE="text" NAME="14-e-mail" MAXLENGTH="30">
</TD>
</TR>
```

```
<TR>
<TD>
URL:
</TD>
<TD>
<INPUT TYPE="text" NAME="15-URL" MAXLENGTH="30"> Request Link:
<INPUT TYPE="checkbox" NAME="16-link" VALUE="on">
</TD>
</TR>

<TR>
<TD COLSPAN="2">
<FONT SIZE="+1">Credit Card Information:</FONT>
</TD>
</TR>

<TR>
<TD COLSPAN="2">
<INPUT TYPE="radio" NAME="17-type_of_card" VALUE="visa">Visa
<INPUT TYPE="radio" NAME="17-type_of_card"
VALUE="mastercard">Mastercard
<INPUT TYPE="radio" NAME="17-type_of_card" VALUE="discover">Discover
</TD>
</TR>

<TR>
<TD>
Name on Card:
</TD>
<TD>
<INPUT TYPE="text" NAME="19-cardname" SIZE="30" MAXLENGTH="30">
</TD>
</TR>

<TR>
<TD>
Number:
</TD>
<TD>
<INPUT TYPE="text" NAME="20-card_number" MAXLENGTH="20">
</TD>
</TR>
```

```
<TR>
<TD>
Exp. Date:
</TD>
<TD>
<INPUT TYPE="text" NAME="21-ex_date" SIZE="10" MAXLENGTH="10">
</TD>
</TR>

</TABLE>
</CENTER>

<CENTER>
<P>
Allow 3-4 weeks for delivery. Shipping prices and delivery times may
vary when shipping to cities outside the continental US.
<P>
<INPUT TYPE=reset>
<INPUT TYPE=submit NAME = "submit_order_form_button"
            VALUE = "Submit Secure Order"><BR>
</CENTER>
</FORM>
</BODY></HTML>
```

Notice that the bottom of the HTML form contains an <INPUT> submit button. You can change the caption on this button to whatever you want. For example, you may wish to simply call it "Submit Order" if your server is not really a secure server. However, you absolutely must keep the **NAME** of the <INPUT> tag equal to **submit_order_form_button**.

To summarize, there are four things to keep in mind when editing the **outlet_order_form.html** file. First, the <FORM> tag must exist so that the web_store.cgi script can replace it with the appropriate form tag along with hidden variables that need to be passed along such as the user's cart id. Second, the **<H2>CART CONTENTS HERE</H2>** must exist so that it can be replaced with the actual user's cart contents. Third, the form variables for the order form that are specified in the Setup file must exist in the order form HTML file so that the user can fill them out. (The Setup file will be discussed in greater detail below.) Fourth, the **submit_order_form_button** submit tag must be in the form so that the form can actually be sent to the **web_store.cgi script**.

Changes to the Setup File

Like most of the other parameters for the Web store, the ordering logic is specified inside the Setup file. The following is a list of variable inside the Setup file that affect order processing. Example values for these fields will be displayed below the total descriptions for these fields.

- **$sc_mail_lib_path** is the location of **mail-lib.pl**, which is used to mail nonencrypted email.

- **$sc_order_lib_path** is the location of **web_store_order_lib.pl**, which contains the routines that process orders.

- **$sc_pgp_lib_pl** is the location of **pgp-lib.pl**, which has a routine to automatically encrypt final cart orders for sending in email or logging to a file. You must have installed PGP on your Web server and configured it for use previously. Setting up and using PGP with the Web store will be discussed further in Chapter 9.

- **%sc_order_form_array** is the associative array of form variables that are used on the order form to send in an order. These variables may ask for the user's name, address, or other information. The array maps a form field name with a descriptive name so that a well-formatted email will be produced later.

The form field names must begin with a two-digit number followed by a dash. For example, the descriptive field name **First Name** might correspond with a field name **01-fname**. The prefixed numbers tell the Web store script what order to process the form variables when the orders finally get emailed or logged to a file. Thus, **01-fname** would be processed before **02-lname**. The prefixed number is used so that the Web store can sort the values from the form. If the example order form from the previous section was to be sent, this variable would look like the following code:

```
%sc_order_form_array =('01-name', 'Name',
    '02-b_street_address', 'Billing Address Street',
    '03-b_city', 'Billing Address City',
    '04-b_state', 'Billing Address State',
```

```
'05-b_zip', 'Billing Address Zip',
'06-b_country', 'Billing Address Country',
'07-m_street_adress', 'Mailing Address Street',
'08-m_city', 'Mailing Address City',
'09-m_state', 'Mailing Address State',
'10-m_zip', 'Mailing Address Zip',
'11-m_country', 'Mailing Address Country',
'12-phone', 'Phone Number',
'13-fax', 'Fax Number',
'14-e-mail', 'Email',
'15-URL', 'URL',
'16-link', 'Link',
'17-type_of_card', 'Type of Card',
'18-cardname', 'Name Appearing on Card',
'19-card_number', 'Card Number',
'20-ex_date', 'Card Expiration',
'22-shipping', 'Shipping Method');
```

NOTE

Remember to always define the numbers as *two* digits. This should be done because the array elements are sorted on their string value rather than their numeric value. Thus, a string like **12** actually comes before **3** because the ASCII value of the first character in the string **12** is less than **3**. To avoid this problem, all the numbers in this array should have two digits. In a string comparison, **12** is greater than **03**.

- **@sc_order_form_required_fields** is an array containing the form field names (as defined in **%sc_order_form_array**) that are required fields. The order will not be processed without these field names being entered on the form. If the user fails to enter any of these fields into the order form, the script will inform them of which fields they failed to enter.

- **$sc_order_with_hidden_fields** is **yes** or **no**. If you want to submit orders to another server or to a MAILTO: URL, then you can use this option to make sure that hidden fields are actually generated with the contents of the cart in them. Chapter 9 goes into more detail regarding situations where you may wish to submit the cart information with hidden fields.

The following variables determine the shipping logic. While a brief overview of them is given below, subsequent sections in this chapter will go into greater detail as to examples of their use:

- **$sc_calculate_discount_at_display_form** is a numerical variable that tells the script how to calculate discounts at the display of the order form. If this value is **0**, it tells the script not to process discounts at the display of the order form at all. If the value is **1, 2,** or **3** then the script will process discounts relative to the numbers that are set for other order-processing variables.

- **$sc_calculate_discount_at_process_form** is just like the above variable but instead of telling the script how to process discounts at the stage where the order form is displayed, it tells the script how to process discounts at the stage where the order form has been submitted and is currently being processed.

- **$sc_calculate_shipping_at_display_form** is a numerical variable that tells the script how to calculate shipping costs at the display of the order form. If this value is **0**, it tells the script not to process shipping at the display of the order form at all. If the value is **1, 2,** or **3,** then the script will calculate shipping relative to the numbers that are set for other order-processing variables.

- **$sc_calculate_shipping_at_process_form** is just like the preceding variable but instead of telling the script how to process shipping at the stage where the order form is displayed, it tells the script how to process shipping at the stage where the order form has been submitted and is currently being processed.

- **$sc_calculate_sales_tax_at_display_form** is a numerical variable that tells the script how to calculate sales tax at the display of the order form. If this value is 0, it tells the script not to process sales tax at the display of the order form at all. If the value is 1, 2, or 3 then the script will process sales tax relative to the numbers that are set for other order processing variables.

- **$sc_calculate_sales_tax_at_process_form** is just like the above variable but instead of telling the script how to process sales tax at the stage where the order form is displayed, it tells the script how to process sales tax at the stage where the order form has been submitted and is currently being processed.

- **@sc_order_form_shipping_related_fields** is an array containing the names of the form variables on the order form that will be used in calculating shipping. If you are calculating shipping without regard to form values, leave this array empty. The field names here correspond to the form field names in the **%sc_order_form_array**.

- **@sc_order_form_discount_related_fields** is an array containing the names of the form variables on the order form that will be used in calculating a discount for the user. If you are calculating a discount without regard to form values, leave this array empty. The field names here correspond to the form field names in the **%sc_order_form_array**.

- **@sc_shipping_logic** is an array containing the logic for applying the shipping cost to the order. Each criteria is a separate list element. The fields within the criteria are pipe-delimited (|).

The values of the criteria are equal whole values (such as UPS or 5 or 11) or they can be ranges separated by hyphens (for example, 1–5, 1–, –5). If a second number is left off the hyphen, then the range is open-ended up to the value defined by the hyphen. For example, "5–" means anything greater than or equal to 5.

The first fields correspond to the fields in the **@sc_order_form_shipping_related_fields** array. If this array is empty, then no fields in **@sc_shipping_logic** will correspond to the shipping.

The next field is the subtotal amount to compare against if you are determining shipping cost based on the total sum of money needed to purchase what is in the cart.

The following field after that is the quantity of items to compare against to determine shipping based on quantity.

The next field after quantity is the measured total of items based on the measured field index determined in the cart setup above.

The final field is the amount of money the shipping will be if the criteria is matched in the above fields. If the value is followed by a % symbol, then the value of the shipping will be a percentage of the current subtotal.

- **@sc_discount_logic** is an array containing the logic for applying a discount to the order. The discount is calculated as a dollar amount. Do not make the amounts negative. The Web store automatically subtracts the values in this array from the subtotal when the discount is calculated.

- **$sc_sales_tax** is the value of sales tax. For example, Maryland has a 5 percent sales tax, so this value would be **.05** or (5/100).

- **$sc_sales_tax_form_variable** is the name of a form variable that will be used on the order form to determine if the sales tax is applicable. For example, **05-b_state** could be a form variable that would determine whether the customer needs to have sales tax applied. This variable corresponds to the **%sc_order_form_array** form field names.

- **@sc_sales_tax_form_value** are the possible, case insensitive values that the form variable above (**$sc_sales_tax_form_variable**) should be equal to in order to apply sales tax. For the Maryland sales tax example, this would be an array containing **md** and **maryland**.

- **$sc_order_email** is the email address to send orders to. Do not forget to "escape" the @ symbols with a backslash character:

  ```
  "you@yourdomain.com"
  ```

  must be written as:

  ```
  "you\@yourdomain.com"
  ```

- **$sc_send_order_to_email** should be set equal to **yes** if you want orders sent to the above email address.

- **$sc_send_order_to_log** should be set equal to **yes** if you want the orders to be recorded in a local log file.

- **$sc_order_log_file** is the path and filename of the logfile where you want orders recorded if the above variable is **yes**.

- **$sc_order_check_db** should be set equal to **yes** if you want to use the database routines to double-check that the user has not attempted to fool around with the database by entering in values for items based on form manipulation. The Web store script double-checks to see if the price in the cart for the item being ordered is the same as the recorded price in the database file.

- **$sc_use_pgp** should be set equal to **yes** if you want to use the PGP library to communicate with PGP for encrypting orders. You must have previously installed PGP on your system and set up your public/private key pairs. This process will be discussed in more detail in Chapter 9.

- **$sc_pgp_temp_file_path** is the path where you want the PGP program to generate temporary files. This should be a directory that is writable to the Web server.

The following is a list of example values for the variables that have been discussed above:

```
$sc_mail_lib_path = "./Library/mail-lib.pl";
$sc_order_lib_path = "./Library/web_store_order_lib.pl";
$sc_pgp_lib_path = "./Library/pgp-lib.pl";
$sc_order_lib_path = "./Library/web_store_order_lib.pl";
$sc_order_script_url = "web_store.cgi";

%sc_order_form_array =('01-name', 'Name',
    '02-b_street_address', 'Billing Address Street',
    '03-b_city', 'Billing Address City',
    '04-b_state', 'Billing Address State',
    '05-b_zip', 'Billing Address Zip',
    '06-b_country', 'Billing Address Country',
    '07-m_street_adress', 'Mailing Address Street',
    '08-m_city', 'Mailing Address City',
    '09-m_state', 'Mailing Address State',
    '10-m_zip', 'Mailing Address Zip',
    '11-m_country', 'Mailing Address Country',
    '12-phone', 'Phone Number',
    '13-fax', 'Fax Number',
    '14-e-mail', 'Email',
    '15-URL', 'URL',
    '16-link', 'Link',
    '17-type_of_card', 'Type of Card',
    '18-cardname', 'Name Appearing on Card',
    '19-card_number', 'Card Number',
    '20-ex_date', 'Card Expiration',
    '22-shipping', 'Shipping Method');

@sc_order_form_required_fields =
    ("01-name",
    "02-b_street_address",
```

```
        "03-b_city",
        "04-b_state",
        "05-b_zip",
        "12-phone",
        "14-e-mail");

$sc_order_with_hidden_fields = "yes";

$sc_calculate_discount_at_display_form = 1;
$sc_calculate_discount_at_process_form = 1;

$sc_calculate_shipping_at_display_form = 0;
$sc_calculate_shipping_at_process_form = 1;

$sc_calculate_sales_tax_at_display_form = 1;
$sc_calculate_sales_tax_at_process_form = 1;

@sc_order_form_shipping_related_fields =
    ("22-shipping");

@sc_order_form_discount_related_fields =
    ();

@sc_shipping_logic =
    ("ups||1-10||5",
     "ups||11-||10",
     "fedex||1-10||20",
     "fedex||11-||30");

@sc_discount_logic = ("|1-||1");

$sc_sales_tax = ".05"; # 5%
$sc_sales_tax_form_variable = "04-b_state";
@sc_sales_tax_form_values = ("md", "Maryland");

$sc_order_email = "you\@yourdomain.com";
$sc_send_order_to_email = "yes";
$sc_send_order_to_log = "no";
$sc_order_log_file = "./Admin_files/order.log";
$sc_order_check_db = "yes";

$sc_use_pgp = "no";
$sc_pgp_temp_file_path = "./Admin_files";
```

Defining Shipping, Discount, and Sales Tax Calculation Order

The Web store shipping costs, discounts, and sales tax can be calculated either when the order form is displayed or after the order form has been submitted by the customer. All three types of calculations have the flexibility of being configured to rely on what the customer types into the order form.

For example, some Web stores may be set up such that the shipping is always done through UPS with rigid logic. Other Web stores may allow the user to choose the type of shipping on the order form itself. Allowing the user to choose the type of shipping will generally affect the cost. Thus, each of these calculations also have the ability to be configured such that they only calculate after the order form has been submitted. In addition, each calculation has the flexibility of being able to be calculated in conjunction with, before, or after any other calculation is applied to the subtotal. All these options are discussed below.

The key to specifying the calculations that are performed lies in the following variables:

```
$sc_calculate_discount_at_display_form
$sc_calculate_discount_at_process_form
$sc_calculate_shipping_at_display_form
$sc_calculate_shipping_at_process_form
$sc_calculate_sales_tax_at_display_form
$sc_calculate_sales_tax_at_process_form
```

These variables are numeric variables valued from 0 to 3. If any of them is equal to 0, then the Web store does not calculate that value. Each type of value (shipping, discount, and sales tax) has two variables: **at_display_form** and **at_process_form**. The **at_display_form** variable corresponds to whether the calculation occurs at the display of the order form to the user. The **at_process_form** variables corresponds to whether the calculation is performed after the order form has been submitted (the order form is being processed).

The order of the calculation is determined by the value of the variables (1 to 3). The following is an illustration of the basic algorithm.

1. *Stage One.* All three variables are checked to see if they are equal to 1. If any variable is equal to 1, then the current subtotal is used to calculate their appropriate values. At the end of all the calculations, the subtotal is adjusted to reflect the calculations done at stage 1. The fact that all the calculations are done before the subtotal value is affected is very important. If you wish the calculations to be applied to the subtotal before the next calculation is performed, you merely need to make sure that the values of the variables are not equal. An example will be given below.

2. *Stage Two.* All three variables are checked to see if they are equal to 2. If any variable is equal to 2, then the current subtotal after Stage One is used to calculate the appropriate values. At the end of all the Stage Two calculations, the subtotal is adjusted to reflect these calculations.

3. *Stage Three.* Finally, all three variables are checked to see if they are equal to 3, if any variable is equal to 3, then the current subtotal after Stage Two is used to calculate the appropriate values. At the end of all the Stage Three calculations, the subtotal is adjusted to reflect these calculations.

The following are examples of the application of this algorithm and how you would set up the above variables to accomplish your goal. Various different scenarios are presented.

All Calculations Done at the Same Time

If all calculations are to be performed at the same time, you need only set up the variables so that all the numbers are equal to 1:

```
$sc_calculate_discount_at_display_form = 1;
$sc_calculate_discount_at_process_form = 1;
$sc_calculate_shipping_at_display_form = 1;
$sc_calculate_shipping_at_process_form = 1;
$sc_calculate_sales_tax_at_display_form = 1;
$sc_calculate_sales_tax_at_process_form = 1;
```

If you follow the algorithm above, only Step One will actually calculate any values since all the variables are equal to 1. Furthermore, all the values (discount, shipping, and sales tax) will all be calculated based on the Stage One subtotal. Only after all these values have been calculated independent of each other will the subtotal be changed to reflect the new values.

Thus, if the subtotal of all the items in an order was $10.00, and the shipping came out to $1.00, a discount came to $2.00, and the sales tax of 5 percent came to 50 cents, then the new subtotal is $9.50 after all the calculations are applied to the subtotal after Step One of the algorithm.

Calculations Done at Different Times

If the shipping is to be performed before sales tax which is to be performed before the discount is applied, then the relative variables should be set to **1**, **2**, and **3**, respectively. An example of these values appears below.

```
$sc_calculate_discount_at_display_form = 3;
$sc_calculate_discount_at_process_form = 3;
$sc_calculate_shipping_at_display_form = 1;
$sc_calculate_shipping_at_process_form = 1;
$sc_calculate_sales_tax_at_display_form = 2;
$sc_calculate_sales_tax_at_process_form = 2;
```

If you follow the three steps in the calculation algorithm, then shipping will be calculated at Stage One. Then, the subtotal will have shipping added to it. Next, at Stage Two, the sales tax will be calculated based on the subtotal plus the shipping from the end of Stage One. Then, the subtotal will have the sales tax added to it. At Stage Three, the discount will be calculated based off of the subtotal from Stage Two (with the added sales tax and shipping). Finally, the subtotal from Stage Two will have the discount subtracted from it. This will be the final subtotal.

Thus, if the subtotal for all the items was $10.00 and the shipping was $1.00, the new subtotal after Stage One is $11.00. Then, if a 5 percent sales tax is applied to the new $11.00 subtotal at Stage Two, a sales tax of 55 cents will be calculated and added to the subtotal. This results in a subtotal of $11.55. Finally, if the discount came to $2.00 at Stage Three, the new subtotal will be $9.55 after the discount is applied.

Notice how a slight change in the logic adjusts the final result subtotal from when we calculated all the calculations at once. Since, this time around, we are calculating the sales tax after the shipping was applied, the sales tax is being calculated on the basis of the larger value of the $11.00 subtotal instead of the $10.00 subtotal in the previous scenario.

Some Calculations Done After Submitting the Order Form

Sometimes you will want to produce logic where certain calculations are performed only after the order form has been submitted. For example, many online stores calculate shipping differently depending on whether the user chooses UPS, FedEx, or some other shipping method at the level of the order form. Since it is obvious that shipping depends on an order form variable, in this case we cannot calculate shipping at this time. In addition, the sales tax may depend on what the user has typed into the order form as their state. A person who is out of state should not have state sales tax applied.

The first example where everything was calculated at once would be affected by making the shipping and sales tax variables at the display of the order form equal to 0. The discount will still be calculated just like before. An example of these variables appears below:

```
$sc_calculate_discount_at_display_form = 1;
$sc_calculate_sales_tax_at_display_form = 0;
$sc_calculate_sales_tax_at_process_form = 1;
```

The case of the second example where the sales tax is calculated after the shipping and then the discount is applied after the shipping and sales tax is more interesting. In this case, although discount does not directly rely on a form variable, we do not want to calculate it at the display of the order form since the discount is clearly dependent on the resulting subtotals after shipping and sales tax have been applied. However, if sales tax and shipping cannot be applied at the display of the order form, then we can not apply the discount here either. The following is a list of what the variables would be given this new twist on the scenario:

```
$sc_calculate_discount_at_display_form = 0;
$sc_calculate_discount_at_process_form = 3;
$sc_calculate_shipping_at_display_form = 0;
$sc_calculate_shipping_at_process_form = 1;
$sc_calculate_sales_tax_at_display_form = 0;
$sc_calculate_sales_tax_at_process_form = 2;
```

Defining Shipping and Discount Logic

Shipping and discount logic are defined in exactly same way except that the value calculated from the discount logic is subtracted, rather than added, to the current subtotal. Thus, our examples of how we define shipping and discount logic will focus on defining the shipping logic variables.

Logic Where Shipping Is Independent of Any Form Variable

If shipping is independent of any form variable value from the order form, then **@sc_order_form_shipping_related_fields** is set equal to an empty list. In the example below, **@sc_shipping_logic** is set so that the shipping is always equal to $5.00:

```
@sc_order_form_shipping_related_fields = ();
@sc_shipping_logic = ("|1-||5");
```

Recall that **@sc_shipping_logic** is an array of elements that correspond to logic performed to get the final shipping value. Each logical element is a pipe-delimited list that determines whether the logic is satisfied and the amount of shipping to be applied if that logic is satisfied. The first elements of the pipe-delimited list correspond to the **@sc_order_form_ shipping_related_fields** array. If there are no elements in that array, then the first element of the list is the subtotal to compare against, the second element is the quantity, and the third field is the measured quantity to compare against. The last field is the actual shipping cost to apply if the previous fields are matched.

In the above example, the first field is empty so there is no match done on the subtotal. The second field consists of **1-**, which is an open-ended range. This means that quantities of 1 or greater have this shipping logic applied to them. Finally, since the third field is empty so there is no measured quantity to compare against. Since the quantity of **1-** applies to all orders with any items, the shipping will always be $5.00 (the value of the last field).

Logic Where Shipping Is a Percentage of the Subtotal

In this example, the shipping is calculated the same way as in the example above. Except that instead of a flat amount for shipping ($5.00), we calculate the shipping as a percentage of the subtotal. This is done by simply adding a % symbol to the shipping amount in the field. An example of applying a 10 percent shipping charge is given below:

```
@sc_order_form_shipping_related_fields = ();
@sc_shipping_logic = ("|1-||10%");
```

Notice that the value to apply is listed as the number **10** followed by a **%** sign. The % sign tells the Web store to apply the shipping as a percentage rather than a whole shipping amount.

Logic Where Shipping Is Dependent on Shipping Type

When the shipping logic is dependent on the shipping type that the user selected in the order form, we need to set the **@sc_order_form_shipping_related_fields** to show that this form field needs to be compared against. In the example below, the array is set to the form variable field name **22-shipping**. In this case, the first pipe-delimited field in each element of the **@sc_shipping_logic** array now gets compared against this form variable:

```
@sc_order_form_shipping_related_fields =  ("22-shipping");
@sc_shipping_logic =  (     "ups|1-10|||5",
"ups|11-19|||10",
"ups|20-|||12",
"fedex|1-10|||7",
"fedex|11-19|||14",
"fedex|20-|||21"     );
```

In the preceding example, if the value filled into **22-shipping** form field is **ups**, then the first three elements of **@sc_shipping_logic** are compared. If the value filled into **22-shipping** is **fedex**, then the last three values of

@sc_shipping_logic will be examined further. Since the first field after the shipping type field has values to compare against this time instead of the second field, this means that we are comparing subtotal amounts instead of quantities. The measured amount is also left blank.

Based on the above variable settings, there are several examples to examine. First, if the **22-shipping** field is **ups** and the subtotal is $15.00, then we match the element that says **ups|11-19|||10**. This means that the shipping would be calculated as $10.00. If the **22-shipping** field is fedex and the subtotal is $50.00, then the shipping would become $21.00 since this matches **fedex|20-||||21**.

Logic Where Shipping Is Dependent on Shipping Type and Zip Code

This example is just like the previous one except that the shipping will be dependent on the zip-code field that the user enters as well as the shipping type field. Notice below that the **@sc_order_form_shipping_related_fields** has the zip code added to it. In addition, the zip code range to match against is now added to the pipe-delimited logical elements in the **@sc_shipping_logic array**. The shipping logic is no longer dependent on the subtotal amount in this example. Notice that this is indicated by leaving the three fields after the shipping type and zip code empty—since the fields after the **@sc_order_form_shipping_related_fields** correspond to subtotal, quantity, and measured-quantity comparisons.

```
@sc_order_form_shipping_related_fields =
("22-shipping", "05-b_zip");
@sc_shipping_logic = (      "ups|-10000||||5",
"ups|10001-20000||||10",
"ups|20001-||||12",
"fedex|-10000||||7",
"fedex|10001-20000||||14",
"fedex|20001-||||21"  );
```

If the zip code is 09000 and the shipping type is **ups**, then the shipping will be $5.00 since this matches the element that has a shipping type of **ups** and open ended range for the zip code **-10000**. If the zip code is 20855, and the shipping type is **fedex**, then the shipping will be $21.00 since this matches element with a shipping type of **fedex** and the open-ended zip code range **20001-**.

Logic Where Shipping Is Dependent on Measured Quantity

This example has no dependency on form variables. Instead, the shipping costs will be dependent on the weight of what was ordered. For this example, assume that **$sc_cart_index_of_measured_value** is set equal to a field in the cart that corresponds to the weight of the items being ordered. Also, assume that the weight is measured in kilograms. It really does not matter what the weight field unit is, as long as it is consistent throughout the catalog. When this field is set, the Web store automatically keeps track of this field and keeps a running subtotal of it. Since this example does not depend on any order form variables, **@sc_order_form_shipping_related_fields** consists of an empty list (nothing). The **@sc_shipping_logic** array consists of shipping prices for the various weights. The third field is the measured quantity (weight). The first two fields (Subtotal and Total quantity) are left blank because they will not be affecting the shipping cost in this example. The code for the Measured quantity example appears below:

```
@sc_order_form_shipping_related_fields = ();
@sc_shipping_logic = (        "||-10|1",
"||11-20|2",
"||21-30|3",
"||31-50|4",
"||51-75|5",
"||76-|20");
```

Thus, if the weight is **5 kg**, the shipping will be $1.00 because the open-ended comparison (**-10**) corresponds to **5 kg**. If the weight is **40 kg**, then the shipping will be $4.00 since **40 kg** falls in the comparison range **31-50**.

Shipping and Discount Logic Summary

@sc_order_form_shipping_related_fields and the **@sc_shipping_logic** Setup variables are key to determining how shipping is calculated. Flat-rate shipping can be indicated by simply having one element in **@sc_shipping_logic**, which is not dependent on any form variable. Complex shipping tables including zip codes can also be represented easily by adding form variables to the

@sc_order_form_shipping_related_fields array and then representing their different values and options in the **@sc_shipping_logic** array elements.

The same flexibility of logic that can be applied to calculating shipping can also be applied to discounts. The **@sc_order_form_discount_related_fields** and **@sc_discount_logic** arrays correspond exactly to the arrays related to shipping logic. All the rules that apply to configuring shipping logic apply to configuring discount logic as well.

Setting Up Mail-lib.pl

Setting up **mail-lib.pl** for emailing nonencrypted orders is very simple. The only variables that need to be set are **$sc_mail_lib_path**,which should be set to the path and filename of the mail library you are using, **$sc_send_order_to_email** should be **yes**, and **$sc_order_email** should be set to your email address. Note that **$sc_order_email** should have a backslash (\) appear before the @ symbol.

The **mail-lib.pl** distributed with the system by default is UNIX-specific. It uses the UNIX **sendmail** command located at **/usr/lib/sendmail** by default. If you find your UNIX-based Web store is not sending email, you may need to change the path of **sendmail** in the **mail-lib.pl** file. At line 42, the variable to change is **$mail_program** in this file.

Windows NT and Windows 95 Server Considerations

If you are using a Windows NT–based Web server, you should be using **smtp-mail-lib.pl**. To use this version of the library instead of the sendmail version, copy the **smtpmail-lib.pl** file over the **mail-lib.pl** that is distributed with the UNIX version of the script. Then, edit the **mail-lib.pl** file so that **$mail_os** is set equal to **NT**. If you are using Windows 95, you will need to do an additional adjustment to the source code so that the line that reads:

```
$SMTP_PORT = (getservbyname('smtp','tcp'))[2];
```

is changed to

```
$SMTP_PORT = 25;
```

As of this writing, the Windows 95 version of Perl has trouble with the **get-servbyname** socket call.

In addition, if you are using the SMTP version of the **mail-lib.pl** file, then you will need to make sure that the email address that you are sending orders to is the direct email host that is processing the SMTP mail.

Very large sites typically give you an email address that fits the large domain name such as **you@yourdomain.com**. However, in a large domain, there may be too many email addresses for any one server to handle all the Internet traffic. Therefore, the **yourdomain.com** part of the email address is usually just an alias for another machine that does the actual mail handling. This machine name is usually more specific than **yourdomain.com**, such as **mailserver.your-domain.com**. Figure 8.2 shows an example of how it is possible that the server that actually processes the mail may not always be the hostname that you are sending mail to.

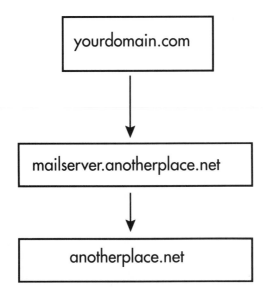

Figure 8.2   Emailing to someone@anotherplace.net does not always go directly to anotherplace.net.

It is recommended that you first try to use your normal email address. If it does not work, then contact your Internet service provider and ask if they are using another machine to actually process email.

CHAPTER NINE

SECURE SHOPPING SETUP

Ultimately, the Web store deals with money that needs to get safely from your customer to you. Thus, it is imperative that security is implemented in any online store. There are two main areas of security to be concerned about. First, we want to make sure that the user's financial information/credit cards do not travel over the Internet to the Web server unencrypted and second, once we have the user's financial information, we want to make sure that it stays secure on our end.

Once users have chosen the items that they wish to order, they need to actually pay for them. Unfortunately, traditional methods of payment such as check, money order, or cash cannot be used over the Internet unless the customer finished the deal by using physical mail to send the money. The concept of sending real cash over the Internet is like faxing a pizza: it cannot be done, or worse, the process will be messy.

Thus, credit cards are a natural means of paying for items relatively instantaneously on the Web. However, with this option comes some responsibility. We should assume that customers do not want their credit card information transmitted over the Internet as plain text from the browser to the Web server where the store is housed. The first section of this chapter discusses solutions to this problem.

Finally, once the order has been completed, most store administrators like to have the order actually emailed to them. Unfortunately, because so much attention is focused on security in submitting the credit card information in the first place, little attention is usually placed on what happens with the information when it is submitted. If your store owner's email address, for example, resides on another Internet service provider (ISP) or on another machine, emailing the order can be very insecure. Remember, email is sent as plain text. Thus, if the email includes credit card information, it can be picked up as plain text. Figure 9.1 illustrates the pipeline involved in ordering a product over the Internet and where something can go wrong. The second part of this chapter discusses how to encrypt your orders so that they will not be subject to prying eyes on the Internet.

Customer Fills Out Order Form

First Name	: John
Last Name	: Smith
Credit Card #	: WWWW-XXXX-YYYY-ZZZZ
Exp Date	: 10/98

If SSL or some other encryption is not used here, the order form is sent as plain text which can be snooped for on the Internet.

WebServer Processes Order Form Using web_store.cgi Script

If PGP or some other e-mail encryption is not used here, the order processed by the CGI script is sent to the store employee in plain text.

Order is E-Mailed To Store Employee For Actual Processing

Figure 9.1   Security problems with ordering over the Internet.

Using SSL and Other Secure Protocols

Getting the credit card information from the user's Web browser to your Web store script is not that hard. All you need is a "secure" server that supports a popular Web encryption protocol such as SSL (Secure Sockets Layer). Most commercial Web servers, as well as many public domain Web servers support SSL or some other Web-related encryption protocol.

If your Web store is being hosted by an ISP, you will need to piggyback onto their existing secure server—assuming they have one. If your ISP lacks a secure server, then you are not entirely out of luck, but your options become more limited. Basically, you will need to find a third-party secure server that will accept the orders on your behalf. Sometimes, you will want this option anyway, because if you are unable to accept credit cards as a vendor, then this third party can be used to charge the customer's credit card for you and then send the money directly to your bank account. To use a third party in this way, you will need to turn on the setup variable **$sc_order_with_hidden_fields** so that the cart contents will be stored in hidden fields that can be submitted to the third party. The reason you need to use hidden fields to store cart information if a third party is involved is because they probably will not have direct access to the cart or database information. Therefore the order form must contain all the cart information as hidden fields so that all the ordering information will be sent to the third party as form data.

The problem with this approach is that it introduces a third party who may or may not be reputable, and your third party will not be able to double-check the orders against a live database of items. Remember, the Web store, data, and cart files all reside on your server, not on the third party's server. If your customers figure out that they can create their own form with "fake" items and submit it to your third party, they may be short-changing you by also faking the price and subtotal calculations that get sent to the third party as hidden variables. You may have to reconcile all your orders closely. For example, a user might easily change a price from 17.95 to 15.95 and order 100 of them at their new "discount". If you have a lot of products, it can be time consuming and difficult to reconcile these prices.

Even if your ISP has a secure server, there is no guarantee that it will be on the same physical machine as the Web server you are renting space on. If this is the case, you will need to make sure that the Web store is set up on the secure server as well, just for handling orders. Additionally, all the data-related directories from the original Web store setup should be available on the secure server as directories mounted over the network. If your ISP is using a UNIX server, making the data related directories accessable from the secure server will be done using NFS (network file system) or AFS (Andrew file system). Figure 9.2 shows an example of how your ISP might be set up if the secure server is physically located on a machine other than where the Web store is set up.

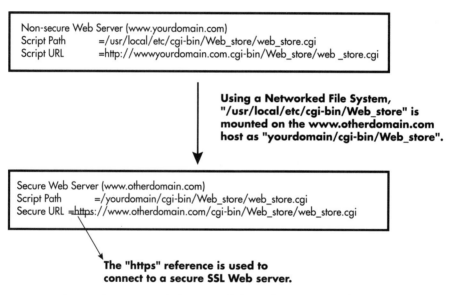

Figure 9.2   Network diagram of physically separate Web servers.

While it is more convenient to have the secure server located on the same machine as the nonsecure Web server, it usually costs more money to maintain a secure server. For example, the certificates that authorize a secure server for action have the DNS name (descriptive Internet name) registered to the certificate. Thus, even if you were running **www.buysneakers.com**, your order form would need to post to **www.yourisp.com** unless you specifically purchased a certificate for your domain name that your ISP would set up for you. Depending on how deep your pockets are, the extra cost of getting your domain name registered with a secure certificate may or may not be a problem. Most people opt to just use the secure server that an ISP has for secure orders, and use the regular Web server for all the other Web store functions.

If you are running your own Web server, you will need to obtain a version of your Web server software that handles encryption. For example, if you are using Netscape server, you will need to obtain either Netscape Commerce Server or Netscape Enterprise Server. If you are using the freeware Apache server, you will need to obtain the special patch that lets it run the SSL protocol. Next, you will need to apply for a "secure certificate" yourself from a signature authority such as Verisign and set it up on your new secure server. Detailed instructions for obtaining a secure certificate are generally distributed with your Web server documentation.

Regardless of how you are going to access a secure server, it is important to understand what you must do in order to enable secure server processing. First of all, you do not need to run the whole Web store in secure mode. Doing so will only slow down the user's browser, since it will be encrypting their entire browsing experience. In addition, the actual order form that the user fills out does not have to be secure. When the empty form is transmitted to the customer's browser, the user enters data locally on the form. No financial information has been exchanged.

However, when the customer actually presses the **Submit Order** button, the server that the form information is posted to must be secure because now the customer's information really *is* being transmitted to the Web server. The URL that is used by the Web store to post data is in the setup file and is called **$sc_order_script_url**. If your Web server is using the SSL protocol, this variable will typically be set to the same URL as before except with an HTTPS instead of HTTP protocol signature. For example, if **$sc_main_script_url** is:

```
http://www.yourdomain.com/cgi-bin/Web_store/web_store.cgi"
```

then $sc_order_script_url should be set to something like: https://www.your domain.com/cgi-bin/Web_store/web_store.cgi

Of course, if your secure server is located on another machine or name, you will need to make the appropriate modifications to the **$sc_order_script_url** variable. Figure 9.3 illustrates how the hand-off works from the nonsecure order form to the secure order form processing.

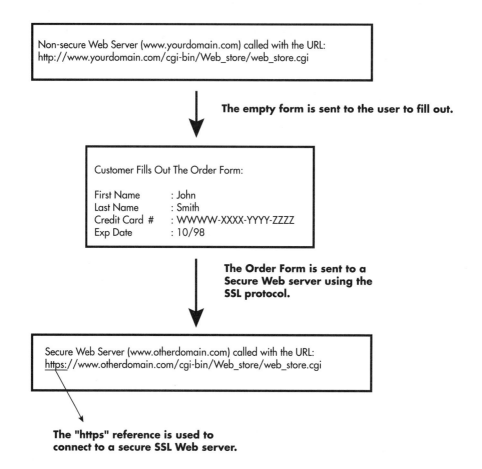

Figure 9.3   The process of moving from nonsecure to secure Web server.

In summary, to set up a secure server you must pay attention to the Setup variable **$sc_order_script_url** and make sure that it points to the secure server. Second, the secure server must have access to Web store cgi script and the related data files. If you are using a third party secure server, then **$sc_order_script_url** should point to that third-party secure server and **$sc_order_with_hidden_fields** should be set to **yes** so that the cart contents will be embedded in the order form as hidden fields that will be sent to the third-party secure server.

Setting up PGP For Emailing Orders Securely

Once the order has been sent to the Web store script, the script has several choices about how to handle the data. The script can either log the data to a file, email the data, or both. In addition, the data can be logged or emailed either encrypted (secure) or as plain text (insecure).

Logging the data to a file is not recommended, especially on a shared Web server. The likelihood is high that other people will be able to figure out how to get into the log file and get information about the orders. E-Mailing the orders is reasonable, but if that email is traveling to a machine other than where the Web server is located, then there is a possibility that someone else may be able to intercept and snoop into the email packets. Such a scenario like this would basically undo all the protection you have been trying to set up by using a secure Web server. The solution to security problems in either case is to use an encryption tool to encrypt the data.

One of the best and most widely available encryption tools is called PGP (Pretty Good Privacy), written by Phil Zimmerman. Keep in mind though, that PGP is only freeware for noncommercial use. You will have to obtain an official license to use it if you are using it for running a for-profit online store.

NOTE

The main PGP tool is useful only if you are inside the boundaries of the United States or Canada. At the time of this writing, the U.S. government is very particular about the exportation of encryption technology, so none of the sites that carry PGP allow people to download it outside this continent.

If you are in Europe, Australia, or some other country, then you will need to get PGP 2.6ui. The "ui" version is developed outside of the U.S. and is fully compatible with the regular PGP v2.6 inside the United States. Yes, it does seem kind of silly that the United States does not allow the exportation of technology already widely available outside of our boundaries. For more details regarding the massive policy debate surrounding the export of cryptography, see http://www.eff.org/pub/Privacy/.

Why do we want to use PGP instead of another encryption tool such as "crypt"? The UNIX crypt tool was simply not made for high security and its encryption can easily be broken. In addition, to use crypt and most other encryption tools, you have only one password, which is used as a key for both encrypting and decrypting. If the same key is used on your Web server to encrypt the messages, then it is possible that someone snooping around may find that key and use it to decrypt your log file or emails. It is inherently inse-cure to use the exact same key to both encrypt and decrypt messages.

PGP uses a different mechanism. It actually breaks up the key into two parts: a public key and a private key. You keep the private key on your local machine. However, you take your public key and configure the Web server so that it encrypts the email using your public key. Even if someone else gets a hold of your public key, they will not be able to decrypt any of your messages. Once something is encrypted with the public key, it can be decrypted only by using the private key. Figure 9.4 illustrates the use of public/private keys.

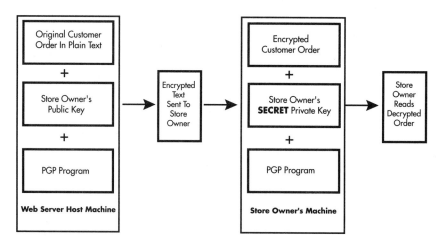

Figure 9.4 The use of public/private keys.

In fact, when you create a private key for yourself using PGP, you typically want as many people as possible to get your public key. Then, all your friends can send you messages that are encrypted so that only you can decrypt them with your private key. Likewise, you want to obtain your friend's public keys so that you can send them encrypted replies that only they can decrypt. Without the special mechanism of having two-part keys, you would always have to keep all your keys secret. With public/private key encryption, you only need to keep your one private key a secret. A detailed discussion of how private/public key encryption works can be found in O'Reilly & Associates, Inc., PGP: Pretty Good Privacy, by Simson Garfinkel.

To set up the Web store with PGP, you need to generate a private key for yourself and the corresponding public key that the Web server will use to encrypt email. In addition, you will need to set up the PGP related variables and do some editing to **pgp-lib.pl** in order to set it up for interfacing with pgp on your system.

Setting up a PGP Receiver (Private-Key)

The first thing that you need to do to use PGP is set up your private key on the machine you expect to be receiving email on. If you are using Windows/DOS at home to dial in to your ISP, then the first thing you need to do is download the DOS version of PGP. As of this writing, the latest copy of PGP is located at http://web.mit.edu/network/pgp-form.html. This is a form that makes you acknowledge that you are a United States citizen or someone else who is legally allowed to download PGP. The International version of PGP can be found at http://www.ifi.uio.no/~staalesc/PGP/ if you are outside the United States. As of this writing, if you are planning on using PGP for commercial purposes, you can purchase it from Pretty Good Privacy, Inc. which is located at http://www.pgp.com/.

Although you can obtain a Windows GUI version of PGP, the instructions here work for the command-line MS-DOS and UNIX versions. If you prefer using the Windows GUI, the concepts are the same, except that you use menus and buttons to do the same thing as command-line options.

When you download PGP for DOS, you will receive it as a normal zip file. You should unzip this file inside a subdirectory called **pgp262**. Unzipping this file will reveal another zip file. If you are using the DOS version of PKUNZIP, use the **-d** option to unzip the file with full directory names. A sample session for installing PGP on a DOS machine appears below. The characters that you type appear in bold:

```
C:\>mkdir pgp262
C:\>cd pgp262
C:\pgp262\>pkunzip ..\pgp262.zip
  Exploding: setup.doc
```

```
  Extracting: pgp262i.asc
  Extracting: pgp262i.zip
C:\pgp262\>pkunzip -d pgp262i.zip
  Exploding: config.txt
  Exploding: doc/pgformat.doc
  Exploding: doc/keyserv.doc
  Exploding: doc/setup.doc
  Exploding: doc/pgpdoc2.txt
  Exploding: doc/pgpdoc1.txt
  Exploding: doc/politic.doc
  Exploding: doc/appnote.doc
  Exploding: doc/changes.doc
  Exploding: doc/blurb.txt
  Exploding: es.hlp
  Exploding: fr.hlp
  Exploding: keys.asc
  Exploding: language.txt
  Exploding: mitlicen.txt
  Exploding: pgp.exe
  Exploding: pgp.hlp
  Exploding: readme.doc
  Exploding: rsalicen.txt
C:\pgp262\>dir

  Volume in drive C is MAIN
  Volume Serial Number is 1F3A-09FE
  Directory of C:\pgp262
  .                 <DIR>        12-15-96  2:31p .
  ..                <DIR>        12-15-96  2:31p ..
  SETUP    DOC       16,253      10-22-94  6:53p SETUP.DOC
  PGP262I  ASC          293      10-22-94  7:38p PGP262I.ASC
  PGP262I  ZIP      275,146      10-22-94  7:38p PGP262I.ZIP
  CONFIG   TXT        4,042      10-11-94  5:26p CONFIG.TXT
  DOC               <DIR>        12-15-96  2:33p DOC
  ES       HLP        4,379      05-06-94  3:58p ES.HLP
  FR       HLP        4,467      05-06-94  3:58p FR.HLP
  KEYS     ASC        5,895      09-03-94 12:52a KEYS.ASC
  LANGUAGE TXT       70,744      05-23-94  6:40p LANGUAGE.TXT
  MITLICEN TXT        2,589      05-24-94 11:56a MITLICEN.TXT
  PGP      EXE      243,097      10-22-94  7:37p PGP.EXE
  PGP      HLP        3,983      06-19-94  5:15p PGP.HLP
  README   DOC        6,768      10-18-94  5:38p README.DOC
  RSALICEN TXT        7,630      05-23-94 10:39p RSALICEN.TXT
          13 file(s)         645,286 bytes
           3 dir(s)       49,987,584 bytes free
C:\pgp262>
```

Now, you should be ready to use PGP on your DOS machine. The installation for UNIX is generally more difficult and involves compiling PGP from source-code files. The installation for UNIX also differs depending on the flavor of UNIX you have. It is recommended that your ISP should have previously installed PGP for you if you feel uncomfortable with compiling public-domain programs on your UNIX server.

The next step is to actually generate your very own private key. PGP contains a list of "k" command line options used to maintain your keys. Typing pgp -k at the command line will give you a list of these options. The sample output from **pgp -k** appears below:

```
C:\pgp262\pgp -k
Distributed by the Massachusetts Institute of Technology.
Export of this software may be restricted by the U.S. government.
Current time: 1996/12/15 22:45 GMT

Key management functions:
To generate your own unique public/secret key pair:
   pgp -kg
To add a key file's contents to your public or secret key ring:
   pgp -ka keyfile [keyring]
To remove a key or a user ID from your public or secret key ring:
   pgp -kr userid [keyring]
To edit your user ID or pass phrase:
   pgp -ke your_userid [keyring]
To extract (copy) a key from your public or secret key ring:
   pgp -kx userid keyfile [keyring]
To view the contents of your public key ring:
   pgp -kv[v] [userid] [keyring]
To check signatures on your public key ring:
   pgp -kc [userid] [keyring]
To sign someone else's public key on your public key ring:
   pgp -ks her_userid [-u your_userid] [keyring]
To remove selected signatures from a userid on a keyring:
   pgp -krs userid [keyring]
```

The first option (**-kg**) is what you want to use in order to generate a private/public key pair. The following is a sample session of making a key. The characters that you type appear in bold:

```
C:\pgp262\>pgp -kg
WARNING: Environmental variable TZ is not defined, so GMT timestamps
may be wrong.  See the PGP User's Guide to properly define TZ in
```

```
AUTOEXEC.BAT file.
Pretty Good Privacy(tm) 2.6.2 - Public-key encryption for the masses.
(c) 1990-1994 Philip Zimmermann, Phil's Pretty Good Software. 11 Oct
94
Uses the RSAREF(tm) Toolkit, which is copyright RSA Data Security,
Inc.
Distributed by the Massachusetts Institute of Technology.
Export of this software may be restricted by the U.S. government.
Current time: 1996/12/15 22:47 GMT
Pick your RSA key size:
            1)  512 bits- Low commercial grade, fast but less
                    secure
            2)  768 bits- High commercial grade, medium speed,
                    good security
        3)  1024 bits- "Military" grade, slow, highest
                    security
Choose 1, 2, or 3, or enter desired number of bits: 3
Generating an RSA key with a 1024-bit modulus.

You need a user ID for your public key.  The desired form for this
user ID is your name, followed by your E-mail address enclosed in
<angle brackets>, if you have an E-mail address.
For example:  John Q. Smith <12345.6789@compuserve.com>
Enter a user ID for your public key:
yourname

You need a pass phrase to protect your RSA secret key.
Your pass phrase can be any sentence or phrase and may have many
words, spaces, punctuation, or any other printable characters.

Enter pass phrase:yourpassword
Enter same pass phrase again:yourpassword
Note that key generation is a lengthy process.

We need to generate 1016 random bits.  This is done by measuring the
time intervals between your keystrokes.  Please enter some random text
on your keyboard until you hear the beep:
1016[RANDOM TEXT ENTERED]

key generation completed.
C:\pgp262\>
```

That's all there is to it. You are now ready to receive and decrypt email. If you receive something that is encrypted, use the command that follows. Let's assume that you received something that was encrypted. The following code outlines steps for decrypting the file along with a quick example as well as a display of what the encrypted data actually looks like before the decryption is done. As before, the characters you type appear in bold. The main step is simply to type **pgp** followed by the filename that you wish to decrypt. But first, the encrypted file sample is displayed using the DOS **type** command:

```
C:\pgp262\>type order.txt
-----BEGIN PGP MESSAGE-----
Version: 2.6.2

hEwDS3ppBLlMyp0BAf90zBPMdkJ3IxEOCrUqnfb7im/U1ilDr2
1s2apl61RnXSvS5k+SrCszHlpE5FHgflsLYoI2tspgAAAbvm7/
+jyMdI8Ob99e06GrjecBSA2ZBz8tYbcYI19OqxJApbmeFE/E/D
XzdBxFko7uCZZCOGr8yW5gU/tPhuqDRTDOoejRJQUf/Z+IH/+W
bwkDyXB+zw4OLWY5Jaest59fTlzaaLAUmKk3slMcb7ZiPzZtAo
lakcnlNnRqmM9H5n2z5OYT0i/bcCQgT7WCwwAW1+2rnsa16f44
5eFJaTw7aF6O4ou0B4vlRRu44UQqCwnsOgIdP+++nVRW2r1Nnz
6PgB3Gu2YdmQpHyM4hD3JXjxGoSS9ndZm2xUkOpBkiek1frXpp
X8zcuuBJIVehFwb4J50ptoAVg5F1Mu4nohq0/Va5zBKGZE23Td
6/UGEyj9p1Gz7ex/m3VAU2Uspdy0NAGmvGHI0P2proKW/h6sa0
02TB8gZTO0eCgNTBr/G4uFXYVs8b8y7JO5gok+NSXtKU/2sQIt
C5FwhrxCZND+q74y0oiycacJD8QHFkJ9yMrZFX+WO91AT1oyoa
3XuJAD0GWAbdzbkXcUTw===jUwS
-----END PGP MESSAGE-----
```

The step below actually performs the decryption:

```
C:\pgp262\>pgp order.txt
WARNING: Environmental variable TZ is not defined, so GMT timestamps
may be wrong.  See the PGP User's Guide to properly define TZ in
AUTOEXEC.BAT file.
Pretty Good Privacy(tm) 2.6.2 - Public-key encryption for the masses.
(c) 1990-1994 Philip Zimmermann, Phil's Pretty Good Software. 11 Oct
94
Uses the RSAREF(tm) Toolkit, which is copyright RSA Data Security,
Inc.
Distributed by the Massachusetts Institute of Technology.
Export of this software may be restricted by the U.S. government.
Current time: 1996/12/15 23:01 GMT

File is encrypted.  Secret key is required to read it.
Key for user ID: yourname
1024-bit key, Key ID C669795D, created 1996/12/15
```

```
You need a pass phrase to unlock your RSA secret key.
Enter pass phrase: yourpassword
Pass phrase is good.  Just a moment......
Plaintext filename: order
```

After the file has been decrypted, the **type** command is used to look at the resulting file:

```
C:\pgp262>type order
Description         = The letter A
Options             = Times New Roman 0.00, Red 0.00
Price After Options = $15.98

Description         = The letter E
Options             = Times New Roman 0.00, Red 0.00
Price After Options = $12.98

Subtotal:           = $171.74

Shipping:           = $5.00

Discount:           = $1.00

Sales Tax:          = $8.60

Grand Total:        = $184.34
C:\pgp262>
```

At this point you would have your decrypted order in hand. The next step is to set up your account on the Web server so that it can encrypt files using your public key. Before we configure this, we need to export the public key from your "key ring" on the DOS machine. This is done using the command line option (**-kxa**). **kx** extracts the key and **a** tells pgp to export the key as ASCII text to make it easier to transfer from machine to machine:

```
C:\pgp262\pgp -kxa
WARNING: Environmental variable TZ is not defined, so GMT timestamps
may be wrong.  See the PGP User's Guide to properly define TZ in
AUTOEXEC.BAT file.
Pretty Good Privacy(tm) 2.6.2 - Public-key encryption for the masses.
(c) 1990-1994 Philip Zimmermann, Phil's Pretty Good Software. 11 Oct
94
```

```
Uses the RSAREF(tm) Toolkit, which is copyright RSA Data Security,
Inc.
Distributed by the Massachusetts Institute of Technology.
Export of this software may be restricted by the U.S. government.
Current time: 1996/12/15 23:10 GMT


A user ID is required to select the key you want to extract.
Enter the key's user ID:yourname


Extracting from key ring: 'pubring.pgp', userid "yourname".


Key for user ID: yourname
1024-bit key, Key ID C669795D, created 1996/12/15


Extract the above key into which file? yourname.asc


Transport armor file: yourname.asc


Key extracted to file 'yourname.asc'.
C:\pgp262\>type yourname.asc
-----BEGIN PGP PUBLIC KEY BLOCK-----
Version: 2.6.2

mQCNAzK0gWEAAAEEAO5CCH8cYH99dECtptItvPEyHUmbo8DLtbrG7rfMuphlxW5j58eYYT
LInVUSLpQQXAea6k7f6uuWYhT8ofbKWKT0YNb1x8YC++EoR6tLxYYsEY11Yj2cbZTng4b9
z/oXLL1BCHkrvXjD5D3dtuBUH/9BwOC55yK0U0VGhonGaXldAAURtAh5b3VybmFtZQ===7
BFj
-----END PGP PUBLIC KEY BLOCK-----
C:\pgp262\>
```

Now that you have your public key extracted from your key ring, all you need
to do is transfer it to the machine that is housing your Web server. At this
point, we will switch to assuming that your Web server is running on a UNIX-
based machine and has PGP configured for it. If you are using a Windows NT
based server, the steps to take would be similar with changes made that are
unique to the DOS version of PGP.

Setting Up a PGP Sender (Public-Key)

On your UNIX system, you need to initially set up your PGP files. First, set
up a separate dummy private key on your UNIX machine account. This will
let your UNIX account act as a real PGP user that can encrypt messages with

other user's public keys. You set up the private account by using the (**-kg**) option in the same manner that was explained before. After you have set up a private account, you are ready to import the ASCII public key into your UNIX server account's key ring. You do this using the (**-ka**) parameter:

```
UNIX:/home/yourhome>pgp -ka yourname.asc
Pretty Good Privacy(tm) 2.6.2 - Public-key encryption for the masses.
(c) 1990-1994 Philip Zimmermann, Phil's Pretty Good Software. 11 Oct
94
Uses the RSAREF(tm) Toolkit, which is copyright RSA Data Security,
Inc.
Distributed by the Massachusetts Institute of Technology.
Export of this software may be restricted by the U.S. government.
Current time: 1996/12/15 20:19 GMT


Looking for new keys...
pub  1024/C669795D 1996/12/15   yourname


Checking signatures...


Keyfile contains:
   1 new key(s)


One or more of the new keys are not fully certified.
Do you want to certify any of these keys yourself (y/N)?y
Key for user ID: yourname
1024-bit key, Key ID C669795D, created 1996/12/15
Key fingerprint =  3E D9 D0 89 A3 53 5F 44  3C DE AD 43 36 70 C2 9F
This key/userID association is not certified.


Do you want to certify this key yourself (y/N)?y


READ CAREFULLY:  Based on your own direct first-hand knowledge, are
you absolutely certain that you are prepared to solemnly certify that
the above public key actually belongs to the user specified by the
above user ID (y/N)?y
You need a pass phrase to unlock your RSA secret key.
Key for user ID "gunther"


Enter pass phrase: Pass phrase is good.  Just a moment....
Key signature certificate added.


Make a determination in your own mind whether this key actually
```

belongs to the person whom you think it belongs to, based on available evidence. If you think it does, then based on your estimate of that person's integrity and competence in key management, answer the following question:

Would you trust "yourname"
to act as an introducer and certify other people's public keys to you?
(1=I don't know. 2=No. 3=Usually. 4=Yes, always.) ?**4**
UNIX:/home/yourhome>

The next step is to test your account to make sure that you can encrypt files with your public key. In this case, assume we have made a dummy text file called **foobar.txt**.

```
UNIX:/home/yourhome>pgp -feat <foobar.txt >foobar.enc
Pretty Good Privacy(tm) 2.6.2 - Public-key encryption for the masses.
(c) 1990-1994 Philip Zimmermann, Phil's Pretty Good Software. 11 Oct
94
Uses the RSAREF(tm) Toolkit, which is copyright RSA Data Security,
Inc.
Distributed by the Massachusetts Institute of Technology.
Export of this software may be restricted by the U.S. government.
Current time: 1996/12/15 20:29 GMT


A user ID is required to select the recipient's public key.
Enter the recipient's user ID: yourname


Key for user ID: yourname
1024-bit key, Key ID C669795D, created 1996/12/15
UNIX:/home/yourhome>cat foobar.enc
-----BEGIN PGP MESSAGE-----
Version: 2.6.2


hIwDRUaGicZpeV0BBACZ3ek41DmwQF3lhWJMWetf+lO9YOU2Y9Q86f27b1GSfjX+HsDh6l
jzz/TqunTFsAXY2H1vTIwCi+M8P4z72Z2t7Bpfw0YnN521W2E31JDXk6xOjsjF8FRkNGfo
ViIPN4iSIQ13KmKK9twles1qkHGsluFnfu7IFuFoGzsXDEeTj6YAAAAtF4tdHVH0cNtgqi
uYurM3qeNiUNj0suEzwjAciNl342It5qfIjX5PhG02Y2gB=/+bR
-----END PGP MESSAGE-----
UNIX:/home/yourhome>
```

If printing out **foobar.enc** reveals a message similar to what is shown immediately above, then your environment is set up correctly for encrypting files. The next step is to set up your Web server so that it can encrypt files using the PGP information that you just set up.

Setting up the PGP Sender Files (Public-Key) on Your Web Server

By default, your PGP-related files are stored in a hidden subdirectory under your UNIX home directory called **.pgp**. Your UNIX home directory is typically the directory you start in when you first telnet into your UNIX server.

NOTE The directory name for the PGP files is called **.pgp** by default. The period in front of the directory name is important because it tells UNIX to hide the file when you do a normal directory listing. If you wish to see hidden files, use the (**-a**) command-line parameter **ls** to list all files.

Under the **Web_store** distribution, there is a directory called **Pgpfiles**. Take the resulting files from your **.pgp** directory and copy them into the **Pgpfiles** directory. To do this on UNIX, make sure you are currently in the **Pgpfiles** directory under **Web_store** and issue the command **cp ~/.pgp/* .** . The **cp** command copies all files under the **.pgp** directory under your home directory (indicated by a tilde (~) into the current directory (indicated by a single period).

The files that can be found in the **.pgp** directory are **config.txt**, **pubring.bak**, **pubring.pgp**, **randseed.bin**, and **secring.pgp**. Although you are going to copy all these files to the **Pgpfiles** directory, recall that the setup described here only specified making your real private key on your DOS machine. You export only the public key from your DOS machine and import it to your UNIX account. Your UNIX account should not have your private key in it when you copy the files to the **Pgpfiles** directory.

Make sure that the Web server has permission to read these files using the instructions previously illustrated in Chapter 1. Finally, edit the **pgp-lib.pl** file to make sure that the settings are correct for your Web server. Specifically, you must edit the following variables:

- **$pgp_path** is the path and filename where the PGP executable is located.

- **$pgp_public_key_user_id** is the username of the public key you are going to use to encrypt the data. To be consistent with the examples given here, we would make **$pgp_public_key_user_id = "yourname"**.

- **$pgp_config_files** is the full path to where the Web_store/Pgpfiles directory is located on your UNIX server.

Finally, you must edit the Setup file and change the PGP-related variables to suit your environment. The following is a list of PGP-related variables in the Setup file:

- **$sc_pgp_lib_path** is the path and filename where **pgp-lib.pl** is located.

- **$sc_use_pgp** is set to yes if you wish to start using PGP encryption.

- **$sc_pgp_temp_file_path** is set to the path where you wish to store PGP files temporarily. You must set this to a directory that is writable by the Web server. The default is to store the PGP temporary files inside the **Admin_files** directory.

Summary

After all these steps, you should finally be able to use PGP to encrypt your orders. Keep in mind that the Web server account, not your account, is running the CGI scripts. Your Web server must have permission set up so that it can access the PGP executable as well as the PGP configuration files.

CHAPTER TEN

LOG ANALYSIS

One of the benefits of utilizing CGI in your Web site is the ability of a CGI script to gather and store information about your customers and what they have been doing. Two particularly important types of information are who accessed your site and when and what types of errors, if any, they found.

The Web store application attempts to document this information in two files located in the **Admin_files** subdirectory: **error.log** and **access.log**. These two files are used by the application to store information that might be useful for you in debugging or upgrading the Web store.

For example, by analyzing the access log, you might discover that you tend to be hit at certain peak hours and from certain locations. With this information you might adjust your backup schedules or the content of your pages, or even streamline server speed by getting together with your sysadmin to compare peak statistics. Similarly, by analyzing the error log, you can quickly determine what types of errors may be occurring and/or if you are being hacked and by whom.

This chapter will take a brief look at the log files and discuss how you can utilize the log analysis script to use them to the best of your advantage.

The Access Log

The **access.log** file generates server-known statistics about every customer who accesses your store. Specifically, it appends the current time and date to the list of HTTP environment variables known by the server.

The environment variables are shown in Table 10.1:

Table 10.1 Environment Variables

GATEWAY_INTERFACE	(What type of gateway interface you are using, probably CGI)
DOCUMENT_ROOT	(The directory that your Web Server sees as root)
REMOTE_ADDR	(IP address of your customer)
SERVER_PROTOCOL	(Protocol used by the server)
REQUEST_METHOD	(GET or POST)
REMOTE_HOST	(Domain name of your customer)
QUERY_STRING	(The information coming in as form data)
HTTP_USER_AGENT	(The type of browser your customer uses)
PATH	(The Web server's known paths)
TZ	(Time Zone)
HTTP_CONNECTION	(Type of HTTP Connection)
HTTP_ACCEPT	(Types of Documents allowed by your server)
SCRIPT_NAME	(Location of **web_store.cgi**)
SERVER_NAME	(Your web server's URL)
SERVER_PORT	(The port your Web server is running on)
HTTP_HOST	(The URL of your host)

You can use these variables or others that your specific server is defining to learn more about the use of your store. Although many of the environment variables will be only valuable for specific uses, several can be picked out as broadly useful. These include **DOCUMENT_ROOT**, **REMOTE_ADDR**, **REMOTE_HOST**, **HTTP_USER_AGENT**, and **SCRIPT_NAME**. Further, if your server is enabled with its own authentication environment, you can gather more detailed information about your users through the **REMOTE_USER** variable.

The Error Log

The error log also collects information about the Web server environment and the date and time of the error. Plus, it records the line number that the error occurred on and the type of error. There are currently three types of errors documented by this script:

- **File Open Errors** occur when the script has trouble opening a requested file. This will typically happen if you have set the wrong permissions for files that the Web store application needs, or if you have incorrectly specified a path. Thus, once you have correctly installed the application on your server, you should not get this error. If you do, it almost definitely means that you have modified the permissions accidentally. You should execute **web_store_check_setup.cgi** to determine where the problem is.

- **Page Load Warnings** occur when a customer has attempted to call a page that is restricted. As noted in Chapter 2, the Setup file defines only a limited set of acceptable file extensions to display. If the customer attempts to read a file other than one specified there, the script will die. These are interesting errors to view because they will alert you when someone is trying to manipulate the script for fun or for malice.

- **Randomizing errors** occur when the script has a problem creating a unique cart id for new customers. It is most likely that this error will occur because you have set the wrong permissions for the **User_carts** subdirectory. It is also possible that your server does not support the Perl **rand** function. If this is the case, you should disable this routine by commenting out the code.

The Log Analysis Script

For quick analysis of the log files, we have created the log analysis script which allows you to do simple keyword searching of the log file so that you can compare rows in the log database against each other for similarities. Figure 10.1 shows the Log Analysis query form.

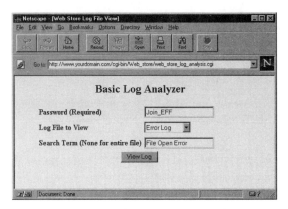

Figure 10.1   Log Analysis query form.

Rows that satisfy your search criteria are returned as tabular-view database rows with all the fields represented in table cells. Figure 10.2 shows a sample output from a nonkeyword filtered request.

For example, you may want to know how many hits you get from a certain IP address or how many hits you get on a single day. Similarly, you may want to see all the occurrences of Page Load Warnings and determine if they are from a sole source.

To use the log analysis script, you must point your Web browser to the script, enter your desired password, select a log file to review, and a keyword with which to filter.

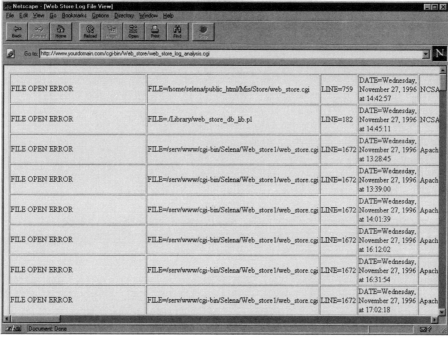

Figure 10.2   Raw dump of log file.

PART TWO

UNDERSTANDING
THE NUTS AND BOLTS

CHAPTER ELEVEN

THE MAIN SCRIPT

Defining the Operating Environment

Like any Perl script, the first line of the main script lets the Web server know to execute this script using the Perl interpreter and where it is located. As discussed in Chapter 1, you may have to modify this line to reflect the location of the Perl interpreter on your local server.

```
#!/usr/local/bin/perl
```

Next, Perl is told to bypass its own buffer so that the information generated by this script will be sent immediately to the browser.

```
$| = 1;
```

Then, the HTTP header is sent to the browser. This is done early for two reasons. First, it will be easier to debug the script while making modifications or customizing because we will be able to see exactly what the script is doing and avoid the unhelpful "500 Server Error" warnings.

Secondly, the HTTP header is sent out early so that the browser will not "time out" in case the script takes a long time to complete its work.

```
print "Content-type: text/html\n\n";
```

Next, the script executes a few subroutines that define the environment in which the script will operate. First, the **web_store.setup** file is read in order to assign global setup variables. Notice that, in the distribution, we have six setup files by default. We will use **web_store.setup.frames.javascript** as our basic example.

Secondary supporting libraries are loaded using **require_supporting_ libraries**, which is passed the current filename as well as the current line number. This subroutine uses these values to generate useful error messages in case the script is unable to read in the files requested.

- **web_store.setup.*** defines many global variables for this script relative to the local server and installation.
- **$sc_cgi_lib_path** is the location of **cgi-lib.pl**, used to parse incoming form data.
- **$sc_html_setup_file_path** is the location of **web_store_html_lib.pl**, used to define various customizable HTML interface headers, footers, and pages.
- **$sc_mail_lib_path** is the location of **mail-lib.pl**, used to mail nonencrypted mail to the administrator about use of the script.

```
&require_supporting_libraries (__FILE__, __LINE__,
     "./Library/web_store.setup.db");
&require_supporting_libraries (__FILE__, __LINE__,
                 "$sc_cgi_lib_path",
                 "$sc_html_setup_file_path",
                 "$sc_mail_lib_path");
```

The incoming form data is then read and parsed using **&read_and_parse_form_data** which simply uses the ReadParse subroutine in **cgi-lib.pl** to parse the incoming form data into the associative array, **%form_data**:

```
&read_and_parse_form_data;
```

This subroutine is discussed in greater detail later. Once we have parsed the incoming form data, we can assign the values of administrative variables to scalars, local to this script.

- **$page** will contain the path location of any pages that this script is required to display. This may be the store frontpage, order form, or any number of product or category pages used for store navigation.

- **$search_request** is the value of the form button used when a customer submits search terms used to generate a dynamic custom product page.

- **$cart_id** is the i.d. number of the customer's unique cart containing all of the items they have ordered so far. The specifics of cart generation and maintenance are covered in greater depth in the next section.

- **$sc_cart_path** is the actual path of the shopping cart combining both **$sc_user_carts_directory_path** defined in **web_store.setup** and **$cart_id** that may be coming in as form data.

All four of these variables are crucial state variables which must be passed as form data from every instance of this script to the next.

```
$page = $form_data{'page'};
$search_request = $form_data{'search_request_button'};
$cart_id = $form_data{'cart_id'};
$sc_cart_path = "$sc_user_carts_directory_path/$cart_id.cart";
```

The incoming form data is then submitted to some security checks. **error_check_form_data** is a subroutine that checks the just-parsed incoming form data to make sure that the script is only being used to display proper pages (typically **.html**, **.html**, or **.htm**).

This is an important security precaution. Later in this script, we are going to use a variable called **page** to communicate the page in our store we want to display to the customer.

The danger lies in the fact that a customer might "fake" a request to the script by editing the **page** variable in the HTML or in the encoded URL. For example, they might manually reassign a page from, say, **Vowels.html** to "../../../etc/passwd"! As you can imagine, this could end up displaying your password file to the browser window if you are running a UNIX-based Web server. Thus, we need to make sure that only appropriate files can be displayed by the store. Typically, these are only HTML pages you will have designed. The subroutine itself will be discussed in greater detail later.

```
&error_check_form_data;
```

Finally, the script assigns a unique cart i.d. if none has been submitted as form data. Every customer who is using the application must be assigned a unique cart that will contain their specific shopping list. Obviously, customers will not share carts.

These carts are actually short, flat file, text databases stored by default in the **User_carts** subdirectory in the format **[SOME RANDOM NUMBER].cart**. These files contain information about which items the customer has ordered and how many of each item they ordered.

Once customers enters the store, they are assigned their own unique cart. For the rest of their stay, the script will make sure that it matches customers with their carts, no matter which page they go to.

It does this matching by continually passing along the location of the cart (**$cart_id**) as either hidden form data or URL encoded information, depending on whether the customer uses a Submit button or a hyperlink to navigate through the store. As long as the customer follows the path provided by the application, she will never lose her cart.

Thus, before anything else, the script must check to see if the customer has already received a unique shopping cart. If so, it will be coming in as form data and have been just assigned to **$cart_id**. If the script has not received a shopping cart i.d. number as form data (**$cart_id eq ""**), it means that the customer has not yet received a unique shopping cart.

In such a case, the script must assign a new cart i.d. number. However, as a matter of good housekeeping, the script will first delete old carts that have been abandoned by using the **delete_old_carts** subroutine documented later in this script. Then, it will assign customers their own fresh new cart using **assign_a_unique_shopping_cart_id**, which is also discussed later.

```
if ($cart_id eq "")
  {
  &delete_old_carts;
  &assign_a_unique_shopping_cart_id;
  }
```

Decoding the Main Script Logic

Now that the script has created the entire environment in which it must operate, it is time to provide the logic for it to determine what it should do. Figure 11.1 shows the logic of this determination.

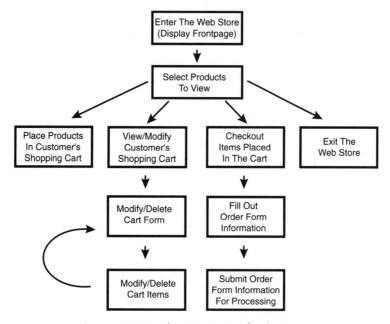

Figure 11.1 The Main Logic of web_store.cgi.

The logic is broken down into a series of "if" tests. Specifically, the script checks the values of incoming administrative form variables (mainly supplied from the Submit buttons on dynamically generated HTML forms) and performs its operations depending on whether those administrative variables have values associated with them or not. The basic format for such an "if" test follows the syntax:

```
if (the value of some submit button is not equal to
    nothing)
  {
  process that type of request;
  exit;
  }
```

For example, consider the first case in which the customer has clicked on the **Add to Cart** Submit button denoted with the NAME value of the **add_to_cart_button**.

```
elsif ($form_data{'add_to_cart_button'} ne "")
  {
  &add_to_the_cart;
  exit;
  }
```

Because the Submit button will have some caption value like **Add this item to my cart**, when the script reaches this line, it will answer true to the test. Since the customer can only click on one Submit button at a time, we can be assured that only one operation will answer true because only one submit NAME variable will have a value.

The beauty of using the not equal (**ne**) test is that, regardless of what the Submit button actually says (it might say, "Add a wiener dog to the chopping block"), the if test will still be satisfied if the customer has clicked the button, since whatever the VALUE is, it will certainly not be equal to "nothing". Of course, this assumes that you do not rename the NAME argument of the Submit buttons. If you do so, you must harmonize the variable you use on the input forms, with the variables used here to test. To repeat, the NAME of the buttons cannot change, but you can change the caption VALUE of them.

Similarly, if you wish to have graphical Submit buttons instead of the ugly default buttons supplied by the browser, you will have to modify the if tests so that they follow the standard image map test:

```
if ($form_data{'some_button.x'} ne "")
 {
&do some subroutine;
 exit;
 }
```

```
where the HTML code looks like the following:
<INPUT TYPE = "image" NAME = "some_button"
       SRC = "Images/button.gif" BORDER = "0">
```

Thus, if the button actually has an X-dimension value (any x-dimension value at all), it means that the button had been clicked.

Finally, note that every if test is concluded with an exit statement. This is because once the script has executed the routine specified in the Submit button, it is through with its work and should exit immediately and wait for the next request.

Get used to the idea that this script is self-referencing. The application itself contains many miniroutines that all refer back this script. Every instance of the script executes maybe only 20 percent of the routines in the whole file, but in the lifetime of the application, most, if not all, of the routines are executed. Next, let us look at each of the routines that this application must execute. There are ten cases that might apply to a customer's request.

1. **Adding an Item to the Shopping Cart** One request that the script may have to handle is that of adding an item to a shopping cart. Once the customer has decided to purchase an item, he or she will have added a quantity to the text box and clicked on the **add this item** Submit button. So we must be prepared to add items to the customer's cart. Additions are handled with the **add_to_the_cart** subroutine to be discussed later.

2. **Displaying the Customer's Cart with Cart Manipulation Options** On the other hand, the customer may have already been adding items, realized she went over budget, and decided to reduce the quantities of some of the items she had chosen or even delete them altogether from her cart.

    We need to send her an HTML form with which she can choose whether to delete or modify, as well as send her a table depicting the current contents of the shopping cart. This is all done using the **display_cart_contents** subroutine at the end of this file.

3. **Displaying the Change Quantity Form** Yet another function that this script may be asked to perform is modifying the quantities of some of the items in the customer's cart. If the customer has asked to make a quantity modification, the script must give her a form so that she can specify the changes she wants made.

    The form is fairly simple. We will use the same basic table presentation that we used in the **display_cart_contents** subroutine, except that we will add another column of text input fields to submit a new quantity for every row in the cart. These text input fields, however, will use as their NAME argument, the unique cart row number for every row. Consider the following cell definition:

    ```
    <TD><INPUT TYPE = "text" NAME = "219" SIZE ="3"></TD>
    ```

    When the customer submits a quantity change, they will be submitting a **cart_row_number "219"** associated with a quantity value (the value submitted in the text field). We will use the cart row number to figure out exactly which item in the cart should be modified.

4. **Changing the Quantity of Items in the Cart** Once the customer has typed in some quantity changes and submitted the information back to this script, we must make the modifications to the database. This is done with the **modify_quantity_of_items_in_cart** subroutine discussed below.

5. **Displaying the Delete Item Form** Instead, perhaps the customer asked to delete an item rather than modify the quantity. If this is the case, the script must display a form very similar to the one for modification. The only difference is that we will use checkboxes for each item instead of text boxes because in the case of deletion, the customer need only select items to delete rather than specify a specific quantity.

As in the case of modification, the script associates the NAME argument of the checkboxes with the cart row number of the item they represent. Thus, the syntax will resemble the following:

```
<TD><INPUT TYPE = "checkbox" NAME = "220"></TD>
```

where **"220"** is the cart row number of some element that can be deleted. We will handle the display of the delete item form using the **output_delete_item_form** subroutine to be discussed later.

6. **Deleting Items from the Cart** Once the customer submits some items to delete, the script must also be able to delete them from the cart. This is done with the **delete_from_cart** subroutine to be discussed later.

7. **Displaying the Order Form** Further, the script must be able to display the order form for the customer if that is what she wants to see. The script uses the **display_page** subroutine, which will be discussed later, to display a predesigned order form.

8. **Submitting the Order** Once the customer fills out the order form, she may submit the order for final processing. Final processing involves calculating order logic (shipping method, tax rates, discounts, etc.), sending the order to the order processing administrator, and letting the customer know that all was completed successfully. All orders are processed by the **process_order_form** subroutine, which is designed to handle all of these chores.

There is one catch to order processing: secure servers. Many stores have secure server functionality in which specific directories are designed to handle encrypted communication between server and browser. In this case, the CGI script handling the order processing must be physically located inside the secure directory.

If this is your situation, then you must make a mirror copy of the application directories and place them all inside the secure area. Then, you will set **$sc_order_script_url** in the Setup file equal to the secured mirror of the script. Then, the script will dynamically reference the secured location instead of the insecure location for order processing. In actuality, only the order-processing routine will be executed in the Secure directory, but we copy the whole script there for simplicity's sake. If you are not running a secure server, you may just set **$sc_order_script_url** equal to **web_store.cgi** and continue the regular self-referencing behavior. This is discussed in greater detail in Chapter 8.

9. **Displaying Products, Categories, and Miscellaneous Pages** If the script is getting in a value for page or for product, it means that it is being asked to navigate through the store. The page variable is used to locate a pre-designed HTML page that the store should display to the customer. In the case of an HTML store, the page value will be used to point to both pages with products as well as pages with lists of products. Also in the case of the HTML store, there will be no need for the product variable since the product variable is specific to the Database store, which must be able to interpret between a list-of-products–type page and an actual product page. This is because when the database version creates a page to view, it needs to generate the page on the fly. Thus, the database searches for the product in the database. If the script needs to display a list-of-products–type page with sublinks to actual product pages within a similar group, it should not go to the database. Instead, it actually needs to display a list page just as the HTML store would do.

The product value will be used by the database shopping cart to pull out the list of products that the customer is interested in seeing. Think of this as a type of hard-coded search of the database where the administrator may define a category to search for in the URL string that requests a product page view. Consider the following hyperlinks as examples.

```
web_store.cgi?page=Letters.html&cart_id=98.123
web_store.cgi?page=Numbers.html&cart_id=8708496.3559
web_store.cgi?product=Numbers&cart_id=2196655.5107
```

The first case could be used in either the HTML- or Database-based version. The script would display the HTML page **Letters.html** which would be a list of products type of page. In our distribution example page, **Letters.html** contains links to both **Vowels.html** and **Consonants.html**.

The second URL would be used for an HTML-based store. It would cause this script to display the pre-designed product page, **Numbers.html**.

Finally, the last line would be used for a Database-based cart system and would cause this script to search through the database for all items with **Numbers** in the category field (by default, this is the second field in **data.file**)

Thus, there are two ways that products can be displayed with this script. The first way is for the store administrator to create a delimited data file with all the data to be displayed incorporated in database rows. The contents of these rows will be displayed according to the format defined in the **$sc_product_page_row** variable in **web_store_html_lib.pl**. The second way is for the administrator to create HTML pages directly with the same data already incorporated into some desired interface.

The administrator specifies which method she will use by setting the variable **$sc_use_html_product_pages** in the Setup file. If this variable is set to "yes", it means that the script should simply output a predesigned HTML product page. Anything else, and it will expect a database.

The **display_products_for_sale** subroutine (to be discussed later) does just that. However, there is one catch to the presentation of an HTML page. If the customer is doing a keyword search, we will have to generate a list of pages on which their keyword was found using the **html search** subroutine located in **web_store_html_search.pl**.

10. **Display the Front Page** Finally, if all else has failed, it means that we are simply being asked to display the store front page, because no other routines remain to test. To display the store front page, we will access the **output_frontpage** subroutine discussed later.

Now that we have defined the cases, let us go through them one by one as code.

```
if ($form_data{'add_to_cart_button'} ne "")
   {
   &add_to_the_cart;
   exit;
   }

elsif ($form_data{'modify_cart_button'} ne "")
   {
   &display_cart_contents;
   exit;
   }

elsif ($form_data{'change_quantity_button'} ne "")
   {
   &output_modify_quantity_form;
   exit;
   }

elsif ($form_data{'submit_change_quantity_button'} ne "")
   {
   &modify_quantity_of_items_in_cart;
   exit;
   }

elsif ($form_data{'delete_item_button'} ne "")
   {
   &output_delete_item_form;
   exit;
   }

elsif ($form_data{'submit_deletion_button'} ne "")
   {
   &delete_from_cart;
   exit;
   }

elsif ($form_data{'order_form_button'} ne "")
   {
   &require_supporting_libraries (__FILE__, __LINE__,
                                  "$sc_order_lib_path");
   &display_order_form;
   exit;
   }
```

```
elsif ($form_data{'submit_order_form_button'} ne "")
   {
   &require_supporting_libraries (__FILE__, __LINE__,
                               "$sc_order_lib_path");
   &process_order_form;
   exit;
   }

elsif (($page ne "" || $form_data{'product'} ne "") &&
      ($form_data{'return_to_frontpage_button'} eq ""))
   {
   &display_products_for_sale;
   exit;
   }

else
   {
   &output_frontpage;
   exit;
   }
```

Well, that's it. That is just the end of the main body of logic. From here on, we will define the logic of the subroutines called with the "if" tests above.

Load Supporting Libraries

The subroutine **require_supporting_libraries** is used to load some of the supporting files that this script will take advantage of. The subroutine takes a list of arguments beginning with the current filename, the current line number, and the list of files that must be loaded using the following syntax:

```
&require_supporting_libraries (__FILE__, __LINE__,
                         "file1", "file2",
                         "file3"...);
```

NOTE __FILE__ and __LINE__ are special Perl variables that contain the current file-name and line number respectively. We will continually use these two variables throughout the rest of this script in order to generate useful error messages.

```
sub require_supporting_libraries
   {
```

The incoming file and line arguments are split into the local variables **$file** and **$line**, while the file list is assigned to the local list array **@require_files**. **$require_file**, which will just be a temporary holder variable for our processing, is also defined as a local variable.

```
local ($file, $line, @require_files) = @_;
local ($require_file);
```

Next, the script checks to see if every file in the **@require_files** list array exists (**-e**) and can be read (**-r**). If so, the script goes ahead and loads it with the require command.

```
foreach $require_file (@require_files)
    {
    if (-e "$require_file" && -r "$require_file")
      {
      require "$require_file";
      }
```

If not, the scripts sends back an error message that will help the administrator isolate the problem with the script.

```
else
      {
      print "I am sorry but I was unable to require
             $require_file at line $line in $file.
             Would you please make sure that you have
             the path correct and that the permissions
             are set so that I have read access?  Thank
             you.";
      exit;
      }
    } # End of foreach $require_file (@require_files)
  } # End of sub require_supporting_libraries
```

Read and Parse Form Data

read_and_parse_form_data is a short subroutine responsible for calling the **ReadParse** subroutine in **cgi-lib.pl** to parse the incoming form data. The script also tells **cgi-lib** to prepare that information in the associative array named **%form_data**, which we will be able to use for the rest of this script.

read_and_parse_form_data takes no arguments and is called with the following syntax:

```
&read_and_parse_form_data;
```

The code reads as follows:

```
sub read_and_parse_form_data
  {
  &ReadParse(*form_data);
  }
```

Error Check Form Data

error_check_form_data is responsible for checking to make sure that only authorized pages are viewable using this application. It takes no arguments and is called with the following syntax:

```
&error_check_form_data;
```

The routine simply checks to make sure that the page variable extension is not one defined in the Setup file as an appropriate extension such as **.html** or **.htm**, or that there is no customer-definable page being requested for display. If, however, these conditions exist, the script will send a warning to the customer, append the error log, and exit.

@acceptable_file_extensions_to_display is an array of acceptable file extensions defined in the Setup file. To be more—or less—restrictive, just modify this list. Specifically, for each extension defined in the Setup file, if the value of the page variable coming in from the form (**$page**) is like the extension (**=~ /$file_extension/**) or (**||**) there is no value for page (**eq ""**), we will set **$valid_extension** equal to "yes."

```
sub error_check_form_data
  {
  foreach $file_extension
        (@acceptable_file_extensions_to_display)
    {
    if ($page =~ /$file_extension/ || $page eq "")
```

```
        {
        $valid_extension = "yes";
        }
    }
```

Next, the script checks to see if **$valid_extension** has been set to "yes."

If the value for page satisfied any of the extensions in **@acceptable_file_extensions_to_display**, the script will have set **$valid_extension** equal to "yes" in the previous routine. If the value is set to "yes," the subroutine will go on with it's work. Otherwise it will exit with a warning and write to the error log if appropriate.

Notice that we pass three parameters to the **update_error_log** subroutine. The subroutine gets a warning, the name of the file, and the line number of the error.

$sc_page_load_security_warning is a variable set in **web_store.setup**. If you want to give a more or less informative error message, you are welcome to change the text there.

```
if ($valid_extension ne "yes")
    {
    print "$sc_page_load_security_warning";
    &update_error_log("PAGE LOAD WARNING", __FILE__,
                      __LINE__);
    exit;
    }
  }
```

Deleting Old Carts

delete_old_carts is a subroutine used to prune the Carts directory, cleaning out all the old carts after a time interval defined in the Setup file. It takes no arguments and is called with the following syntax:

```
&delete_old_carts;
```

The code is explained below:

```
sub delete_old_carts
  {
```

The subroutine begins by grabbing a listing of all of the customer-created shopping carts in the **User_carts** directory. It then opens (**opendir**) the directory and reads the contents (**readir**) using grep and pattern-matching for **.cart** to grab every file in the **User_carts** directory. Then it closes the directory. If the script has any trouble opening the directory, it will output an error message using the **file_open_error** subroutine to be discussed later. To the subroutine, it will pass the name of the file that had trouble, as well as the current routine in the script having trouble, the filename, and the current line number.

```
opendir (USER_CARTS, "$sc_user_carts_directory_path")
   || &file_open_error("$sc_user_carts_directory_path",
                       "Delete Old Carts", __FILE__,
                    __LINE__);
@carts = grep(/\.cart/,readdir(USER_CARTS));
closedir (USER_CARTS);
```

Then, for every cart in the directory, the script deletes the cart if it is older than half a day. The **-M** file test returns the number of days since the file was last modified. Since the result is in terms of days, if the value is greater than the value of **$sc_number_days_keep_old_carts** set in **web_store.setup**, the file is deleted using the unlink function.

```
foreach $cart (@carts)
   {
   if (-M "$sc_user_carts_directory_path/$cart" >
          $sc_number_days_keep_old_carts)
     {
     unlink("$sc_user_carts_directory_path/$cart");
     }
   }
} # End of sub delete_old_carts
```

Assigning a Shopping Cart

assign_a_unique_shopping_cart_id is a subroutine used to assign a unique cart i.d. to every new customer. It takes no arguments and is called with the following syntax:

```
&assign_a_unique_shopping_cart_id;
```

The code is explained below:

```
sub assign_a_unique_shopping_cart_id
  {
```

First, the script checks to see if the administrator has asked it to log all new customers. If so, it gets the current date using the **get_date** subroutine discussed later, opens the access log file for appending, and prints all of the environment variable values as well as the current date and time to the access log file.

However, to protect ourselves from multiple, simultaneous writes to the access log, the script uses the **lockfile** routine documented at the end of this file, passing it the name of a temporary lock file to use.

NOTE   Remember that there may be multiple simultaneous executions of this script because there may be many people shopping all at once. It would not do if one customer was able to overwrite the information of another customer if both accidentally wanted to access the log file at the same exact time.

```
if ($sc_shall_i_log_accesses eq "yes")
    {
    $date = &get_date;
    &get_file_lock("$sc_access_log_path.lockfile");
    open (ACCESS_LOG, ">>$sc_access_log_path");
```

Using the Keys function, the script grabs all the keys of the **%ENV** associative array and assigns them as elements of **@env_keys**. It then creates a new row for the access log, which will be a pipe-delimited list of the date and all the environment variables and their values, using the **.=** operator to continually append fields to the **$new_access** variable.

```
@env_keys = keys(%ENV);

    $new_access = "$date\|";
    foreach $env_key (@env_keys)
      {
      $new_access .= "$ENV{$env_key}\|";
      }
```

The script then takes off the final pipe, adds the new access to the log file, closes the log file, and removes the lock file.

```
chop $new_access;
print ACCESS_LOG "$new_access\n";
close (ACCESS_LOG);
&release_file_lock("$sc_access_log_path.lockfile");
}
```

Now that the new access is recorded, the script assigns the customers their own unique shopping carts. To do so, it generates a random (**rand**) 8-digit (100000000) integer (**int**) and then appends to that string the current process i.d. (**$$**) separated by a period. Additionally, the **srand** function is seeded with the time and the current process i.d. in order to produce a more random random number. **$sc_cart_path** is also defined, now that we have a unique cart i.d. number.

```
srand (time|$$);
$cart_id = int(rand(10000000));
$cart_id .= ".$$";
$sc_cart_path = "$sc_user_carts_directory_path/$cart_id.cart";
```

However, before we can be absolutely sure that we have created a unique cart, the script must check the existing list of carts to make sure that there is not one with the same value.

It does this by checking to see if a cart with the randomly generated i.d. number already exists in the **User_carts** subdirectory. If one does exist (**-e**), the script grabs another random number using the same routine as above and checks again.

Using the **$cart_count** variable, the script executes this algorithm three times. If it does not succeed in finding a unique cart i.d. number, the script assumes that there is something seriously wrong with the randomizing routine and exits, warning the customer on the Web and the administrator using the **update_error_log** subroutine discussed later.

```
$cart_count = 0;
while (-e "$sc_cart_path")
  {
  if ($cart_count == 3)
```

```
          {
          print "$sc_randomizer_error_message";
          &update_error_log("COULD NOT CREATE UNIQUE CART
                          ID", __FILE__,
                             __LINE__);
          exit;
          }

     srand (time|$$);
     $cart_id = int(rand(10000000));
     $cart_id .= ".$$";
     $cart_count++;


     } # End of while (-e $sc_cart_path)
```

Now that we have generated a truly unique i.d. number for the new customer's cart, the script may go ahead and create it in the **User_carts** subdirectory. If there is a problem opening the new cart, we will output an error message with the **file_open_error** subroutine discussed later.

```
open (CART, ">$sc_cart_path") ||
        &file_open_error("$sc_cart_path",
                           "Assign a Shopping Cart",
  __FILE__, __LINE__);
  }
```

Displaying the Frontpage

output_frontpage is used to display the frontpage of the store. It takes no arguments and is accessed with the following syntax:

```
&output_frontpage;
```

The subroutine simply utilizes the **display_page** subroutine, which is discussed later, to output the frontpage file, the location of which is defined in **web_store.setup**. **display_page** takes four arguments: the frontpage HTML file path, the routine calling it, the current filename, and the current line number.

```
sub output_frontpage
```

```
{
&display_page("$sc_store_front_path",
            "Output Frontpage", __FILE__,
            __LINE__);
}
```

Adding to the Shopping Cart

The **add_to_the_cart** subroutine is used to add items to the customer's unique cart. It is called with no arguments with the following syntax:

```
&add_to_the_cart;
```

The code is explained below:

```
sub add_to_the_cart
  {
```

The script must first figure out what the customer has ordered. It begins by using the **%form_data** associative array given to it by **cgi-lib.pl**. It takes all of the keys of the **form_data** associative array and drops them into the **@items_ordered** array.

 An associative array *key* is like a variable name, whereas an associative array *value* is the value associated with that variable name. The benefit of an associative array is that you can have many of these key/value pairs in one array.

N O T E

Conveniently enough, you will notice that input fields on HTML forms will have associated NAMES and VALUES corresponding to associative array KEYS and VALUES. Since each of the text boxes in which the customer could enter quantities were associated with the database i.d. number of the item that they accompany (as defined in the **display_page** routine at the end of this script), the HTML should read

```
<INPUT TYPE = "text" NAME = "1234">
```

for the item with database i.d. number **"1234"** and

```
<INPUT TYPE = "text" NAME = "5678">
```

for item **"5678"**.

If the customer orders **"2"** of **"1234"** and **"9"** of **"5678"**, then the incoming data will be a list of **"1234"** and **"5678"** such that **"1234"** is associated with **"2"** in the **%form_data** associative array and **"5678"** is associated with **"9"**. The script uses the keys function to pull out just the keys. Thus, **@items_ordered** would be a list like (1234, 5678, ...).

```
@items_ordered = keys (%form_data);
```

Next the script goes through the list of items ordered one by one.

```
foreach $item (@items_ordered)
   {
```

However, there are some incoming items that do not need to be processed. Specifically, we do not care about **cart_id**, **page**, **keywords**, **add_to_cart**, or whatever incoming administrative variables exist because these are all values set internally by this script. They will be coming in as form data just like the customer-defined data, and we will need them for other things, just not to fill up the customer's cart. In order to bypass all of these administrative variables, we use a standard method for denoting incoming items. All incoming items are prefixed with the tag **item-**. When the script sees this tag, it knows that it is seeing an item to be added to the cart.

Similarly, items that are actually options information are prefixed with the word **option**. We will also accept those for further processing. And of course, we will not need to worry about any items which have empty values. If the shopper did not enter a quantity, then we will not add it to the cart.

```
if (($item =~ /^item-/i ||
    $item =~ /^option/i) &&
    $form_data{$item} ne "")
   {
```

Once the script has determined that the current element (**$item**) of **@items_ordered** is indeed a nonadministrator item, it must separate out the items that have been ordered from the options which modify those items. If $item begins with the keyword **option**, which we set specifically in the HTML defining the option, the script will add (**push**) that item to the array called **@options**. The script also removes the **item-** flag since it will not be necessary now that the item has passes the "if" test above.

```
$item =~ s/^item-//i;
if ($item =~ /^option/i)
  {
  push (@options, $item);
  }
```

On the other hand, if it is not an option, the script adds it to the array **@items_ordered_with_options**, but adds both the item and its value as a single array element.

The value will be a quantity and the item will be something like **item-0001 | 12.98 | The letter A** as defined in the HTML file. Once we extract the initial **item-** tag from the string using regular expressions (**$item =~ s/^item-//i;**) and append the quantity, the resulting string would be something like the following:

```
2|0001|12.98|The letter A
```

where **2** is the quantity.

However, the quantity value must satisfy a few conditions before it is considered valid. First, it must be a digit. That is, we do not want the customers trying to enter values like "a", "-2", ".5" or "1/2". They might play havoc on the ordering system. A sneaky customer might even gain a discount because you were not reading the order forms carefully. Second, the script will disallow any zeros (**$form_data{$item} == 0**). In both cases the customer will be sent to the subroutine **bad_order_note** located in **web_store_html_lib.pl**.

```
else
  {
  if (($form_data{"item-$item"} =~ /\D/) ||
      ($form_data{"item-$item"} == 0))
    {
    &bad_order_note;
    }
  else
    {
    $quantity = $form_data{"item-$item"};
    push (@items_ordered_with_options,
          "$quantity\|$item\|");
    }
  }
  } # End of if ($item ne "$variable"
} #End of foreach $item (@items_ordered)
```

Next, the script goes through the array **@items_ordered_with_options** one item at a time in order to modify any item that has had options applied to it. Recall that we just built the **@options** array with all the options for all the items ordered. Now the script will need to figure out which options in **@options** belong to which items in **@items_ordered_with_options**.

```
foreach $item_ordered_with_options
        (@items_ordered_with_options)
    {
```

First, clear out a few variables that we are going to use for each item. **$options** will be used to keep track of all of the options selected for any given item. **$option_subtotal** will be used to determine the total cost of each option. **$option_grand_total** will be used to calculate the total cost of all ordered options. **$item_grand_total** will be used to calculate the total cost of the item ordered factoring in quantity and options.

```
$options = "";
$option_subtotal = "";
$option_grand_total = "";
$item_grand_total = "";
```

Then, the script splits out **the $item_ordered_with_options** variable into its fields.

NOTE

We have defined the index location of some important fields in **web_store.setup**. Specifically, the script must know the index of quantity, item i.d. and item price within the array. It will need these values in particular for further calculations.

The script also changes all occurrences of **~qq~** to a double quote (") character, **~gt~** to a greater than sign (>), and **~lt~** to a less than sign (<). The reason that this must be done is so that any double quote, greater than, or less than characters used in URL strings can be stuffed safely into the cart and passed as part of the NAME argument in the Add Item form. Consider the following item name which must include an image tag.

```
<INPUT TYPE = "text"  NAME = "item-0010|Vowels|15.98|The letter
A|~lt~IMG SRC = ~qq~Html/Images/a.jpg~qq~ ALIGN = ~qq~left~qq~~gt~"
```

Notice that the URL must be edited. If it were not, how would the browser understand how to interpret the form tag? The form tag uses the double quote, greater than, and less than characters in its own processing.

```
$item_ordered_with_options =~ s/~qq~/\"/g;
$item_ordered_with_options =~ s/~gt~/\>/g;
$item_ordered_with_options =~ s/~lt~/\</g;

@cart_row = split (/\|/, $item_ordered_with_options);
$item_quantity = $cart_row[$sc_cart_index_of_quantity];
$item_id_number = $cart_row[$sc_cart_index_of_item_id];
$item_price = $cart_row[$sc_cart_index_of_price];
```

Then, for every option in **@options**, the script splits up each option into its fields. Once it does both splits, the script can compare the name of the item with the name associated with the option. If they are the same, it knows that this is an option meant to enhance this particular item.

```
foreach $option (@options)
  {
  ($option_marker, $option_number,
   $option_item_number) = split
     (/\|/, $option);
```

If the script finds a match, it records the option information contained in the **$option** variable.

```
if ($option_item_number eq "$item_id_number")
  {
```

Since it must apply this option to this item, the script splits out the value associated with the option and appends it to **$options**. Once it has gone through all of the options, using **.=**, the script will have one big string containing all the options so that it can print them out. Note that in the form on which the customer chooses options, each option is denoted with the form

```
NAME = "A|B|C" VALUE = "D|E"
```

where

- "A" is the option marker "option."

- "B" is the option number. You might have multiple options all modifying the same item. Option number identifies each option uniquely .

- "C" is the option item number, the unique item i.d. number that the option modifies.

- "D" is the option name—the descriptive name of the option.

- "E" is the option price.

For example, consider this option from the default **Vowels.html** file that modifies item number **0001**:

```
<INPUT TYPE = "radio" NAME = "option|2|0001"
       VALUE = "Red|0.00" CHECKED>Red<BR>
```

This is the second option modifying item number **0001**. When displayed in the display cart screen, it will read **Red 0.00**, and will not affect the cost of the item.

```
($option_name, $option_price) =
        split (/\|/,$form_data{$option});
$options .= "$option_name $option_price,";
```

But the script must also calculate the cost changes due to options. To do so, it takes the current value of **$option_grand_total** and adds to it the cost of the current option. It then formats the result to two decimal places using the **format_price** subroutine discussed later and assigns the new result to **$option_grand_total**.

```
$unformatted_option_grand_total = $option_grand_total
                                 + $option_price;
$option_grand_total =
    &format_price($unformatted_option_grand_total);

} # End of if ($option_item_number eq
} # End of foreach $option (@options)
```

Next, the script takes off the last comma in **$options**. Look a few lines up; you will see that a comma is added to the end of each option. The last option should not display the last comma.

```
chop $options;
```

Then, the script adds a space after each comma so that the display looks more neatly formatted.

```
$options =~ s/, /, /g;
```

The counter subroutine, discussed later, is then called and sent the location of the counter file defined in the Setup file as well as the file name and current line number.

This routine will return one variable called **$item_number**, that the script can use to identify a shopping cart item. This must be done so that when we modify and delete from the cart, we will know exactly which item to affect. We cannot rely simply on the unique database i.d. number because a customer may purchase two of the same item but with different options. Unless there is a separate, unique cart row i.d. number, how would the script know which to delete if the customer asked to delete one of the two? Thus, the counter subroutine assures that each cart row can be uniquely identified.

```
$item_number = &counter ($sc_counter_file_path,
                    __FILE__, __LINE__);
```

Finally, the script makes the last price calculations and appends every ordered item to **$cart_row**.

A completed cart row might look like the following:

```
2|0001|Vowels|15.98|Letter A|Times New Roman 0.00|15.98|161
```

The code is shown below:

```
$unformatted_item_grand_total = $item_price +
                                $option_grand_total;
$item_grand_total =
    &format_price("$unformatted_item_grand_total");

  foreach $field (@cart_row)
    {
    $cart_row .= "$field\|";
    }

$cart_row .= "$options\|$item_grand_total\|$item_number\n";
    } # End of foreach $item_ordered_with_options.....
```

When the script is through appending all the items to **$cart_row**, it opens the customer's shopping cart and adds the new items. If there is a problem opening the file, it will call **file_open_error** subroutine to handle the error reporting.

```
open (CART, ">>$sc_cart_path") ||
    &file_open_error("$sc_cart_path",
                     "Add to Shopping Cart",
                     __FILE__, __LINE__);
print CART "$cart_row";
close (CART);
```

Then, the script sends the customer back to a previous page. There are two pages that the customer can be sent to: the last product page they were on or the page displaying the customer's cart. Which page the customer is sent to depends on the value of **$sc_should_i_display_cart_after_purchase**, which is defined in the Web store Setup file. If the customer should be sent to the display cart page, the script calls **display_cart_contents**; otherwise it calls **display_page** if this is an HTML store cart or **create_html_page_from_db** if this is a Database store cart.

```
if ($sc_use_html_product_pages eq "yes")
   {
   if ($sc_should_i_display_cart_after_purchase
       eq "yes")
     {
     &display_cart_contents;
     }
   else
     {
     &display_page("$sc_html_product_directory_path/$page",
                   "Display Products for Sale");
     }
   }
else
   {
   if ($sc_should_i_display_cart_after_purchase eq "yes")
     {
     &display_cart_contents;
     }
   else
     {
     &create_html_page_from_db;
     }
   }
}
```

Output Modify Quantity Form

output_modify_quantity_form is the subroutine responsible for displaying the form that customers can use to modify the quantity of items in their cart. It is called with no arguments with the following syntax:

```
&output_modify_quantity_form;
```

The subroutine is explained below:

```
sub output_modify_quantity_form
  {
```

The subroutine begins by outputting the HTML header using **standard_page _header**, adds the modify form using **display_cart_table**, and finishes off the HTML page with **modify_form_footer**. All of these subroutines and their parameters are discussed in **web_store_html_lib.pl**.

```
  &standard_page_header("Change Quantity");
  &display_cart_table("changequantity");
  &modify_form_footer;
  }
```

Modify Quantity of Items in the Cart

The **modify_quantity_of_items_in_cart** subroutine is responsible for making quantity modifications in the customer's cart. It takes no arguments and is called with the following syntax:

```
&modify_quantity_of_items_in_cart;
```

The subroutine is discussed below:

```
sub modify_quantity_of_items_in_cart
  {
```

First, the script gathers the keys as it did previously for the **add_to_cart** routine, checking to make sure the customer entered a positive integer (not fractional and not less than one).

```
@incoming_data = keys (%form_data);
foreach $key (@incoming_data)
    {
    if ((($key =~ /[\d]/) &&
        ($form_data{$key} =~ /\D/)) ||
        $form_data{$key} eq "0")
      {
      &update_error_log("BAD QUANTITY CHANGE",
                        __FILE__, __LINE__);
      &bad_order_note;
      }
```

Just as in the **add_to_cart** routine previously, the script will create an array (**@modify_items**) of valid keys.

```
    unless ($key =~ /[\D]/ &&
            $form_data{$key} =~ /[\D]/)
      {
      if ($form_data{$key} ne "")
        {
        push (@modify_items, $key);
        }
      }
    } # End of foreach $key (@incoming_data)
```

Then, the script must open up the customer's cart and go through it line by line. Problems opening the file are, as usual, handled by **file_open_error**.

```
  open (CART, "$sc_cart_path") ||
    &file_open_error("$sc_cart_path",
                     "Modify Quantity of Items in the
                     Cart", __FILE__, __LINE__);
```

As the script goes through the cart, it will split each row into its database fields placing them as elements in **@database_row**. It will then grab the unique cart row number and subsequently replace it in the array.

The script needs this number to check the current line against the list of items to be modified. This list will be made up of all the cart items that are being modified.

Finally, the script chops the newline character off the cart row number.

```
while (<CART>)
  {
  @database_row = split (/\|/, $_);
  $cart_row_number = pop (@database_row);
  push (@database_row, $cart_row_number);
      chop $cart_row_number;
```

Next, the script checks to see if the item number submitted as form data is equal to the number of the current database row.

```
  foreach $item (@modify_items)
    {
    if ($item eq $cart_row_number)
      {
```

If so, it means that the script must change the quantity of this item. It will append this row to the **$shopper_row** variable and begin creating the modified row. That is, it will replace the old quantity with the quantity submitted by the customer (**$form_data{$item}**). Recall that **$old_quantity** has already been shifted off the array.

```
    $shopper_row .= "$form_data{$item}\|";
```

Now the script adds the rest of the database row to **$shopper_row** and sets two flag variables. **$quantity_modified** lets us know that the current row has had a quantity modification for each iteration of the while loop.

```
  foreach $field (@database_row)
    {
    $shopper_row .= "$field\|";
    }

  $quantity_modified = "yes";
  chop $shopper_row; # Get rid of last pipe symbol but
       # not the newline character

  } # End of if ($item eq $cart_row_number)
} # End of foreach $item (@modify_items)
```

If the script gets this far and **$quantity_modified** has not been set to "yes," it knows that the above routine was skipped because the item number submitted from the form was not equal to the current database i.d. number. Thus, it knows that the current row is not having its quantity changed and can be added to **$shopper_row** as is. Remember, we want to add the old rows as well as the new modified ones.

```
if ($quantity_modified ne "yes")
  {
  $shopper_row .= $_;
  }
```

Finally, the script clears out the **quantity_modified** variable so that next time the while loops start, it will have a fresh test.

```
$quantity_modified = "";
  } # End of while (<CART>)
close (CART);
```

At this point, the script has gone all the way through the cart. It has added all of the items without quantity modifications as they were, and has added all the items with quantity modifications but made the modifications. The entire cart is contained in the **$shopper_row** variable.

The actual cart still has the old values, however. To change the cart completely the script must overwrite the old cart with the new information and send the customer back to the view cart screen with the **display_cart_contents** subroutine (to be discussed below). Notice the use of the write operator (**>**) instead of the append operator (**>>**).

```
open (CART, ">$sc_cart_path") ||
&file_open_error("$sc_cart_path",
             "Modify Quantity of Items in the Cart",
             __FILE__, __LINE__);
print CART "$shopper_row";
close (CART);

&display_cart_contents;
} # End of if ($form_data{'submit_change_quantity'}...
```

Displaying the Delete Item

The **output_delete_item_form** subroutine is responsible for displaying the HTML form that the customers can use to delete items from their cart. It takes no arguments and is called with the following syntax:

```
&output_delete_item_form;
```

As it did when it printed the modification form, the script uses several subroutines in **web_store_html_lib.pl** to generate the header, body, and footer of the Delete form.

```
sub output_delete_item_form
  {
  &standard_page_header("Delete Item");
  &display_cart_table("delete");
  &delete_form_footer;
  } # End of if ($form_data{'delete_item'} ne "")
```

Deleting Items from the Cart

The job of **delete_from_cart** is to take a set of items submitted by the customer for deletion and actually delete them from the customer's cart. The subroutine takes no arguments and is called with the following syntax:

```
&delete_from_cart;
```

As with the modification routines, the script first checks for valid entries. This time it only needs to make sure that it filters out the extra form keys. It is not necessary to make sure that it has a positive integer value as well, because unlike with a text entry, customers have less ability to enter bad values with checkbox submit fields.

```
sub delete_from_cart
  {
  @incoming_data = keys (%form_data);
  foreach $key (@incoming_data)
    {
```

We still want to make sure that the key is a cart row number and that it has a value associated with it. If the key is actually an item which the customer has asked to delete, the script will add it to the **@delete_items** array.

```
unless ($key =~ /[\D]/)
   {
   if ($form_data{$key} ne "")
      {
      push (@delete_items, $key);
      }
   } # End of unless ($key =~ /[\D]/...
} # End of foreach $key (@incoming_data)
```

Once the script has gone through all the incoming form data and collected the list of all items to be deleted, it opens up the cart and gets the **$cart_row_number** and **$db_id_number** as it did in the modification routines previously.

```
open (CART, "$sc_cart_path") ||
   &file_open_error("$sc_cart_path",
                    "Delete Item From Cart",
                    __FILE__, __LINE__);
while (<CART>)
   {
   @database_row = split (/\|/, $_);
   $cart_row_number = pop (@database_row);
   $db_id_number = pop (@database_row);
   push (@database_row, $db_id_number);
   push (@database_row, $cart_row_number);
   chop $cart_row_number;
```

Unlike modification, all we need to do for deletion is check to see if the current database row matches any submitted item for deletion. If it does not match, the script adds it to **$shopper_row**. If it is equal, it does not. Thus, all the rows will be added to **$shopper_row** except for the ones that should be deleted.

```
$delete_item = "";
foreach $item (@delete_items)
   {
   if ($item eq $cart_row_number)
      {
```

```
    $delete_item = "yes";
    }
  } # End of foreach $item (@add_items)
 if ($delete_item ne "yes")
   {
   $shopper_row .= $_;
   }
 } # End of while (<CART>)
close (CART);
```

Then, as it did for modification, the script overwrites the old cart with the new information and sends the customer back to the view cart page with the **display_cart_contents** subroutine, which will be discussed later in this chapter.

```
open (CART, ">$sc_cart_path") ||
    &file_open_error("$sc_cart_path",
                     "Delete Item From Cart",
 __FILE__, __LINE__);
 print CART "$shopper_row";
 close (CART);
 &display_cart_contents;
 } # End of if ($form_data{'submit_deletion'} ne "")
```

Displaying Products for Sale

display_products_for_sale is used to dynamically generate the product pages that the customer will want to browse through. However, there are two cases within it.

First, if the store is an HTML-based store, this routine will either display the requested page or, in the case of a search, perform a search on all the pages in the store for the submitted keyword. Second, if this is a Database-based store, the script will use the **create_html_page_from_db** to output the product page requested or to perform the search on the database. The subroutine takes no arguments and is called with the following syntax:

```
&display_products_for_sale;
```

The script first determines which type of store this is. If it turns out to be an HTML-based store, the script will check to see if the current request is a keyword search or simply a request to display a page. If it is a keyword search, the script will require the HTML search library and use the **html_search** subroutine within it to perform the search.

```
sub display_products_for_sale
  {
  if ($sc_use_html_product_pages eq "yes")
    {
    if ($form_data{'search_request_button'} ne "")
      {
      &standard_page_header("Search Results");
      require "$sc_html_search_routines_library_path";
      &html_search;
      &html_search_page_footer;
      exit;
      }
```

However, if the store is HTML-based but there is no current keyword, the script simply displays the page as requested with **display_page**, which will be discussed below.

```
&display_page("$sc_html_product_directory_path/$page",
              "Display Products for Sale", __FILE__,
          __LINE__);
    }
```

On the other hand, if **$sc_use_html_product_pages** was set to "no," it means that the administrator wants the script to generate HTML product pages on the fly, using the format string and the raw database rows. The script will do so using the **create_html_page_from_db** subroutine, which will be discussed in the next section.

```
  else
    {
    &create_html_page_from_db;
    }
  }
```

Creating Dynamically Generated Product Pages from the Database

create_html_page_from_db is used to generate the navigational interface for database-based stores. It is used to create both product pages and list of products pages. The subroutine takes no arguments and is called with the following syntax:

```
&create_html_page_from_db;
```

First, the subroutine defines a few working variables that will remain local to this subroutine.

```
sub create_html_page_from_db
  {
  local (@database_rows, @database_fields, @item_ids,
        @display_fields);
  local ($total_row_count, $id_index, $display_index);
  local ($row, $field, $empty, $option_tag,
        $option_location, $output);
```

Next, the subroutine checks to see if there is actually a page that must be displayed. If there is a value for the page variable incoming as form data (for example, a list of products page), the script will simply display that page with the **display_page** subroutine and exit.

```
  if ($page ne "" &&
      $form_data{'search_request_button'} eq "")
    {
    &display_page
("$sc_html_product_directory_path/$form_data{'page'}",
                "Display Products for Sale",
                __FILE__, __LINE__);
    exit;
    }
```

If there is no page value, then the script knows that it must generate a dynamic product page using the value of the product form variable to query the database. First, the script uses the **product_page_header** subroutine in order to dynamically generate the product page header. The subroutine takes the value of the page we have been asked to display so that it can display something useful in the <TITLE></TITLE> area.

The **product_page_header** subroutine is located in **web_store_html_lib.pl** and **$sc_product_display_title** is defined in the Setup file.

```
  &product_page_header($sc_product_display_title);
    if ($form_data{'add_to_cart_button'} ne "" &&
    $sc_shall_i_let_client_know_item_added eq "yes")
      {
      print "$sc_item_ordered_message";
      }
```

Next, the database is queried for rows containing the value of the incoming product variable in the correct category as defined in the Web Store setup file. The script uses the **submit_query** subroutine in **web_store_db_lib.pl**, passing to it a reference to the list array **@database_rows**.

submit_query returns a descriptive status message if there is a problem and a total row count for diagnosing if the maximum rows returned variable is exceeded.

```
if (!($sc_db_lib_was_loaded =~ /yes/i)) {
   &require_supporting_libraries (__FILE__, __LINE__,
                                 "$sc_db_lib_path");
}
($status,$total_row_count) = &submit_query(*database_rows);
```

Now that the script has the database rows to be displayed, it will display them.

First, the script goes through each database row contained in **@database_rows** splitting it into its fields. For the most part, in order to display the database rows, the script will simply need to take each field from the database row and substitute it for a **%s** in the format string defined in the Web store Setup file.

However, in the case of options that will modify a product, the script must grab the code from an Options file. The special way that options are denoted in the database are by using the format **%%OPTION%%option.html** in the data file. The use of this flag is covered in more detail in Chapter 4 and includes two important items of information, as follows.

First, it begins with **%%OPTION%%**. This is a flag that will let the script know that it needs to deal with this database field as if it were an option. When the script sees the flag, it will then look what follows the flag to see which file it should load. Thus, in this example, the script would load the file **option.html** for display.

NOTE

Why go through all the trouble? Basically, because we need to create a system that will handle large, very likely similar, chunks of HTML code within the database. If there are options on product pages, it is probable that they will be repeated fairly often. For example, every item in a database might have an option like tape, cd, or lp. By creating one **options.html** file, we could easily put all the code into one shared location and not need to worry about typing it in for every single database entry.

```
foreach $row (@database_rows)
  {
  @database_fields = split (/\|/, $row);
  foreach $field (@database_fields)
    {
```

For every field in every database row, the script simply checks to see if it begins (^) with **%%OPTION%%**. If so, it splits the string into three pieces of information: an empty string, an OPTION tag, and the location of the option to be used. Then the script resets **$field** to null because it is about to overwrite it.

```
if ($field =~ /^%%OPTION%%/)
  {
  ($empty, $option_tag, $option_location) =
  split (/%%/, $field);
  $field = "";
```

The Option file is opened and read. Every line of the Option file is appended to the **$field** variable and the file is closed again. However, the current product i.d. number is substituted for the **%%PRODUCT_ID%%** flag, which is a mandatory tag contained in all options files.

```
open (OPTION_FILE,
"$sc_options_directory_path/$option_location") ||
&file_open_error ("$sc_options_directory_path/$option_location",
"Display Products for Sale", __FILE__,
__LINE__);

while (<OPTION_FILE>)
  {

s/%%PRODUCT_ID%%/$database_fields[$sc_db_index_of_product_id]/g;
  $field .= $_;
  }
close (OPTION_FILE);
} # End of if ($field =~ /^%%OPTION%%/)
} # End of foreach $field (@database_fields)
```

Finally, the database fields (including the Option field that has been recreated) are stuffed into the format string **$sc_product_display_row** and the entire formatted string is printed to the browser along with the footer.

In doing so, however, we must format the fields correctly. Initially, **@display_fields** is created containing the values of every field to be displayed, including a formatted price field.

```
@display_fields = ();
@temp_fields = @database_fields;
foreach $display_index (@sc_db_index_for_display)
  {
  if ($display_index == $sc_db_index_of_price)
    {
    $temp_fields[$display_index] =
      &display_price($temp_fields[$display_index]);
    }
  push(@display_fields,
      $temp_fields[$display_index]);
  }
```

Then, the elements of the NAME field are created so that customers will be able to specify an item to purchase. We are careful to substitute double quote marks (") and greater and less than signs (>,<) for the tags **~qq~**, **~gt~**, and **~lt~**. The reason that this must be done is so that any double quote, greater than, or less than characters used in URL strings can be stuffed safely into the cart and passed as part of the NAME argument in the "add item" form. Consider the following item name that must include an image tag.

```
<INPUT TYPE = "text"  NAME = "item-0010|Vowels|15.98|The letter
A|~lt~IMG SRC = ~qq~Html/Images/a.jpg~qq~ ALIGN = ~qq~left~qq~~gt~"
```

Notice that the <IMG SRC> reference was edited. If it were not, how would the browser understand how to interpret the form tag? The form tag uses the double quote, greater than, and less than characters in its own processing, so the value of NAME of the tag cannot contain these special characters without this substitution.

```
@item_ids = ();
foreach $id_index (@sc_db_index_for_defining_item_id)
  {
  $database_fields[$id_index] =~ s/\"/~qq~/g;
  $database_fields[$id_index] =~ s/\>/~gt~/g;
  $database_fields[$id_index] =~ s/\</~lt~/g;
  push(@item_ids, $database_fields[$id_index]);
  }
```

Finally, **$sc_product_display_row** is created with the two arrays using **printf** to apply the formatting.

```
printf ($sc_product_display_row,
        join("\|",@item_ids),
        @display_fields);
} # End of foreach $row (@database_rows)
&product_page_footer($status,$total_row_count);
exit;
}
```

Displaying the Contents of the Cart

display_cart_contents is used to display the current contents of the customer's cart. It takes no arguments and is called with the following syntax:

```
&display_cart_contents;
```

The subroutine begins by defining some working variables as local to the subroutine.

```
sub display_cart_contents
  {
  local (@cart_fields);
  local ($field, $cart_id_number, $quantity,
         $display_number, $unformatted_subtotal,
         $subtotal, $unformatted_grand_total,
         $grand_total);
```

Next, as when we created the modification and deletion forms for cart manipulation, we will use the routines in **web_store_html_lib.pl** to generate the header, body, and footer of the cart page. However, unlike with the modification and deletion forms, we will not need an extra table cell for the checkbox or text field. Thus, we will not pass anything to **display_cart_table**. We will simply get a table representing the current contents of the customer's cart.

```
&standard_page_header("View/Modify Cart");
&display_cart_table("");
&cart_footer;
exit;
} # End of sub display_cart_contents
```

Handling File Open Errors

If there is a problem opening a file or a directory, it is useful for the script to output some information clarifying what problem has occurred. This subroutine is used to generate those error messages. **file_open_error** takes four arguments: the file or directory that failed, the section in the code in which the call was made, the current file name, and the line number. It is called with the following syntax:

```
&file_open_error("file.name", "ROUTINE", __FILE__, __LINE__);
```

The subroutine simply uses the **update_error_log** subroutine discussed later to modify the error log and then uses **CgiDie** in **cgi-lib.pl** to gracefully exit the application with a useful debugging error message sent to the browser window.

```
sub file_open_error
  {
  local ($bad_file, $script_section, $this_file,
         $line_number) = @_;
  &update_error_log("FILE OPEN ERROR", $this_file,
                    $line_number);
  &CgiDie ("I am sorry, but I was not able to access
           $bad_file in the $script_section routine of
           $this_file at line number $line_number.
           Would you please make sure the path is
           correctly defined in web_store.setup and
           that the permissions are correct.")
  }
```

Displaying a Pre-designed HTML Page

display_page is used to filter HTML pages through the script and display them to the browser window. **display_page** takes four arguments: the file directory that failed, the section in the code in which the erroneous call was made, the current file name, and the line number, and is called with the following syntax:

```
&file_open_error("file.name", "ROUTINE", __FILE__, __LINE__);
```

The subroutine begins by opening the requested file for reading, exiting with **file_open_error** if there is a problem as usual.

```
sub display_page
  {
  local ($page, $routine, $file, $line) = @_;
  open (PAGE, "$page") ||
        &file_open_error("$page", "$routine", $file,
        $line);
```

It then reads in the file one line at a time. However, on every line it looks for special tag sequences that it knows must be replaced in order to maintain the state information necessary for the workings of this script. Specifically, every form must include a page and a **cart_id** value and every URL hyperlink must have a **cart_id** value added to it.

Raw pre-designed HTML pages must include the following tag lines if they are to filter properly and pass along this necessary state information. All forms must include two hidden field lines with the substitution "tags" embedded as follows:

```
<INPUT TYPE = "hidden" NAME = "cart_id"
       VALUE = "%%cart_id%%">
<INPUT TYPE = "hidden" NAME = "page"
       VALUE = "%%page%%">
```

When the script reads in these lines, it will see the tags "**%%cart_id%%**" and "**%%page%%**" and substitute them for the actual **page** and **cart_id** values which came in as form data. Similarly, it might see the following URL reference:

```
<A HREF = "web_store.cgi?page=Letters.html&cart_id=">
```

In this case, it will see the **cartid=** flag and substitute the correct and complete **cartid=[SOME NUMBER]**.

```
  while (<PAGE>)
    {
    s/cart_id=/cart_id=$cart_id/g;
    s/%%cart_id%%/$cart_id/g;
    s/%%page%%/$form_data{'page'}/g;
```

Next, it checks to see if the **add_to_cart_button** button has been clicked. If so, it means that we have just added an item and are returning to the display of the product page. In this case, we will sneak in an additional confirmation message right after the **<FORM>** tag line so that the customer will know that the item was successfully added.

```
if ($form_data{'add_to_cart_button'} ne "" &&
    $sc_shall_i_let_client_know_item_added eq
    "yes")
  {
  if ($_ =~ /<FORM/)
    {
    print "$_";
    print "$sc_item_ordered_message";
    }
  }
```

If it is any other line, simply print it out to the browser window. Once we have gone through all of the lines in the file, the HTML will be complete and filtered.

```
    print $_;
    }

close (PAGE);
} # End of sub display_page
```

Getting a Unique Cart Row Number with Counter

The **counter** subroutine is used to keep track of unique cart database i.d. numbers so that every item in every cart will be uniquely identifiable. The subroutine takes three arguments, the name of the counter file defined in the Setup file, the current filename, and the current line number. It is called with the following syntax:

```
&counter ($sc_counter_file_path, __FILE__, __LINE__);
```

First, the subroutine assigns to the local variable **$counter_file**, the filename that we passed to this subroutine from the main script. It also defines **$file**, **$line**, and **$item_number** as local.

```
sub counter
  {
local($counter_file, $file, $line) = @_;
local ($item_number);
```

Next, the script checks to see if the Counter file exists. If it does not, it attempts to create it.

```
if (!(-e $counter_file))
  {
  open(COUNTER_FILE, ">$counter_file") ||
      &file_open_error("$counter_file", "Counter",
      $file, $line);
  print COUNTER_FILE "1\n";
  close(COUNTER_FILE);
  }
```

Next, the script opens the Counter file. If the Counter file cannot be opened, however, **&file_open_error** is called as usual.

```
open (COUNTER_FILE, "$counter_file") ||
    &file_open_error("$counter_file", "Counter",
    $file, $line);
```

Then, the script checks to see what number the counter is currently on and assigns that value to **$item_number**.

```
while (<COUNTER_FILE>)
  {
  $item_number = "$_";
  }
close (COUNTER_FILE);
```

It then adds 1 to that number, changes the Counter file to reflect the addition, returns the number to the main script, and closes the Counter file.

```
$item_number += 1;
open (NOTE, ">$counter_file") ||
    &file_open_error("$counter_file", "Counter",
    $file, $line);
```

```
print NOTE "$item_number\n";
close (NOTE);
return $item_number;
} # End of sub counter
```

Updating the Error Log

update_error_log is used to append to the error log if there has been a process executing this script and/or email the administrator. The subroutine takes three arguments: the type of error, the current filename, and the current line number. It is called with the following syntax:

```
&update_error_log("WARNING", __FILE__, __LINE__);
```

The subroutine begins by assigning the incoming arguments to local variables and defining some other local variables to use during its work.

- **$type_of_error** will be a text string explaining what kind of error is being logged.
- **$file_name** is the current filename of this script.
- **$line_number** is the line number on which the error occurred. Note that it is essential that the line number, stored in **__LINE__** be passed through all levels of subroutines so that the line number value will truly represent the line number of the error and not the line number of some subroutine for error handling.

```
sub update_error_log
  {
  local ($type_of_error, $file_name, $line_number) = @_;
  local ($log_entry, $email_body, $variable, @env_vars);
```

The list of the HTTP environment variables is culled into the **@env_vars** list array and **get_date** is used to assign the current date to **$date**.

```
  @env_vars = keys(%ENV);
  $date = &get_date;
```

Now, if the administrator has instructed the script to log errors by setting **$sc_shall_i_log_errors** in the Web store Setup file, the script will create an error log entry.

```
if ($sc_shall_i_log_errors eq "yes")
   {
```

First, the new log entry row is created as a pipe-delimited list beginning with the error type, filename, line number, and the current date.

```
$log_entry = "$type_of_error\|FILE=$file_name\|LINE=$line_num-
ber\|";
$log_entry .= "DATE=$date\|";
```

Then, the error log file is opened securely by using the lock file routines in **get_file_lock** discussed later in this chapter.

```
&get_file_lock("$sc_error_log_path.lockfile");
open (ERROR_LOG, ">>$sc_error_log_path") ||
    &CgiDie("The Error Log Could Not Be Opened");
```

Next, the script adds to the log entry row, the values associated with all of the HTTP environment variables, and prints the whole row to the log file it then closes and opens for use by other instances of this script by removing the lock file.

```
foreach $variable (@env_vars)
  {
  $log_entry .= "$ENV{$variable}\|";
  }

print ERROR_LOG "$log_entry\n";
close (ERROR_LOG);
&release_file_lock("$sc_error_log_path.lockfile");
} # End of if ($sc_shall_i_log_errors eq "yes")
```

Finally, the script checks to see if the administrator has instructed it to also send an email error notification to the administrator by setting the **$sc_shall_i_email_if_error** in the Web store Setup file.

If so, it prepares an e-mail with the same information contained in the log file row and mails it to the administrator using the **send_mail** routine in **mail-lib.pl**. Note that a common source of email errors lies in the administrator not setting the correct path for **sendmail** in **mail-lib.pl** on line 42. Make sure that you set this variable there if you are not receiving your mail and you are using the **sendmail** version of the mail-lib package.

```
if ($sc_shall_i_email_if_error eq "yes")
  {
  $email_body = "$type_of_error\n\n";
  $email_body .= "FILE = $file_name\n";
  $email_body .= "LINE = $line_number\n";
  $email_body .= "DATE=$date\|";
  foreach $variable (@env_vars)
    {
    $email_body .= "$variable = $ENV{$variable}\n";
    }
  &send_mail("$sc_administrator_email",
             "$sc_administrator_email", "Web Store
             Error", "$email_body");
  } # End of if ($sc_shall_i_email_if_error eq "yes")
}
```

Getting the Date

get_date is used to get the current date and time and format it into a readable form. The subroutine takes no arguments and is called with the following syntax:

```
$date = &get_date;
```

Since it will return the value of the current date, you must assign it to a variable in the calling routine if you are going to use the value.

```
sub get_date
  {
```

The subroutine begins by defining some local working variables

```
local ($sec,$min,$hour,$mday,$mon,$year,
       $wday,$yday,$isdst,$date);
local (@days, @months);
@days = ('Sunday','Monday','Tuesday',
         'Wednesday','Thursday', 'Friday','Saturday');
@months = ('January','February','March','April',
           'May','June','July', 'August','September',
           'October', 'November','December');
```

Next, it uses the **localtime** command to get the current time from the value returned by the time command, splitting it into variables.

```
($sec,$min,$hour,$mday,$mon,$year,$wday,$yday,$isdst) = localtime(time);
```

Then the script formats the variables and assign them to the final **$date** variable. Note that $**sc_current_century** is defined in **web_store.setup**. Since the 20th century is really 1900–1999, we will need to subtract 1 from this value in order to format the year correctly.

```
if ($hour < 10)
  {
  $hour = "0$hour";
  }
if ($min < 10)
  {
  $min = "0$min";
  }
if ($sec < 10)
  { $sec = "0$sec";
  }
$year = ($sc_current_century-1) . "$year";
$date = "$days[$wday], $months[$mon] $mday, $year at
        $hour\:$min\:$sec";
return $date;
}
```

Displaying the Price

display_price is used to format the price string so that the store can take into account differing methods for displaying prices. For example, some countries use **$xx.yy**. Others may use **xx.yy UNIT**. This subroutine will use the **$sc_money_symbol_placement** and the **$sc_money_symbol** variables defined in **web_store.setup** to format the entire price string for display. The subroutine takes one argument, the price to be formatted, and is called with the following syntax:

```
$price = &display_price(xx.yy);
```

Where **xx.yy** is some number like "23.99".

NOTE The main routine calling this subroutine must prepare a variable for the returned formatted price to be assigned to.

```
sub display_price
  {
  local ($price) = @_;
  local ($format_price);

  if ($sc_money_symbol_placement eq "front")
    {
    $format_price = "$sc_money_symbol $price";
    }
  else
    {
    $format_price = "$price $sc_money_symbol";
    }

  return $format_price;
  }
```

Making a Lockfile

get_file_lock is a subroutine used to create a lockfile. Lock files are used to make sure that no more than one instance of the script can modify a file at one time. A lockfile is vital to the integrity of your data. Imagine what would happen if two or three people were using the same script to modify a shared file (such as the error log) and each accessed the file at the same time. At best, the data entered by some of the customers would be lost. Worse, conflicting demands could possibly result in the corruption of the file.

Thus, it is crucial to provide a way to monitor and control access to the file. This is the goal of the lockfile routines. When an instance of this script tries to access a shared file, it must first check for the existence of a lockfile by using the **file lock** checks in **get_file_lock**.

If **get_file_lock** determines that there is an existing lockfile, it instructs the instance that called it to wait until the lockfile disappears. The script then waits and checks back after some time interval. If the lockfile still remains, it continues to wait until some point at which the administrator has given it permission to just overwrite the file because some other error must have occurred.

If, on the other hand, the lockfile has disappeared, the script asks **get_file_lock** to create a new lock file and then goes ahead and edits the file.

The subroutine takes one argument, the name to use for the lock file, and is called with the following syntax:

```
&get_file_lock("file.name");
```

The code is explained below:

```
sub get_file_lock
  {
  local ($lock_file) = @_;
  local ($endtime);
  $endtime = 60;
  $endtime = time + $endtime;
```

We set endtime to wait 60 seconds. If the lockfile has not been removed by then, there must be some other problem with the file system. Perhaps an instance of the script crashed and could never delete the lock file.

```
  while (-e $lock_file && time < $endtime)
    {
    # Do Nothing
    }
  open(LOCK_FILE, ">$lock_file");
```

NOTE

If **flock** is available on your system, feel free to use it. **flock** is an even safer method of locking your file because it locks it at the system level. The above routine is "pretty good" and it will server for most systems. But if you are lucky enough to have a server with **flock** routines built in, go ahead and uncomment the next line and comment the one above.

```
# flock(LOCK_FILE, 2); # 2 exclusively locks the file
  }
```

Deleting a Lockfile

release_file_lock is the partner of **get_file_lock**. When an instance of this script is through using the file it needs to manipulate, it calls **release_file_lock**

to delete the lockfile that it put in place so that other instances of the script can get to the shared file. It takes one argument, the name of the lock file, and is called with the following syntax:

```
&release_file_lock("file.name");
```

The code is explained below

```
sub release_file_lock
  {
  local ($lock_file) = @_;
  # flock(LOCK_FILE, 8); # 8 unlocks the file
```

As we mentioned in the note in the discussion of **get_file_lock**, **flock** is a superior file locking system. If your system has it, go ahead and use it instead of the version here. Uncomment the above line and comment the two that follow.

```
  close(LOCK_FILE);
  unlink($lock_file);
  }
```

Formatting Prices

format_price is used to format prices to two decimal places. It takes one argument, the price to be formatted, and is called with the following syntax:

```
$price =&format_price(xxx.yyyyy);
```

Notice that the main calling routine must assign the returned formatted price to some variable for its own use. Also notice that this routine takes a value even if it is longer than two decimal places and formats it with rounding. Thus, you can utilize price calculations such as 12.99 * 7.985 (where 7.985 might be some tax value).

```
  sub format_price
  {
```

The incoming price is set to a local variable and a few working local variables are defined.

```
local ($unformatted_price) = @_;
local ($formatted_price);
```

The script then uses the rounding method in EXCEL, which is also used in **sprintf.**

```
$formatted_price = sprintf ("%.2f", $unformatted_price);
return $formatted_price;
}
```

Chapter Twelve

The HTML Library

The features of this library are dealt with in great detail in Chapter 2. Thus, we will simply discuss the code here.

Creating a Product Page Header

The HTML Library begins with the **product_page_header** subroutine. **product_page_header** is used to display the shared HTML header used for database-based product pages. It takes one argument, **$page_title**, which will be used to fill the data between the <TITLE> and </TITLE>. Typically, this value is determined by **$sc_product_display_title** in **web_store.setup** . The subroutine is called with the following syntax:

```
&product_page_header("Desired Title");
```

The subroutine begins by assigning the incoming argument to the local variable **$page_title**.

```
sub product_page_header
  {
  local ($page_title) = @_;
```

Then, it assigns the text of all of the hidden fields that may need to be passed as state information to **$hidden_fields** using the **make_hidden_fields** subroutine, which will be discussed later in this chapter.

```
local ($hidden_fields) = &make_hidden_fields;
```

Next, the HTML code is sent to the browser, including the page title and the hidden fields dynamically inserted.

```
print qq~
<HTML>
<HEAD>
<TITLE>$page_title</TITLE>
</HEAD>
<BODY BGCOLOR = "FFFFFF" TEXT = "000000">
<FORM METHOD = "post" ACTION = "$sc_main_script_url">

$hidden_fields
~;
```

Next, we will grab **$sc_product_display_header** which is a preformatted string defined in **web_store.setup** and use **printf** to put the entire contents of **@sc_db_display_fields** in place of the format tags (**%s**). The purpose of this will be to display the header categories which products will follow. Consider the following example from **web_store.setup.db**:

```
$sc_product_display_header = qq!
<TABLE BORDER = "0">
<TR>
<TH>Quantity</TH>
<TH>%s</TH>
<TH>%s</TH>
</TR>
<TR>
<TD COLSPAN = "3"><HR></TD>
</TR>!;

@sc_db_display_fields = ("Image (If appropriate)",
                         "Description");
```

In this case, the strings **"Image (If appropriate)"** and **"Description"** will be substituted by the **printf** function for the two **"%s"** tags in the TABLE header defined in **$sc_product_display_header**.

```
printf($sc_product_display_header,
       @sc_db_display_fields);
  }
```

Creating a Product Page

The **product_page_footer** subroutine is used to generate the HTML page footer for database-based product pages. It takes two arguments, **$db_status** and **$total_rows_returned** and is called with the following syntax:

```
&product_page_footer($status,$total_row_count);
```

The subroutine begins by defining a few local variables. **$db_status** gives us the status returned from the database search engine and **$total_rows_returned** gives us the actual number of rows returned. **$warn_message**, which is first initialized to be blank, will be used to generate a warning that the customer should narrow their search in case too many rows were returned.

```
sub product_page_footer
  {

  local($db_status, $total_rows_returned) = @_;
  local($warn_message);
  $warn_message = "";
```

If the database returned a status, the script checks to see if it was like the string **max.*row.*exceed**. If so, the script lets the customer know that they need to narrow their search.

```
if ($db_status ne "")
  {
  if ($db_status =~ /max.*row.*exceed.*/i)
    {
    $warn_message = qq!
    <CENTER>
    <BLOCKQUOTE>
    Your query returned $total_rows_returned.  This is
    more than the maximum we allow
    ($sc_db_max_rows_returned). You will need to
    restrict your query further.
    </BLOCKQUOTE></CENTER><P>!;
    }
  }
```

Then the script displays the footer information defined with **$sc_product_display_footer** in **web_store.setup** and adds the final basic HTML footer. Notice that one of the Submit buttons, "Return to Frontpage," is isolated into **the $sc_no_frames_button** variable. This is because in the Frames version, we do not want that option as it will cause an endlessly fracturing Frame system. Thus, in a Frame store, you would simply set **$sc_no_frames_button** to "" and nothing would print here. Otherwise, you may include that button in your footer for ease of navigation. The variable itself is defined in **web_store.setup** . The script also will print the warning message if there is a value for it.

NOTE A discussion of recursive Frames appears in Chapter 6 along with an example.

```
print qq~
$sc_product_display_footer
<P>
$warn_message

<CENTER>
<INPUT TYPE = "submit" NAME = "add_to_cart_button"
      VALUE = "Add Items to my Cart">
<INPUT TYPE = "submit" NAME = "modify_cart_button"
      VALUE = "View/Modify Cart">
$sc_no_frames_button
<INPUT TYPE = "submit" NAME = "order_form_button"
      VALUE = "Checkout Stand">
</FORM>
</CENTER>
</BODY>
</HTML>~;
}
```

Defining the HTML Search Page Footer

The **html_search_page_footer** subroutine is used to generate the HTML footer for HTML-based product pages when the script must perform a keyword search and generate a list of hits. It is called with no arguments with the following syntax:

```
&html_search_page_footer;
```

Notice again the use of **$sc_no_frames_button** in place of the "Return to Frontpage" button as discussed in the last section.

```
sub html_search_page_footer
   {
   print qq!
   <CENTER>
   <INPUT TYPE = "submit" NAME = "modify_cart_button"
          VALUE = "View/Modify Cart">
   $sc_no_frames_button
   <INPUT TYPE = "submit" NAME = "order_form_button"
         VALUE = "Checkout Stand">
   </FORM>
   </CENTER>
   </BODY>
   </HTML>!;
   }
```

Defining the Standard Page Header

The **standard_page_header** subroutine is used to generate a standard HTML header for pages within either the HTML-based or Database-based stores. It takes a single argument, the title of the page to be displayed, and is called with the following syntax:

```
&standard_page_header("TITLE");
```

Note, as in the case of **product_page_header**, all state variables must be passed as hidden fields. These hidden fields are generated by **make_hidden_fields** discussed later.

```
sub standard_page_header
   {
   local($type_of_page) = @_;
   local ($hidden_fields) = &make_hidden_fields;
   print qq!
   <HTML>
   <HEAD>
   <TITLE>$type_of_page</TITLE>
   </HEAD>
   <BODY>
   <FORM METHOD = "post" ACTION = "$sc_main_script_url">
   $hidden_fields!;
   }
```

Defining the Modify Form Footer

The **modify_form_footer** subroutine is used to generate the HTML footer code for the Modify Quantity of Items in the Cart form page. It takes no arguments and is called with the following syntax:

```
&modify_form_footer;
```

As usual, we will admit the "Return to Frontpage" button only if we are not using frames by defining it with the **$sc_no_frames_button** in **web_store.setup** .

```
sub modify_form_footer
  {
  print qq!
  <P>
  <INPUT TYPE = "submit" NAME = "submit_change_quantity_button"
         VALUE = "Submit Quantity Changes">
  <INPUT TYPE = "submit" NAME = "continue_shopping_button"
         VALUE = "Continue Shopping">
  $sc_no_frames_button
  <INPUT TYPE = "submit" NAME = "order_form_button"
         VALUE = "Checkout Stand">
  </FORM>
  </CENTER>
  </BODY>
  </HTML>!;
  }
```

Defining the Delete Form Footer

The **delete_form_footer** subroutine is used to generate the HTML footer code for the Delete Items from the Cart form page. It takes no arguments and is called with the following syntax:

```
&delete_form_footer;
```

As usual, we will admit the "Return to Frontpage" button only if we are not using frames by defining it with the **$sc_no_frames_button** in **web_store.setup** .

```
sub delete_form_footer
  {
  print qq!
  <P>
  <INPUT TYPE = "submit"
         NAME = "submit_deletion_button"
         VALUE = "Submit Deletion">
  <INPUT TYPE = "submit"
         NAME = "continue_shopping_button"
         VALUE = "Continue Shopping">
  $sc_no_frames_button
  <INPUT TYPE = "submit" NAME = "order_form_button"
         VALUE = "Checkout Stand">
  </FORM>
  </CENTER>
  </BODY>
  </HTML>!;
  }
```

Defining the Cart Footer

The **cart_footer** subroutine is used to generate the HTML footer code for the View Items in the Cart form page. It takes no arguments and is called with the following syntax:

```
&cart_footer;
```

As before, we will display the "Return to Frontpage" button only if we are not using frames by defining it with the **$sc_no_frames_button** in **web_store.setup** .

```
sub cart_footer
  {
  print qq!
```

```
<INPUT TYPE = "submit"
       NAME = "change_quantity_button"
       VALUE = "Change Quantity">
<INPUT TYPE = "submit" NAME = "delete_item_button"
       VALUE = "Delete Items">
<INPUT TYPE = "submit"
       NAME = "continue_shopping_button"
       VALUE = "Continue Shopping">
$sc_no_frames_button
<INPUT TYPE = "submit" NAME = "order_form_button"
    VALUE = "Checkout Stand">
</FORM>
</CENTER>
</BODY>
</HTML>!;
}
```

Defining the Bad Order Note

The **bad_order_note** subroutine generates an error message for the customer in the case that they have not submitted a valid number for a quantity. It takes no arguments and is called with the following syntax:

```
&bad_order_note;
```

The code is examined below:

```
sub bad_order_note
  {
  &standard_page_header("Wooopsy");
  print qq!

  <CENTER><H2>Wooopsy</H2></CENTER>

  <BLOCKQUOTE>
  I'm sorry, it appears that you did not enter a valid
  numeric quantity (whole numbers greater than zero)
  for one or more of the items you ordered and I am not
  allowed to modify your cart unless you do so. Would
  you try again?  Thanks<P>
```

```
<CENTER>
<INPUT TYPE = "submit" NAME = "try_again"
       VALUE = "Try Again">
</CENTER>

</BLOCKQUOTE>
</BODY>
</HTML>!;
exit;
}
```

Defining the Cart Table Header

The **cart_table_header** subroutine is used to generate the header HTML for views of the cart. It takes one argument, the type of view we are requesting, and is called with the following syntax:

```
&cart_table_header([TYPE OF REQUEST]);
```

First the subroutine takes **$modify_type** and makes it into a table header if it has a value. If it does not have a value, then we don't want to output a needless column. There are really only four values that modify type should be equal to:

1. "" (View/Modify Cart or Order Form Screen)
2. "New Quantity" (Change Quantity Form)
3. "Delete Item" (Delete Item Form)
4. "Process Order" (Order Form Process Confirmation)

These four types distinguish the different types of pages on which a cart will be displayed. Note that although there are more than four reasons to display the cart, the header itself is only added onto for three of the reasons. For most of the reasons such as being at the order form screen or simply viewing the cart, the header itself will stay the same without any additions. We need to know the "modify type" value in order to determine if there will be an extra table header in the cart display. In the case of quantity changes or delete item forms, there must be an extra table cell for the checkbox and text field inputs so that the customer can select items. In the View/Modify cart screen (**$modify_type ne** ""), no extra cell is necessary.

```
sub cart_table_header
  {
  local ($modify_type) = @_;

  if ($modify_type ne "")
    {
    $modify_type = "<TH>$modify_type</TH>";
    }
  print qq!
<CENTER>
<TABLE BORDER = "1">
<TR>
$modify_type!;
```

@sc_cart_display_fields is the list of all of the table headers to be displayed in the cart display table and is defined in **web_store.setup** .

```
  foreach $field (@sc_cart_display_fields)
    {
    print qq!<TH>$field</TH>\n!;
    }
```

The script also adds on table headers for **Quantity** and **Subtotal**.

```
  print qq!<TH>Quantity</TH>\n
        <TH>Subtotal</TH>\n</TR>\n!;
  }
```

Defining the Display Cart Table

The job of **display_cart_table** is to display the current contents of the customer's cart for several different types of screens, all of which display the cart in some form or another. The subroutine takes one argument, which is the reason that the cart is being displayed. It is called with the following syntax:

```
&display_cart_table("reason");
```

There are really only five values that **$reason_to_display_cart** should be equal to:

1. "" (View/Modify Cart Screen)
2. "change quantity" (Change Quantity Form)
3. "delete" (Delete Item Form)
4. "order form" (Order Form)
5. "process order" (Order Form Process Confirmation)

Notice that this corresponds closely to the list in **cart_table_header** because the goal of this subroutine is to fill in the actual cells of the table created by **cart_table_header**. In this list, however, there is one more explicit reason listed for displaying the actual cart table. This is because the cart table display is a little more complex than the cart header display routine. There are more types of changes made to the way the cart table is displayed. These various reasons and how they affect the code will be discussed below.

```
sub display_cart_table
  {
```

Working variables are initialized and defined as local to this subroutine.

```
   local($reason_to_display_cart) = @_;
  local(@cart_fields);
  local($cart_id_number);
  local($quantity);
  local($unformatted_subtotal);
  local($subtotal);
  local($unformatted_grand_total);
  local($grand_total);
  local($price);
  local($text_of_cart);
  local($total_quantity) = 0;
  local($total_measured_quantity) = 0;
  local($display_index);
  local($counter);
  local($hidden_field_name);
  local($hidden_field_value);
  local($display_counter);
  local($product_id, @db_row);
```

Next, the script determines which type of cart display it is being asked to produce. It uses pattern-matching to look for key phrases in the **$reason_to_display_cart**

defined as an incoming argument. Whatever the case, the subroutine calls
cart_table_header to begin outputting the HTML cart display.

```
if ($reason_to_display_cart =~ /change*quantity/i)
  {
  &cart_table_header("New Quantity");
  }

elsif ($reason_to_display_cart =~ /delete/i)
  {
  &cart_table_header("Delete Item");
  }

else
  {
  &cart_table_header("");
  }
```

Next, the customer's cart is read line by line. File open errors are handled by
file_open_error as usual.

```
open (CART, "$sc_cart_path") ||
&file_open_error("$sc_cart_path",
                 "display_cart_contents", __FILE__,
  __LINE__);
while (<CART>)
  {
```

Since every line in the cart will be displayed as a cell in an HTML table, we
begin by outputting an opening <TR> tag.

```
print "<TR>";
```

Next, the current line has its final newline character chopped off.

```
chop;
```

Then, the script splits the row in the customer's cart and grabs the unique
product i.d. number, the unique cart i.d. number, and the quantity. We will use
those values while processing the cart.

```
@cart_fields = split (/\|/, $_);
$cart_row_number = pop(@cart_fields);
push (@cart_fields, $cart_row_number);
```

```
$quantity = $cart_fields[0];
$product_id = $cart_fields[1];
```

Next, we will need to begin to distinguish between types of displays we are being asked for, because each type of display is slightly different. For example, if we are being asked to display a cart for the Delete Item form, we will need to add a checkbox before each item so that the customer can select which items to delete. If, on the other hand, we are being asked for Modify the Quantity of an Item form, we need to add a text field instead, so that the customer can enter a new quantity.

The first case we will handle is if we are being asked to display the cart as part of order processing.

```
if (($reason_to_display_cart =~ /process.*order/i) &&
    ($sc_order_check_db =~ /yes/i))
      {
```

If we are displaying the cart for order processing *and* we are checking the database to make sure that the product being ordered is OK, then we need to load the database libraries if they have not required already.

```
if (!($sc_db_lib_was_loaded =~ /yes/i))
  {
  &require_supporting_libraries (__FILE__, __LINE__,
                                 "$sc_db_lib_path");
  }
```

Then, we call the **check_db_with_product_id** in the database library. If it returns "false," then we output a footer complaining about the problem and exit the program.

```
if (!(&check_db_with_product_id($product_id,*db_row)))
  {
  print qq~
  </TR></TABLE>
  Product ID: $product_id not found in database. Your
  order will NOT be processed without this validation!
  </BODY>
  </HTML>~;
  exit;
  }
```

Otherwise, we check the returned row with the price of the product in the cart. If the prices do not match, then another complaint message is printed and we exit the program.

```
else
  {
  if ($db_row[$sc_db_index_of_price] ne
      $cart_fields[$sc_cart_index_of_price])
    {
    print qq~
    </TR></TABLE>
    Price for product id:$product_id did not match
    database! Your order will NOT be processed without
    this validation!
    </BODY>
    </HTML>~;
    exit;
    }
  } # End of Else
  } # End of if (($reason_to_display_...
```

Remember, we need to use the **display_table_cart** to keep track of totals such as quantity, subtotal, and total measured quantity. Directly below, we keep track of total quantity.

```
$total_quantity += $quantity;
```

Now, we need to fill in the table row for every cart database row. **@sc_display_numbers** defined in the database-specific Setup file will give us the array numbers associated with the fields that we want displayed on this table. Then we will get the value of number from the **cart_fields** array. Hidden fields are generated with the items in the cart if we are displaying the order form and wish the form to be submitted to a different CGI script that merely takes in all form values indiscriminately. The use of hidden fields to store cart information is discussed in Chapter 9.

```
if (($reason_to_display_cart =~ /order*form/i) &&
    ($sc_order_with_hidden_fields =~ /yes/i))
    {
    $counter++;
    $hidden_field_name = "cart-"
      . substr("000", length($counter))
```

```
        . $counter;
$hidden_field_value = join("\|", @cart_fields);
$hidden_field_value =~ s/\"/~qq~/g;
$hidden_field_value =~ s/\>/~gt~/g;
$hidden_field_value =~ s/\</~lt~/g;

print qq!
<INPUT TYPE = "HIDDEN"
       NAME = "$hidden_field_name"
       VALUE = "$hidden_field_value">
!;
}
```

In the case of a Quantity Change form, we will need to create a cell for the text field into which the customer can input a new quantity. The NAME value is set equal to the unique cart i.d. number of the current item so that when we submit this information, the items will be associated with the new quantities.

```
if ($reason_to_display_cart =~ /change*quantity/i)
  {
  print qq!
  <TD ALIGN = "center">
  <INPUT TYPE = "text" NAME = "$cart_row_number"
         SIZE ="3"></TD>!;
  }
```

Similarly, in the case of a Delete Item form, we must include a cell with a checkbox so that the customer can select items to delete from their cart. The NAME value is set equal to the unique cart i.d. number of the current item so that when we submit this information, the items will be associated with the checked checkboxes.

```
elsif ($reason_to_display_cart =~ /delete/i)
  {
  print qq!
  <TD ALIGN = "center">
  <INPUT TYPE = "checkbox" NAME = "$cart_row_number">!;
  }
```

$display_counter is set equal to zero. This variable will be used to keep track of the number of displayed fields.

$text_of_cart is initialized with two newlines. This variable will be used to hold the entire formatted cart contents in one string so that we will be able to send a neatly formatted copy of the cart as plain ASCII to a log file or as email to the admin. We will be using the **.=** operator to append to the variable rather than overwrite it.

```
$display_counter = 0;
$text_of_cart .= "\n\n";
```

Now, for every item in the cart row that should be displayed as defined in the Setup file, we will do two things. First, we will append the data to the **$text_of_cart** variable (formatting it neatly). Then we will display the data as a table cell. However, there are three types of data that must be displayed in table cells but each must be formatted slightly differently. The first type of cell is a cell with no data. To give the table a three-dimensional look, we will substitute all occurrences of no data for the ** ** character in order to get a blank but indented table cell. Of course, this routine simply overwrites the empty value of the data with the ** ** character. It does not actually display the cell; it passes that job on to the next "if" test.

Another case is when a table cell must reflect a price. In that case we must format the data with the monetary symbol defined in **web_store.setup**, using **display_price** as discussed in **web_store.cgi**. Finally, nonprice table cells are displayed (including those passed down from the first case).

```
foreach $display_index (@sc_cart_index_for_display)
   {
```

Reformat blank cells.
```
if ($cart_fields[$display_index] eq "")
   {
```

The text of the cart is entered into a buffer. The actual item being purchased is formatted inside a 25-character-width field.

```
$text_of_cart .= $sc_cart_display_fields[$display_counter] .
        substr((" " x 25),
length($sc_cart_display_fields[$display_counter])) .
        "= nothing entered\n";
$cart_fields[$display_index] = " ";
      }
```

Then the script displays the price or price after options cells.

```
if (($display_index ==
 $sc_cart_index_of_price_after_options)||
    ($display_index ==
 $sc_cart_index_of_price))
  {
  $price = &display_price($cart_fields[$display_index]);
  print qq!<TD ALIGN = "center">$price</TD>\n!;
  $text_of_cart .= $sc_cart_display_fields[$display_counter] .
        substr((" " x 25),
        length($sc_cart_display_fields[$display_counter])) .
        "= $price\n";
  }
```

Next, the script displays all other cells (blank cells have already been reformatted).

```
else
  {
  print qq!<TD ALIGN =
    "center">$cart_fields[$display_index]</TD>\n!;
  $text_of_cart .= $sc_cart_display_fields[$display_counter] .
        substr((" " x 25),
        length($sc_cart_display_fields[$display_counter])) .
        "= $cart_fields[$display_index]\n";
  }
```

If the current display index happens to be a cell that must be measured, we will add the value to **$total_measured_quantity** for later calculation and display.

```
if ($display_index == $sc_cart_index_of_measured_value)
  {
  $total_measured_quantity += $cart_fields[$display_index];
  }

  $display_counter++;
} # End of foreach $display_index...
```

Then, we must use the quantity value we earlier grabbed to fill the next table cell, and, after using another database specific setup variable, calculate the subtotal for that database row and the final cell and close out the table row and the cart file once we have gone all the way through it.

```
$unformatted_subtotal =
        ($quantity*$cart_fields[$sc_cart_index_of_price_after_options]);
$subtotal = &format_price($unformatted_subtotal);
$unformatted_grand_total = $grand_total + $subtotal;
$grand_total = &format_price($unformatted_grand_total);

$price = &display_price($subtotal);
print qq!<TD ALIGN = "center">$quantity</TD>
        <TD ALIGN = "center">$price</TD>
        </TR>!;
$text_of_cart .= "Quantity" .
        substr((" " x 25),
        length("Quantity")) .
        "= $quantity\n";
$text_of_cart .= "Subtotal For Item" .
        substr((" " x 25),
        length("Subtotal For Item")) .
        "= $price\n";

} # End of while (<CART>)
close (CART);
```

Finally, print out the footer with the **cart_table_footer** subroutine in **web_store.html**.

```
$price = &display_price($grand_total);
&cart_table_footer($price);
```

In the case of an order form, we will also have to create a hidden input tag with which to transfer the subtotal state information to the order processing routines.

This is necessary only if the order is being submitted to another server that does not have access to the cart file for processing against.

```
if (($reason_to_display_cart =~ /order*form/i) &&
    ($sc_order_with_hidden_fields =~ /yes/i))
  {
  $hidden_field_name = "subtotal";
  $hidden_field_value = $subtotal;
  print qq!
<INPUT TYPE = "HIDDEN" NAME = "$hidden_field_name"
        VALUE = "$hidden_field_value">!;
  }
```

The **Subtotal** information is also added to **$text_of_cart**:

```
$text_of_cart .= "\n\nSubtotal:" . substr((" " x 25),
length("Subtotal:")) ."= $price\n\n";
```

We need to return the subtotal for routines such as ordering calculations. We also need to return the text of the cart in case we are logging orders to email or to a file:

```
return($grand_total,
       $total_quantity,
       $total_measured_quantity,
       $text_of_cart);
  } # End of display_cart_table
```

Defining the Cart Table Footer

The **cart_table_footer** subroutine is used to display the footer for cart table displays. It takes one argument, the preshipping grand total and is called with the following syntax:

```
&cart_table_footer(PRICE);
```

The code is examined below:

```
sub cart_table_footer
  {
  local($price) = @_;
  print qq!
</TABLE>
<P>
Pre-shipping Grand Total = $price
<P>!;
  }
```

Automatically Generating Hidden Fields

The **make_hidden_fields** subroutine is used to generate the hidden fields necessary for maintaining state. It takes no arguments and is called with the following syntax:

```
&make_hidden_fields;
The code is explained below:
```

```
sub make_hidden_fields
  {
  local($hidden);
  local($db_query_row);
  local($db_form_field);
```

$hidden is defined initially as containing the **cart_id** and page **hidden** tags that are necessary state variables on *every* page in the cart. The script then goes through checking to see which optional state variables it has received as incoming form data. For each of those, the script adds a **hidden** input tag.

```
$hidden = qq!
<INPUT TYPE = "hidden" NAME = "cart_id"
       VALUE = "$cart_id">
<INPUT TYPE = "hidden" NAME = "page"
       VALUE = "$form_data{'page'}">!;
if ($form_data{'keywords'} ne "")
  {
  $hidden .= qq!
  <INPUT TYPE = "hidden" NAME = "keywords"
         VALUE = "$form_data{'keywords'}">!;
  }

if ($form_data{'exact_match'} ne "")
  {
  $hidden .= qq!
  <INPUT TYPE = "hidden" NAME = "exact_match"
         VALUE = "$form_data{'exact_match'}">!;
  }
if ($form_data{'case_sensitive'} ne "")
  {
  $hidden .= qq!
  <INPUT TYPE = "hidden" NAME = "case_sensitive"
         VALUE = "$form_data{'case_sensitive'}">!;
  }

foreach $db_query_row (@sc_db_query_criteria)
  {
  $db_form_field = (split(/\|/, $db_query_row))[0];
  if ($form_data{$db_form_field} ne "" &&
      $db_form_field ne "keywords")
    {
    $hidden .= qq!
```

```
    <INPUT TYPE = "hidden" NAME = "$db_form_field"
          VALUE = "$form_data{$db_form_field}">!;
    }
  }
return ($hidden);
} # End of make_hidden_fields
```

Displaying Results for No Hits Found in HTML Search

The **PrintNoHitsBodyHTML** subroutine is utilized by the HTML-based store search routines to produce an error message in case no *hits* (successful matches) were found, based on the customer-defined keywords It is called with no arguments and the following syntax:

```
&PrintNoHitsBodyHTML;
```

The code is shown below:

```
sub PrintNoHitsBodyHTML
  {
  print qq!
  <P>
  <CENTER>
  <H2>Sorry, No Pages Were Found With Your
      Keyword(s).</H2>
  </CENTER>
  <P>!;
  }
```

Defining the Body in the HTML Search

The **PrintBodyHTML** subroutine is utilized by the HTML-based store search routines to produce a list of hits. These hits will be those pages that had the customer-defined keywords within them. The subroutine takes two arguments, the filename as it will appear in the URL link as well as the text that should be visibly hyperlinked and is called with the following syntax:

```
&PrintBodyHTML("file.name", "Title to be linked");
```

The code is shown below:

```
sub PrintBodyHTML
  {
  local($filename, $title) = @_;
  print qq!
  <LI><B>
  <A HREF =
"$sc_main_script_url?page=$filename&cart_id=$cart_id">$title</A>
  </B>(/$filename)!;
  }
1;
```

CHAPTER THIRTEEN

THE KEYWORD

SEARCH LIBRARY

This subroutine library is used to handle keyword search requests for the HTML-based Web store. Its job is to search every HTML product file for occurrences of the keywords specified in the keyword input field and create an HTML page containing links to every one of those pages.

Thus, it creates an intermediate dynamically generated HTML list of product pages.

Defining the Operating Environment

```
sub html_search
  {
```

The subroutine begins by defining a few important variables coming in as form data:

- **$keywords** will be set equal to the string entered by the customer in the TEXT field form input box named 'keywords'.

- **$exact_match** will be set either to on or null depending on whether or not the customer clicked the checkbox named **exact_match**. It is not necessary for an administrator to even have this checkbox on the form. If the administrator does not include this option on the form, the script will simply search according to whole-word matching.

279

- **$case_sensitive** will similarly be set to on or null depending on whether the customer has clicked the checkbox named **case_sensitive**. Again, the administrator may choose to not give the customer the option if she so chooses.

```
$keywords = $form_data{'keywords'};
$exact_match = $form_data{'exact_match'};
$case_sensitive = $form_data{'case_sensitive'};
```

Then, **@keyword_list** is created by splitting the **$keywords** string on every occurrence of a space. Thus, all the keywords may be individually checked.

NOTE This script searches according to the "and" methodology. That is, every word (defined as characters separated by white spaces) must appear on the page searched for it to register a hit. The script does not support "or" searching.

```
@keyword_list = split(/\s+/, $keywords);
```

Displaying the HTML Header

The HTML header for the results page is sent to the browser:

```
print qq!
<HTML>
<HEAD>
<TITLE>Search Results</TITLE></HEAD>
<BODY BGCOLOR = "FFFFFF" TEXT = "000000">
<UL>!;
```

Performing the Search

Before going further, let us step back and see what the script needs to do in order to perform a keyword search. The routine needs to traverse the directory structure under **$root_web_path** and in doing so, also parse the HTML files to see if they have the keywords we are searching for and, if a match is found, it must determine what the HTML titles are in order to build of a list of successful hits for the client.

As the script goes down a directory looking for entries, if it finds that one of those entries is a directory, then that directory is opened. This directory becomes the new directory to traverse. In order to keep traveling down the directory tree, the script needs to keep track of where it has been. An array called **@dirs** keeps track of thissearch by containing the already open directory names that the script has not yet finished searching. As a directory gets opened for searching, it is appended as a new

element to the end of the **@dirs** array.

The following code sets up the initial variables for the algorithm described above.

- **@dirs** is an array of directories that is used as a placeholder for going back up the directory tree when we run out of files to read in a subdirectory.

- **$cur_dir** is the current directory number as a reference to the element in @dirs for which directory we are currently reading. The directory handles in this program are referred to as the string **DIR** followed by the current directory number indicated by **DIR$cur_dir**.

- **number_of_hits** is the current number of successful hits found while searching the files. The number of hits is equal to the number of files that will be returned as matches for the keyword terms:

```
@dirs = ($sc_root_web_path);
$number_of_hits = 0;
$cur_dir = 0;
```

We initialize the process by opening the directory handle using the reference **DIR$cur_dir** and the path that has been passed to the **@dirs** array. **$end_of_all_files** is a flag that when set to 1, will stop the searching routine since it means that we have finished searching every file in every directory that we can search.

```
$end_of_all_files = 0;
opendir("DIR$cur_dir", $dirs[$cur_dir]);
```

The following while loop does not exit until the script is through searching all of the files. Within this top level while loop, there is a second level while loop that goes on forever unless the **last** command is encountered inside. It is inside this second while loop that the directory tree for HTML documents is traversed:

```
while (!($end_of_all_files))
  {
  while (1)
    {
```

First, the script grabs a reference to the next valid directory or filename into the **$filename** variable. Next, **$fullpath** is set to the current path plus filename:

```
$filename = &GetNextEntry("DIR$cur_dir",
            $dirs[$cur_dir]);
$fullpath = "$dirs[$cur_dir]/$filename";
```

Then, for the entry that was received, the routine goes through multiple cases and does dwhat is appropriate for those cases. Five basic cases are discussed further below.

Case 1: No More Files in Current Directory

In case 1, the file is NULL, but since there are still entries in the **@dirs** variable, the program goes back up the directory tree and continues searching in a previous directory where it left off. Specifically, this involves closing the current directory, subtracting one from the **$cur_dir** variable and then issuing a **next** command to force another iteration through the WHILE(1) loop again:

```
if (!($filename) && $cur_dir > 0)
  {
  closedir("DIR$cur_dir");
  $cur_dir--;
  next;
  }
```

Case 2: The End of the Search

In case 2, there are no more filenames to search on, but the script has already been through all the previous entries in the **@dirs** array. Thus, the search must end. This is done by closing the current directory handle, setting the **$end_of_all_files** to one, and issuing the **last** command to break completely out of the WHILE(1) loop:

```
if (!($filename))
  {
  closedir("DIR$cur_dir");
  $end_of_all_files = 1;
  last;
  }
```

Case 3: The File is a Directory

Case 3 discovers that the filename is actually a directory, so the script descends down into the directory if it is both readable and executable. The program checks if the file is a directory using the -**d** flag. It also checks for Readability and Execute rights by using the -**r** and -**x** flags.

Finally, the program goes down the directory tree if the filename is a directory, by incrementing the current directory counter, **$cur_dir**, by one, pushing a new path onto the **@dirs** array, and opening a new directory handle. Finally, the **next** command is used to force the script to go back to the top of the WHILE(1) loop:

```
if (-d $fullpath)
    {
       if (-r $fullpath && -x $fullpath)
         {
         $cur_dir++;
         $dirs[$cur_dir] = $fullpath;
         opendir("DIR$cur_dir", $dirs[$cur_dir]);
         next;
         }
       else
         {
         next;
         }
    } # End of Case 3 (File is directory
```

Case 4: The File Is Unwanted

In Case 4, the script checks to see if the file about to be searched is actually unwanted. The program starts by setting the **$unwanted_file** flag to 0. Then, each unwanted file in the **@unwanted_files** array is gone through and checked if the filename and path is unwanted by doing a pattern match against it. If it is, then the **$unwanted_file** flag is set to 1. Finally, after all the **@unwanted_files** have been checked, if the **$unwanted_file** flag is equal to 1, the **next** command is issued to reiterate through the WHILE(1) loop again:

```
$unwanted_file = 0;
foreach (@sc_unwanted_files)
    {
      if ($fullpath =~ /"$_"/)
      {
        $unwanted_file = 1;
        }
      } # End of foreach unwanted files
if ($unwanted_file)
      {
      next;
      } # End of Case 4 Unwanted File
```

Case 5: The File Must Be Searched

In this, the last case, the script finds out that the file really is a file that we want to search for keywords in. The **-r** flag is used to check if the file is readable and if it is, the **last** command is issued in order to force a breakout of the WHILE(1) loop. Breaking out of this loop will allow the script to move on and search through the file:

```
    if (-r $fullpath)
      {
      last;
      } # Make sure the file is readable
  } # End of While (1)
```

After the WHILE(1) loop, we check again for the **$end_of_all_files** flag. If it is not set equal to one then the script can continue the file searching:

```
if (!($end_of_all_files))
  {
```

When we search a file, we initially set **@not_found_words** equal to the array of keywords we want to search. This corresponds to the idea that initially all of the words are not found. As we search the file and find keywords later on, those keywords will be deleted from the **@not_found_words** array. When the

@not_found_words array has no elements left in it, we know that all the keywords were found in the file and that we have found a hit:

```
@not_found_words = @keyword_list;
```

In addition to searching for the keyword, we will attempt to parse out the name of the title of the HTML file. The **$are_we_in_head** flag is initially set to zero. If it is zero, we know that we are in the header of the HTML file still. Upon reaching a </HEAD> or </TITLE> flag, the script knows that it is done reading the header. The header is read into the **$headline** variable.

```
$are_we_in_head = 0;
    open(SEARCHFILE, $fullpath);
    $headline = "";
    while(<SEARCHFILE>)
      {
      $line = $_;
      $headline .= $line if ($are_we_in_head == 0);
      $are_we_in_head = 1
        if (($line =~ m!</head>!i) || ($line =~
          </title>!i));
```

The **&FindKeywords** subroutine performs the actual searching of the keywords in each line as it is read in from the file. When the **&FindKeywords** subroutine finds a match, it deletes the keyword from the **@not_found_words** array:

```
&FindKeywords($exact_match, $case_sensitive,
                    $line, *not_found_words);
    } # End of SEARCHFILE
    close (SEARCHFILE);
```

Displaying the Search Hits

If the **@not_found_words** array is less than 1, the script knows that all the keywords were found, so it prints out the matched files. Part of the routine that prints out the match consists of parsing the title of the document out of the HTML code stored in **$headline**:

```
if (@not_found_words < 1)
    {
```

The first thing the routine does is replace all newlines with spaces in **$headline**. Then, it sets up a match against the regular expression <title>(.*)</title>. This expression matches for zero or more characters between the <TITLE> HTML tags. In Perl, the successful match will make the variable **$1** equal to the characters between the <TITLE> tags. The **i** at the end of the match expression indicates that the match is done without regard to case. If the title turns out not to exist in this document, the **$title** variable is set to **"No Title Given"**.

NOTE

We use a special form of the match operator below. Most of the time we use **/**'s to indicate the endpoints of a search. Here, we use the m (match) operator followed by a different character to use as our matching operator. In this case, we use the exclamation point (**!**) to delimit the search. The reason we do this is because we are including **/**'s inside the actual expression to search, and escaping them with the backslash (****) would look messy.

```
$headline =~ s/\n/ /g;
$headline =~ m!<title>(.*)</title>!i;
$title = $1;

if ($title eq "")
  {
  $title = "No Title Given";
  }
```

The program then strips out the **$root_web_path** because it contains information we do not want to pass to the user about the internal directory structure of the Web server. Finally, the script prints out the HTML code related to the hit that we have found and increments the hit counter.

```
$fullpath =~ s!$sc_root_web_path/!!;
&PrintBodyHTML($fullpath, $title);
$number_of_hits++;

  } # If there are no not_found_words
 } # If Not The End of all Files
} # End of While Not At The End Of All Files
```

If there were no results found, the HTML for "getting no hits" is printed out.

```
if ($number_of_hits == 0)
  {
  &PrintNoHitsBodyHTML;
  }
```

```
print qq!</UL></BODY></HTML>!;
} # end of subroutine
```

FindKeywords Subroutine

The **FindKeywords** subroutine is the core routine of the entire search engine and is called with the following syntax:

```
&FindKeywords("on", "on", $line, *not_found_words);
```

As you can see, the subroutine accepts a line of a file and the keywords to search for in that line. If a keyword is found, the routine splices it out of the keyword array (**@not_found_words**). Thus, when the **@not_found_words** array no longer has any elements in it, the script knows that all the keywords have been found in the file:

```
sub FindKeywords
  {
```

There are four parameters. The first, **$exact_match**, is equal to **on** if the type of pattern match we are doing is based on an exact one to one match of each letter in the keyword to each letter in a word contained in the HTML document. Likewise, the **$case_sensitive** variable is on if the customer requested case sensitivity in the search. The third parameter, **$line**, is a line in the HTML file that is currently being searched for the keywords. The fourth and final parameter, ***not_found_words**, is a reference to the array **@not_found_words**, which contain a list of all the keywords not found so far. As keywords get found in the searched file, this array has its words removed. Thus, when the array is empty, we know the file contained all the keywords. In other words, there are no "not found words" if the search is successful:

```
  local($exact_match, $case_sensitive,
$line, *not_found_words) = @_;
  local($x, $match_word);
```

If the exact match and case sensitivity are on, then the program matches all the words in the array by surrounding the keywords with **\b**. This means that the keyword has to be surrounded by word boundaries in order to be a valid match. Thus, the keyword *the* would not match a word like *there* , since *the* is only part of a larger word:

```
if ($case_sensitive eq "on")
  {
  if ($exact_match eq "on")
    {
    for ($x = @not_found_words; $x > 0; $x--)
      {
      $match_word = $not_found_words[$x - 1];
      if ($line =~ /\b$match_word\b/)
        {
```

The **splice** routine used below cuts out the words if they satisfy the search. The **splice** command is a Perl routine that accepts the original array, the element in the array to splice, the number of elements to splice, and a list or array to splice into the original array. Since we are leaving off the fourth parameter of the splice, the routine by default splices "nothing" into the array as the element number. This deletes the element in one convenient little routine:

```
        splice(@not_found_words,$x - 1, 1);
        }
      } # End of for ($x = @not_found_words...
    }
```

If the exact match is not on, then the program will match simply on the basis of the letters in the keyword existing anywhere on the line regardless of if that keyword is part of a larger word or not:

```
else
  {
  for ($x = @not_found_words; $x > 0; $x--)
    {
    $match_word = $not_found_words[$x - 1];
    if ($line =~ /$match_word/)
    {
      splice(@not_found_words,$x - 1, 1);
      } # End of If
    } # End of for ($x = @not_found_words...
  } # End of ELSE
}
```

Next, handle the case-insensitive situation with the exact same routines but performing searches with case-insensitive as indicated by the **i** given after the slashes defining the search term:

```perl
else
{
if ($exact_match eq "on")
   {
   for ($x = @not_found_words; $x > 0; $x--)
      {
      $match_word = $not_found_words[$x - 1];
      if ($line =~ /\b$match_word\b/i)
      {
         splice(@not_found_words,$x - 1, 1);
         } # End of If
      } # End of for ($x = @not_found_words...
   }
   else
   {
   for ($x = @not_found_words; $x > 0; $x--)
      {
      $match_word = $not_found_words[$x - 1];
      if ($line =~ /$match_word/i)
         {
         splice(@not_found_words,$x - 1, 1);
         } # End of If
      } # End of For Loop
   } # End of ELSE
  }
} # End of FindKeywords
```

GetNextEntry Subroutine

The **GetNextEntry** subroutine reads the directory handle for the next entry in the directory. The routine accepts the current directory handle and the current directory path as parameters and is called with the following syntax:

```perl
&GetNextEntry(DIRECTORY_HANDLE, "directory_name");
```

The code is explained below:

```perl
sub GetNextEntry
  {
local($dirhandle, $directory) = @_;
```

If the next entry is a file, the program checks to see if the file has a **.htm** or **.html** extension. This is accomplished by using the regular expression **/htm.?/i**. The **.?** matches any character once after the **htm**. The **i** after the search terms, tells the program to treat upper- and lower-case characters equally:

```
while ($filename = readdir($dirhandle))
  {
  if (($filename =~ /htm.?/i) ||
  (!($filename =~ /^\.\.?$/) && -d
  "$directory/$filename"))
    {
```

If the program satisfies one of these two conditions, the while loop that reads in subsequent directory entries is exited with the **last** command and the found filename/directory name is returned from the subroutine:

```
last;
} # End of IF Filename is html document or a directory
} # End of while still stuff to read
```

The filename will be valid if it is a directory or an HTML file

```
$filename;
} # End of GetNextEntry
1;
```

CHAPTER FOURTEEN

THE DATABASE
SEARCH LIBRARY

The Database Search Library (**web_store_db_lib.pl**) is the Web store's interface to databases. By default, this library provides only an interface to ASCII text file databases. However, because this library acts as a gateway to the text file databases, you can easily change this library to access a real database engine inside the subroutines such as mSQL, Sybase, or Oracle. There are only two routines in this library that are called by the main Web store script: **check_db_with_product_id** and **submit_query**. The rest of the routines in this library are merely supporting routines. If you want to modify the library to access another database engine, the only routines you have to change are **check_db_with_product_id** and **submit_query.**

Global Variables

There is one global variable set inside this library: **$sc_db_lib_was_loaded**. It is set to "yes" so that the main Web store script will know that this library was already loaded once and not to load it a second time if there are multiple references to this script inside the Web store. Since the database library routines are not always used in the Web store, this library is only loaded on an as-needed basis for efficiency. However, because the script is loaded on an as-needed basis, we want to make sure that we do not load the script more than once during the course of running the Web store.

N O T E   The **Require** command itself keeps track of which libraries were loaded and does not load them twice. However, the subroutine that is used by the Web store script to check the permissions and existence of the required file is inefficient to run multiple times. Thus, the **$sc_db_lib_was_loaded** flag to indicates to the script whether the library of routines is already in use.

```
$sc_db_lib_was_loaded = "yes";
```

check_db_with_product_id Subroutine

The **check_db_with_product_id** subroutine is used by the Web store to make sure that the price and other information about the product in the database matches the information about the item that the customer is ordering. This is really a security check to make sure that the customer has not found a way to hack into the HTML interface and change the pricing and other vital information about the item. This routine merely returns the contents of the database row to the calling subroutine. The Web store itself does the field comparisons once the row has been retrieved from the database matching the product i.d.

The routine is called with two parameters: **$product_id** and ***db_row**. **$product_id** is the unique product i.d. number of the row that needs to be retrieved. The contents of the row are passed back to **@db_row**. Because **@db_row** was passed to the routine by reference using the * operator, changes to **@db_row** inside the subroutine are returned back to the original caller of this routine:

```
sub check_db_with_product_id {
  local($product_id, *db_row) = @_;
  local($db_product_id);
```

The first thing that the script does is open the data file. If the open file call fails, the **file_open_error** routine will record the error:

```
open(DATAFILE, "$sc_data_file_path") ||
    &file_open_error("$sc_data_file_path",
      "Read Database",__FILE__,__LINE__);
```

Each line in the data file is read into the variable **$line**. Then, the line is split into fields that are subsequently placed in **@db_row**. If it turns out that the product i.d. matches the product i.d. in the database row, the while loop will stop and **@db_row** will contain the row matching the product i.d. The file is then closed:

```
while (($line = <DATAFILE>) &&
        ($product_id ne $db_product_id)) {
    @db_row = split(/\|/,$line);
    $db_product_id = $db_row[0];
  }

  close (DATAFILE);
```

Finally, the subroutine returns the status of the database search. This is done by testing the Boolean expression "is the given product i.d. equal to the product i.d. of the last row that was retrieved from the database." If this statement is true, then the value of "TRUE" is returned from the subroutine. If this statement is false, then the value of "FALSE" is returned from the subroutine. This returned value is used by the script calling this routine to see whether the database row matching the product ID really was found or not:

```
return ($product_id eq $db_product_id);

} # End of check_db_with_product_id
```

submit_query Subroutine

The **submit_query** subroutine is called in order to return the results of a query on the database file. It is called with only one parameter: ***db_rows. *db_rows** is actually an array of pipe-delimited (|) rows that satisfy the query results. The * operator means that the variable is passed by reference so that when the subroutine changes the array and populates it with rows, these changes will be reflected back to the original variable that was passed in the calling script:

```
sub submit_query
{
  local(*database_rows) = @_;
```

The next few lines of code declare some variables that will be used in this sub-routine but will be invisible outsode of it (local variables). The last two variables (**$exact_match** and **$case_sensitive**) are set equal to the form variables of the same name. Chapter 5 discussed how these form variables affect the behavior of queries involving data types equal to "string" with the equals (=) comparison operator.

```
local($status);
local(@fields);
local($row_count);
local(@not_found_criteria);
local($line); # Read line from database

local($exact_match) = $form_data{'exact_match'};
local($case_sensitive) = $form_data{'case_sensitive'};
```

Since there have been no rows found yet, **$row_count** is initialized to zero:

```
$row_count = 0;
```

The data file is opened for reading. If there is an error while performing this operation, the routine **file_open_error** is called:

```
open(DATAFILE, "$sc_data_file_path") ||
    &file_open_error("$sc_data_file_path",
        "Read Database",__FILE__,__LINE__);
```

Then, every line of the file is read into the **$line** variable using a while loop. As long as the row count does not exceed your configured maximum amount of rows to return (as configured in the Setup file), the data file keeps getting read into **$line** so that the query criteria can be applied to each line:

```
while(($line = <DATAFILE> ) &&
        ($row_count< $sc_db_max_rows_returned+1))
  {
```

Before any processing is done on the line, the newline character at the end is stripped off:

```
chop ($line);
```

Each field is split based on the pipe delimiter (|):

```
@fields = split(/\|/, $line);
```

Now the actual query criteria is applied to the line. First, **$not_found** is initialized to zero. This means that there is nothing "not found" yet. This basically means that we are assuming that the query criteria is satisfied by the row (innocent until proven guilty).

Then, for each criteria specified in the **@sc_db_query_criteria** array from the setup file, the script calls a routine to apply the criteria (**flatfile_apply_criteria**). If the criteria is not satisfied, the routine returns the value **1,** which would increment the **$not_found** variable. Thus, **$not_found** will end up being the number of criteria that were not found. By the end of the foreach loop, if **$not_found** is still zero, this means that the criteria was applied successfully:

```
$not_found = 0;
foreach $criteria (@sc_db_query_criteria)
{
$not_found += &flatfile_apply_criteria(
 $exact_match,
 $case_sensitive,
 *fields,
 $criteria);
    }
```

If **$not_found** is zero, and the row count has not exceeded the maximum amount of rows that are supposed to be returned, then the row is pushed into the **@db_rows** array as a pipe-delimited list of fields:

```
if (($not_found == 0) &&
      ($row_count <= $sc_db_max_rows_returned))
   {
     push(@database_rows, join("\|", @fields));
   }
```

Even if the maximum amount of rows being returned has been exceeded, if **$not_found** is zero, the script increments the row count:

```
if ($not_found == 0) {
     $row_count++;
   }
 } # End of while datafile has data
```

Now that the data file has finished being processed, it is closed by the routine:

```
close (DATAFILE);
```

If the row count exceeds the maximum amount of rows that are allowed to be returned, then the status variable is set equal to an error message related to this fact:

```
if ($row_count > $sc_db_max_rows_returned) {
    $status = "max_rows_exceeded";
}
```

Finally, the status and row count are returned to the calling script and the subroutine ends:

```
return($status,$row_count);

} # End of submit query
```

flatfile_apply_criteria Subroutine

The **flatfile_apply_criteria** subroutine is not actually called by the main Web store script. However, it is the heart of the logic inside this library. It basically does the actual comparison of the query criteria against the rows in the ASCII text flatfile that forms the default database for the Web store. This routine accepts four parameters: **$exact_match**, **$case_sensitive**, ***fields**, and **$criteria**—which will be examined below.

$exact_match and **$case_sensitive** are the values of the corresponding form variables. ***fields** is an array of database fields that are passed by reference.

N O T E   Passing an argument by reference is different from passing by value. *Passing by value* means that the variable that is being passed to the subroutine has a new copy of it allocated in memory that is passed on locally to the subroutine. *Passing by reference,* on the other hand, means that a pointer (location of) the variable is passed to the subroutine. Since the location of the original contents of the variable is passed to the subroutine, it allows the subroutine to make changes to the variable and have the changes take effect on the original contents of the variable. In addition, passing by reference is considered more efficient when dealing with large values such as fields from a database, because making a copy of many bytes of data is time-consuming whereas simply passing a reference to the location of a large block of data is less time consuming to perform.

$criteria is the current criteria from the **@sc_db_query_criteria** array that is being applied to this database row.

> **NOTE** Before reading about what this subroutine does, it is recommended that you go through Chapter 5 in order to get a firm grasp on the logic that is used when applying the criteria defined in the **@sc_db_query_criteria** array.

```
sub flatfile_apply_criteria
{
  local($exact_match, $case_sensitive,
      *fields, $criteria) = @_;
```

$c_name, **$c_fields**, **$c_op**, and **$c_type** are declared local. They will correspond to the fields in the criteria array. The rest of the variables below are declared to be local to the subroutine as well.

```
local($c_name, $c_fields, $c_op, $c_type);
```

@criteria_fields is an array that will hold the index of which fields in the database this criteria will apply to. Recall from the discussion in Chapter 5, that you can define a form field as being able to be matched against more than one field at a time:

```
local(@criteria_fields);
```

$not_found is a flag indicating whether the subroutine found anything:

```
local($not_found);
```

The value for the form field being compared is stored in **$form_value**:

```
local($form_value);
```

The value for the database field currently being compared is stored in **$db_value**:

```
local($db_value);
```

$month, **$year**, **$day**, **$db_date**, and **$form_date** are all date-related variables that are set up for performing date comparisons:

```
local($month, $year, $day);
local($db_date, $form_date);
```

$db_index is a place marker for the current field in the database row that the routine is examining:

```
local($db_index);
```

@word_list is an entire list of words for matching. Keywords entered by the user as search criteria are split into separate words that are also searched for independantly:

```
local(@word_list);
```

The criteria is split into the appropriate variable defined above:

```
($c_name, $c_fields, $c_op, $c_type) =
    split(/\|/, $criteria);
```

Recall that the criteria can match more than one field in the database. Thus, the routine gets the index values of the fields in each row of the database that the form variable will be compared against and places them in the **@criteria_fields** array.

```
@criteria_fields = split(/,/,$c_fields);
```

The value of the form variable that is being compared in the criteria is assigned to **$form_value**:

```
$form_value = $form_data{$c_name};
```

Case 1: Form Variable Contains No Search Value

There are three cases of comparison that will return a value. In the first case, the form field for the criteria was not filled out, so the match is considered a success. Remember, if the user does not enter a keyword, we want the search to be open-ended. The logic used here is that the search is restricted only if the user chooses to enter a search word into the appropriate query field:

```
if ($form_value eq "")
  {
    return 0;
  }
```

Case 2: A Plain Numeric, Date, or String Comparison

In the second case, the data type is a number or a date or if the data type is a string and the operator is not equals (=), then the operator is matched directly based on the data type. Recall from Chapter 5 that a data type equals "string" and the comparison operator is equals (=), then the application of the query criteria becomes more flexible. This is considered case 3and will be discussed further below:

```
if (($c_type =~ /date/i) ||
    ($c_type =~ /number/i) ||
    ($c_op ne "="))
  {
```

$not_found is set to **yes**. In other words, the routine assumes that the data did not match. If any fields do end up matching the data submitted by the user, then the routine will set **$not_found** to **no** later on:

```
$not_found = "yes";
```

For each data field in the **@criteria_fields** array, the routine needs to run the comparison:

```
foreach $db_index (@criteria_fields)
    {
```

The value of the field that is currently being compared is retrieved from the **@fields** array:

```
$db_value = $fields[$db_index];
```

Now, the comparison operators are actually applied to the data. However, the comparison takes on a slightly different flavor for each type of data that can be compared: date, number, string. The first data type that is coded for comparison below is date. Before dates can be compared in Perl, their variables must be rearranged.

In other words, the dates to be compared need to be rearranged so that they form a string of the format "YYYYMMDD," where "YYYY" is a four-digit year, "MM" is a two-digit month, and "DD" is a two-digit day. All of these are padded with zeros if the number does not fill the space. The key trick here is that a date in the form of "YYYYMMDD" can be compared against another date of the same format, using standard numerical operators. Notice that when the date is rearranged this way, numerical comparisons of the dates correspond directly to chronological comparisons. In addition, two-digit years are converted to four-digit years so that this script will not be subject to the "year 2000" problem:

```
if ($c_type =~ /date/i)
    {
```

The first date that is converted is **$db_value**. First, it is split into **$month**, **$day**, and **$year** based on the forward-slash (/) character:

```
($month, $day, $year) =
  split(/\//, $db_value);
```

$month is padded with a zero if it is only one digit long:

```
$month = "0" . $month
  if (length($month) < 2);
```

$day is padded with a zero if it is only one digit long:

```
$day = "0" . $day
  if (length($day) < 2);
```

The year is converted to a four-digit year. Specifically, if the year is greater than 50 but less than 1900, 1900 is added to the year because it is assumed that a year greater than 50 corresponds to the period 1950 to 1999. Otherwise, if the year is still less than 1900, it is assumed that the other options for two-digit years are 2000 through 2049. Of course, if the user entered a year that is already four digits, it is kept the same:

```
if ($year > 50 && $year < 1900) {
  $year += 1900;
}
if ($year < 1900) {
  $year += 2000;
}
```

NOTE The two if tests presented above are used separately instead of using a catch-all else statement to add 2000 to the year in place of the second if. This is because there is a possibility that the year has already been entered by the user as a four-digit year. In this case, both if tests should fail and the year will be kept the same.

$db_date is then assigned as the year plus the month plus the day in the "YYYYMMDD" format that was described earlier:

```
$db_date = $year . $month . $day;
```

The form value is processed in the exact same way as the database field value. In the end, **$form_date** is set equal to the form value that has been processed to comply with the "YYYYMMDD" format:

```
($month, $day, $year) =
  split(/\//, $form_value);
$month = "0" . $month
  if (length($month) < 2);
$day = "0" . $day
  if (length($day) < 2);
if ($year > 50 && $year < 1900) {
  $year += 1900;
}
if ($year < 1900) {
  $year += 2000;
}
$form_date = $year . $month . $day;
```

Now, the dates can be compared with simple Perl numeric comparison operators. If any of the operators matches, a zero is returned to let the **submit_query** routine know that a match was found:

```
if ($c_op eq ">") {
  return 0 if ($form_date > $db_date); }
if ($c_op eq "<") {
  return 0 if ($form_date < $db_date); }
if ($c_op eq ">=") {
  return 0 if ($form_date >= $db_date); }
if ($c_op eq "<=") {
  return 0 if ($form_date <= $db_date); }
if ($c_op eq "!=") {
```

```
    return 0 if ($form_date != $db_date); }
if ($c_op eq "=") {
    return 0 if ($form_date == $db_date); }
```

If the data type is a number, then straight numeric comparisons are performed with no additional work being done to the values. A zero is returned if a match was found:

```
} elsif ($c_type =~ /number/i) {
    if ($c_op eq ">") {
        return 0 if ($form_value > $db_value); }
    if ($c_op eq "<") {
        return 0 if ($form_value < $db_value); }
    if ($c_op eq ">=") {
        return 0 if ($form_value >= $db_value); }
    if ($c_op eq "<=") {
        return 0 if ($form_value <= $db_value); }
    if ($c_op eq "!=") {
        return 0 if ($form_value != $db_value); }
    if ($c_op eq "=") {
        return 0 if ($form_value == $db_value); }
```

If the data type is a string, then the Perl string operators are used to compare the values instead of the numeric operators. For example, instead of **>**, the Perl **gt** string operator is used. A zero is returned if any of the comparisons returned a successful match:

```
} else { # $c_type is a string
    if ($c_op eq ">") {
        return 0 if ($form_value gt $db_value); }
    if ($c_op eq "<") {
        return 0 if ($form_value lt $db_value); }
    if ($c_op eq ">=") {
        return 0 if ($form_value ge $db_value); }
    if ($c_op eq "<=") {
        return 0 if ($form_value le $db_value); }
    if ($c_op eq "!=") {
        return 0 if ($form_value ne $db_value); }
}
        } # End of foreach $form_field
```

Case 3: Full String–Based Keyword Search

Now, consider Case 3. Recall that Case 3 handles situations in which the data type is a string and the operator is =. This is more complex because a fuzzy search is done based on the rules disclosed in Chapter 5. This fuzzy search checks to see whether we need to do case sensitive matches or whether the comparisons should match against whole words. In other words, the variables **$case_sensitive** and **$exact_match** actually affect the search. In addition, each word entered in the form variable is applied to the database field independently. All the words that the user enters must match against the database fields in order for the search to return a success:

```
} else { # End of case 2, Begin Case 3
```

@word_list is the array of words that the user entered into the form variable:

```
@word_list = split(/\s+/,$form_value);
```

Each field defined for comparison is checked against the keywords entered into the form variable:

```
foreach $db_index (@criteria_fields)
    {
```

The database field value that the routine is currently comparing is placed in **$db_value:**

```
$db_value = $fields[$db_index];
```

Initially, **$not_found** is set equal to **yes**, under the assumption that the search failed. If the search finds a match with the fields, this variable will later be set to **no:**

```
        $not_found = "yes";
```

$match_word acts as a place marker for the words that are going to be looked up in the database row. **$x** is used as a place marker inside the for loops that iterate through the keywords that the user entered into the form variable:

```
local($match_word) = "";
local($x) = "";
```

The following routine is the same code that exists for keyword searching in the **FindKeywords** subroutine discussed in Chapter 13:

```
if ($case_sensitive eq "on") {
    if ($exact_match eq "on") {
        for ($x = @word_list; $x > 0; $x--) {
    # \b matches on word boundary
            $match_word = $word_list[$x - 1];
            if ($db_value =~ /\b$match_word\b/) {
                splice(@word_list,$x - 1, 1);
            } # End of If
        } # End of For Loop
    } else {
        for ($x = @word_list; $x > 0; $x--) {
            $match_word = $word_list[$x - 1];
            if ($db_value =~ /$match_word/) {
                splice(@word_list,$x - 1, 1);
            } # End of If
        } # End of For Loop
    } # End of ELSE
} else {
    if ($exact_match eq "on") {
        for ($x = @word_list; $x > 0; $x--) {
# \b matches on word boundary
            $match_word = $word_list[$x - 1];
            if($db_value =~ /\b$match_word\b/i) {
                splice(@word_list,$x - 1, 1);
            } # End of If
        } # End of For Loop
    } else {
        for ($x = @word_list; $x > 0; $x--) {
            $match_word = $word_list[$x - 1];
            if ($db_value =~ /$match_word/i) {
                splice(@word_list,$x - 1, 1);
            } # End of If
        } # End of For Loop
    } # End of ELSE
}
```

After the keyword search routine, the **foreach** loop goes back to check every database field that was specified in the search criteria:

```
} # End of foreach $db_index
```

If there was nothing left in the keyword list that was being compared, then the routine set **$not_found** to **no**, indicating that there were no "not found" words. In other words, the routine found all the words in the word list. This ends Case 3:

```
if (@word_list < 1)
    {
       $not_found = "no";
    }

  } # End of case 3
```

Finally, if **$not_found** is still equal to **yes**, the routine returns a **1**, indicating that the criteria was not satisfied. Otherwise, a **0** is returned, indicating that the routine found a successful match:

```
if ($not_found eq "yes")
  {
    return 1;
  } else {
    return 0;
  }
} # End of flatfile_apply_criteria
```

CHAPTER FIFTEEN

THE ORDER LIBRARY

The Order Library (**web_store_order_lib.pl**) is the Web store's interface to all the order-processing-related routines. This includes everything from the initial display of the order form to the complex processing involved in calculating shipping, discounts, and sales tax.

The two main subroutines that are called from the Web store are **display_order_form** and **process_order_form**. There are also several other routines that act as scaffolding for these two procedures.

Display_order_form Subroutine

The **display_order_form** subroutine displays the order form to the user. It does not use any parameters except for variables that have been configured in the Setup file to affect the order form display. These variables have been previously discussed in Chapter 8.

```
sub display_order_form {
```

$line, $subtotal, $total_quantity, $total_measured_quantity, $text_of_cart,** and **$hidden_fields_for_cart are all declared local to this subroutine.

```
    local($line);
```

```
local($subtotal);
local($total_quantity);
local($total_measured_quantity);
local($text_of_cart);
local($hidden_fields_for_cart);
```

First, the order form HTML file is opened. The filename and path for this file is taken from the **$sc_html_order_form_path** defined in the Setup file. If there is an error opening the file, then it is reported to the script using the **file_open_error** routine.

```
open (ORDERFORM, "$sc_html_order_form_path") ||
    &file_open_error("$sc_html_order_form_path",
      "Display Order Form File
Error",__FILE__,__LINE__);
```

Next, every line of the order form file is read into **$line** using a while loop. This line is then parsed to see if it should display as is or if some piece of cart information needs to be substituted in place of special tags. These special tags will be discussed below.

```
while (<ORDERFORM>) {
    $line = $_;
```

If the <FORM> tag is encountered, then it is replaced with a form tag that is generated based on the value in the Setup file. In addition to this new form tag, hidden fields for the current **cart_id** and **page** that the customer previously visited are placed in the form.

```
    if ($line =~ /<FORM/i) {
      print qq!
      <FORM METHOD = "post" ACTION =
"$sc_order_script_url">
        <INPUT TYPE = "hidden" NAME = "page"
              VALUE = "$form_data{'page'}">
        <INPUT TYPE = "hidden" NAME = "cart_id"
              VALUE = "$form_data{'cart_id'}">\n!;
      $line = "";
    } # End of If Form tag found
```

If there was a tag stating where the cart contents should appear, then the cart contents are inserted in place of the line. The regular expression that is matched against the line is expected to match a string such as "<H2>CART CONTENTS HERE</H2>". This string gets replaced with the customer's cart contents on the order form when it gets displayed.

```
if ($line =~ /<h2>cart.*contents.*h2>/i) {
```

The **display_cart_table** subroutine is called with **orderform** for a parameter to let the routine know that it is dealing with the Display order form routine. The **display_cart_table** subroutine returns the subtotal, total quantity of items in the cart, total measured quantity of the measurement field specified in the Setup file, and the ASCII text of the cart. The ASCII text of the cart is used for logging and emailing the orders.

```
($subtotal,
 $total_quantity,
 $total_measured_quantity,
 $text_of_cart) =
          &display_cart_table("orderform");
```

display_calculations is then called in order to print the shipping, discount, and sales tax calculations where it is appropriate to do so based on the values in the Setup file. The ASCII text of the calculations will be appended to **$text_of_cart** for future logging and emailing of orders.

```
$text_of_cart =
  &display_calculations($subtotal,"before",
       $text_of_cart);
```

Of course, since the script is displaying the cart contents at this time, it needs to make the **$line** blank so that it does not display. The special tags that get replaced with the new form information and the cart contents should not be displayed to the user. They are merely placeholders for the information that the customer actually wants to see.

```
$line = "";
}
```

Finally, the **$line** variable is printed. After the while loop, the routine ends.

```
    print $line;
  } # End of Parsing Order Form

} # End of display_order_form
```

Display_calculations Subroutine

The **display_calculations** subroutine displays all the cart-specific calculations such as shipping costs, discounts, and sales tax. It gets passed the current subtotal, whether we are displaying calculations at the order form or at a point where the order form is being processed, and the actual text of the cart.

```
sub display_calculations {
  local($subtotal,
        $are_we_before_or_at_process_form,
        $text_of_cart) = @_;
```

The first thing that the script does is call the **calculate_final_values** routine, which will calculate the sales tax, shipping, and discount. It also calculates the grand total after all of these calculations have been applied. The reason this subroutine also calculates the grand total is that the shipping, discount, and sales tax are not guaranteed to be applied all at once to the subtotal of the cart. The **calculate_final_values** routine takes care of that type of logic. The routine takes the subtotal, total quantity of items in the cart, the total measured quantity of the measured field specified in the Setup file, and a flag indicating whether the order form is being displayed or processed. These values are necessary for calculating the shipping, discount, and sales tax as well as generating a new grand total.

```
local  ($final_shipping,
        $final_discount,
        $final_sales_tax,$grand_total) =
   &calculate_final_values($subtotal,
                  $total_quantity,
                  $total_measured_quantity,
               are_we_before_or_at_process_form);
```

If there is a final shipping value, then the script prints it and appends it to the text of the cart using the **format_text_field** function to justify the text of the cart.

```
if ($final_shipping > 0) {
  $final_shipping = &display_price($final_shipping);
  print "Shipping: $final_shipping<P>";
  $text_of_cart .= &format_text_field("Shipping:") .
    "= $final_shipping\n\n";
};
```

If there is a final discount value, then it is printed to the user's Web browser and appended to the text of the cart using the **format_text_field** routine.

```
if ($final_discount > 0) {
  $final_discount = &display_price($final_discount);
  print "Discount: $final_discount<P>";
  $text_of_cart .= &format_text_field("Discount:") .
    "= $final_discount\n\n";
}
```

If there is a final sales tax value, it is printed and appended to the text of the cart using the **format_text_field** routine.

```
if ($final_sales_tax > 0) {
  $final_sales_tax = &display_price($final_sales_tax);
  print "Sales Tax: $final_sales_tax<P>";
  $text_of_cart .= &format_text_field("Sales Tax:") .
    "= $final_sales_tax\n\n";
}
```

The real grand total is displayed. Then it is also appended to the text of the cart, just as the calculations above were.

```
$grand_total = &display_price($grand_total);
print "Grand Total: $grand_total<P>";
$text_of_cart .= &format_text_field("Grand Total:") .
  "= $grand_total\n\n";
```

Finally, the ASCII text of the cart is returned to the caller of this subroutine.

```
  return ($text_of_cart);
} # end of display_calculations
```

Format_text_field Subroutine

The **format_text_field** subroutine is a very simple routine. It merely accepts a text field and formats it so that it is left-justified with a field width of 25 char-caters. Basically, a string of 25 characters ("" **x 25**) is truncated by the string contained in svalue using the substr command.

```
sub format_text_field {
  local($value) = @_;

  return($value . substr((" " x 25), length($value)));

} # End of format_text_field
```

An example of what the formatted order looks like follows:

```
Description          = The letter A
Options              = Times New Roman 0.00, Red 0.00
Price After Options = $15.98
Quantity             = 1
Item Subtotal        = $15.98

Description          = The letter E
Options              = Times New Roman 0.00, Red 0.00
Price After Options = $12.98
Quantity             = 1
Item Subtotal        = $12.98

Subtotal:            = $28.96

Shipping:            =  $5.00

Discount:            =  $1.00

Sales Tax:           =  $8.60

Grand Total:         = $41.56
```

Process_order_form Subroutine

The **process_order_form** subroutine takes the contents of the order form that the user filled out previously and processes it as an actual order. This order is then logged and/or emailed to the store owner as specified in the Setup file.

```
sub process_order_form {
```

$subtotal, **$total_quantity**, **$total_measured_quantity**, **$text_of_cart**, and **$required_fields_filled_in** are declared local to this routine. These variables are used in a similar context to the way they were used in the **display_order_form** subroutine. The only different variable is **$required_fields_filled_in**. This variable is added because on the order form that was filled out, there may be some required fields that the user must enter before the form is submitted. If the required fields were not entered, then the script will print an error message letting the user know that they need to fill in more fields on the order form.

```
local($subtotal, $total_quantity,
     $total_measured_quantity,
     $text_of_cart,
     $required_fields_filled_in);
```

The first thing the routine does is print the header of the process order form.

```
print qq!
<HTML>
<HEAD>
<TITLE>Processing The Order Form</TITLE>
</HEAD>
</BODY>
!;
```

Then, the cart table is displayed to the user just as it was displayed in the **display_order_form** subroutine, except the routine is told that it is being called from the part of the Web store currently processing orders by sending it the

"process order" parameter. Then, **display_calculations** is also called in the same manner as the **display_order_form** routine, except that this routine is also passed information letting it know that the order form is being processed.

```
($subtotal,
 $total_quantity,
 $total_measured_quantity,
 $text_of_cart) =
    &display_cart_table("process order");

$text_of_cart =
    &display_calculations($subtotal,"at",
          $text_of_cart);
```

Next, the required fields processing is performed before actually processing the order. By default, **$required_fields_filled_in** is set to "yes," indicating that the routine starts out assuming all the fields were filled in. Then, the script goes through each required field one by one to see if it was filled in. If any one of the fields were not filled in, the **$required_fields_filled_in** flag is set to "no" and a message is displayed to the user letting them know exactly which fields they forgot to fill in.

```
$required_fields_filled_in = "yes";
foreach $required_field (@sc_order_form_required_fields) {
  if ($form_data{$required_field} eq "") {
    $required_fields_filled_in = "no";
    print "<H2>You forgot to fill in " .
      $sc_order_form_array{$required_field} . ".</H2>\n";
  }
} # End of checking required fields
print "<HR>\n";
```

If the required fields were filled in, the rest of the order is actually processed.

```
if ($required_fields_filled_in eq "yes") {
```

The ASCII text of the cart stored in **$text_of_cart** is appended with all the values that the user entered into the order form. The **format_text_field** routine is used to make sure that the form values are lined up and left justified.

```
foreach $form_field (sort(keys(%sc_order_form_array))) {
  $text_of_cart .=
    &format_text_field($sc_order_form_array{$form_field})
    . "= $form_data{$form_field}\n";
}
$text_of_cart .= "\n";
```

If PGP has been configured so that the Web store is using it, then the text of the cart is translated to a PGP-encrypted state using the **pgp-lib.pl** discussed in Chapter 9 and Chapter 18.

```
if ($sc_use_pgp =~ /yes/i) {
  &require_supporting_libraries(__FILE__, __LINE__,
    "$sc_pgp_lib_path");
$text_of_cart = &make_pgp_file($text_of_cart,
              "$sc_pgp_temp_file_path/$$.pgp");
$text_of_cart = "\n" . $text_of_cart . "\n";
}
```

If the order is configured to be sent through email, then the **send_mail** routine in **mail-lib.pl** is used to send the email.

```
if ($sc_send_order_to_email =~ /yes/i) {
  &send_mail($sc_order_email,$sc_order_email,
            "Web Store Order", $text_of_cart);
}
```

If the setup is configured to send the order to a Log file, then the following section of the routine appends the Order log file with the text of the order. Each order is delimited with a line of 40 hyphens (-).

```
if ($sc_send_order_to_log =~ /yes/i) {
  open (ORDERLOG, ">>$sc_order_log_file");
  print ORDERLOG "-" x 40;
  print ORDERLOG $text_of_cart;
  print ORDERLOG "-" x 40 . "\n";
  close (ORDERLOG);
}
```

Then, the user is notified that the order was a success.

```
    print "<H2>Your Order Has Been Sent!</H2>\n";
} else {
```

If the required fields were not filled in, then the user is notified that the order was not sent.

```
    print "<H2>Your Order Has Not Been Sent!</H2>\n";
}
```

Finally, the HTML footer for the process order page is printed and the subroutine is done.

```
print "<HR>\n";
print qq!
</BODY>
</HTML>
!;
} # End of process_order_form
```

Calculate_final_values Subroutine

The **calculate_final_values** routine calculates the shipping, sales tax, and discount logic. It also applies these values to the subtotal in order to produce a genuine grand total for the cart. There are several parameters passed to the script that are needed to determine the calculations. These parameters include the current subtotal, the total quantity of items in the cart, the total measured quantity of the measured field specified in the Setup file, and the status of whether we are calculating these values at the order form or at the point where the contents of the order form are being processed by the Web store.

```
sub calculate_final_values {
  local($subtotal,
        $total_quantity,
        $total_measured_quantity,
        $are_we_before_or_at_process_form) = @_;
```

The following lines of code specify local variables that will be used throughout the processing of this subroutine.

```
local($temp_total) = 0;
local($grand_total) = 0;
local($final_shipping, $shipping);
local($final_discount, $discount);
local($final_sales_tax, $sales_tax);
```

$calc_loop is set to zero. This variable keeps track of looping through the calculations in order to see whether shipping, sales tax, or discount should be calculated at a time where the value of **$calc_loop** reaches either 1, 2, or 3. A description of this logic is provided in Chapter 8.

```
local($calc_loop) = 0;
```

$temp_total is initialized to equal the subtotal of the cart. This total is updated after every cycle through the calculation loop in order to determine what the final grand total is.

```
$temp_total = $subtotal;
```

The reason that there are three cycles of calculation is that there are three things to calculate: shipping, discount, and sales tax. It is conceivable that all three of these values may need to be calculated separately and applied to the subtotal after each calculation. Examples of this situation are given in Chapter 8. The for loop given below starts the three cycles.

```
for (1..3) {
```

At the beginning of the loop, the calculated values of the shipping, discount, and sales tax are set to zero. **$calc_loop** is set equal to the current loop count.

```
$shipping = 0;
$discount = 0;
$sales_tax = 0;
$calc_loop = $_;
```

In addition to the calculation logic being different depending on the cycle number of the loop, the logic is also dependent on whether the order form is being displayed or the contents of the order form have been submitted and are currently being processed. The reason this matters is that some of the calculations may be dependent on values that have been entered onto the form. For example, shipping costs may depend on the user selecting a different shipping type.

```
if ($are_we_before_or_at_process_form =~
    /before/i) {
```

The following code calculates all the items if the routine has been called before the process order form (at the order form display). For each of the possible values to calculate, the Setup file variables that configure which cycle of the loop the values are calculated in are compared. If the cycle number (**$calc_loop**) matches the Setup variable, then that particular type of calculation is performed.

```
if ($sc_calculate_discount_at_display_form ==
    $calc_loop) {
  $discount =
    &calculate_discount($temp_total,
      $total_quantity,
      $total_measured_quantity);
} # End of if discount gets calculated here
if ($sc_calculate_shipping_at_display_form ==
    $calc_loop) {
  $shipping =
    &calculate_shipping($temp_total,
      $total_quantity,
      $total_measured_quantity);
} # End of shipping calculations
if ($sc_calculate_sales_tax_at_display_form ==
    $calc_loop) {
  $sales_tax =
    &calculate_sales_tax($temp_total);
} # End of sales tax calculations
```

The same logic that is explained above is used below, the only exception that the calculations are done at the stage where the order form is being processed instead of being displayed.

```
} else {
  if ($sc_calculate_discount_at_process_form ==
      $calc_loop) {
    $discount =
      &calculate_discount($temp_total,
        $total_quantity,
```

```
        $total_measured_quantity);
  } # End of if discount gets calculated here
  if ($sc_calculate_shipping_at_process_form ==
       $calc_loop) {
    $shipping =
       &calculate_shipping($temp_total,
          $total_quantity,
          $total_measured_quantity);
  } # End of shipping calculations
  if ($sc_calculate_sales_tax_at_process_form ==
       $calc_loop) {
    $sales_tax =
       &calculate_sales_tax($temp_total);
  } # End of sales tax calculations
} # End if we are before or at process order form
```

Finally, for this cycle only, the new temporary total is calculated. In addition, the final discount, shipping, and sales tax values are assigned to other variables if the values have been calculated during this cycle. This assignment is done because the values of the calculations are lost every time the cycle starts again.

```
    $final_discount = $discount if ($discount > 0);
    $final_shipping = $shipping if ($shipping > 0);
    $final_sales_tax = $sales_tax if ($sales_tax > 0);
    $temp_total = $temp_total - $discount
                    + $shipping + $sales_tax;
  } # End of $calc_loop
```

The last thing the routine does is return the final calculated values along with the new grand total.

```
    return ($final_shipping,
          $final_discount,
          $final_sales_tax,
          &format_price($grand_total));
} # end of calculate_final_values
```

Calculate_shipping Subroutine

The **calculate_shipping** subroutine calculates the shipping by taking the shipping logic variables and passing them by reference to a general logic calculation subroutine defined further down in this library. The **calculate_general_logic** routine is also passed all the parameters it needs to perform calculations such as the subtotal, total quantity of items in the cart, and the total measured quantity of the measured field in the cart.

```
sub calculate_shipping {
  local($subtotal,
        $total_quantity,
        $total_measured_quantity) = @_;

  return(&calculate_general_logic(
          $subtotal,
          $total_quantity,
          $total_measured_quantity,
          *sc_shipping_logic,
          *sc_order_form_shipping_related_fields));
} # End of calculate_shipping
```

Calculate_discount Subroutine

The **calculate_discount** routine is defined the same way as the **calculate_shipping** routine described above. The only difference is that references to the discount logic variables are passed to the **calculate_general_logic** routine instead of to shipping-logic-related variables.

```
sub calculate_discount {
  local($subtotal,
        $total_quantity,
        $total_measured_quantity) = @_;

  return(&calculate_general_logic(
          $subtotal,
          $total_quantity,
          $total_measured_quantity,
          *sc_discount_logic,
          *sc_order_form_discount_related_fields));
} # End of calculate_discount
```

Calculate_general_logic Subroutine

The **calculate_general_logic** subroutine calculates shipping or discount values by being passed references to their criteria along with values that affect these calculations such as the subtotal, total quantity of items in the cart, and total measured quantity of the measured field in the cart. ***general_logic** is a reference to an array the contains the criteria used to apply the calculation. ***general_related_form_fields** is a reference to an array containing information about form field values that may affect the criteria in the general logic array.

```
sub calculate_general_logic {
  local($subtotal,
        $total_quantity,
        $total_measured_quantity,
      *general_logic,
        *general_related_form_fields) = @_;
```

The following lines of code declare local variables that will be used throughout this routine.

```
  local($general_value);
  local($x, $count);
  local($logic);
  local($criteria_satisfied);
  local(@fields);
```

@related_form_values is an array that is assigned the values of all the form fields in the **@general_related_form_fields** array using a **foreach** loop to go through all the elements in the array. **$count** is used to keep track of which related form value is currently being assigned.

```
  local(@related_form_values) = ();

  $count = 0;
  foreach $x (@general_related_form_fields) {
    $related_form_values [$count] = $form_data{$x};
    $count++;
  }
```

Each element of the general logic array is processed using another **foreach** loop that places the current logic being processed into the **$logic** variable.

```
  foreach $logic (@general_logic) {
```

The routine starts off assuming that the criteria has been satisfied.

```
$criteria_satisfied = "yes";
```

Next, the definition of the logic being checked currently is split out of the **$logic** variable into the **@fields** array based on the pipe symbol (|) that delimits the logic fields.

```
@fields = split(/\|/, $logic);
```

All the form variables are cycled through to see if any of the criteria matches the form values from the **@related_form_values** array. If any criteria are not satisfied, then **$criteria_satisfied** is set to "no".

```
for (1..@related_form_values) {
  if (!(&compare_logic_values(
      $related_form_values[$_ - 1],
      $fields[$_ - 1]))) {
    $criteria_satisfied = "no";
  }
} # End of loop through form values
```

Now that the related form values have been checked, they are shifted off of the criteria fields array (**@fields**). As each criteria field is applied, it gets shifted off so that the **compare_logic_values** routine that is called below can be called with the first element of the array each time.

```
for (1..@related_form_values) {
  shift(@fields);
}
```

The script is now ready to deal with comparing the general logic with the totals (subtotal, total quantity, total measured quantity). The first field in the logic array after the related form variables fields have been shifted off is the subtotal comparison field. The subtotal is compared against this criteria field. If the match fails, then **$criteria_satisfied** is set to "no."

```
if (!(&compare_logic_values(
    $subtotal,
```

```
        $fields[0]))) {
    $criteria_satisfied = "no";
}
```

The field is shifted off and the next comparison is done. This comparison is based on the total quantity of items.

```
shift (@fields);

if (!(&compare_logic_values(
        $total_quantity,
        $fields[0]))) {
    $criteria_satisfied = "no";
}
```

Again, a field is shifted off the array. This time, the criteria that is left on the array is compared against the total measured quantity value.

```
shift (@fields);
if (!(&compare_logic_values(
        $total_measured_quantity,
        $fields[0]))) {
    $criteria_satisfied = "no";
}
```

The last piece of criteria is shifted off the Fields array. After this occurs, the only item left on the **@fields** array will be the cost to calculate if the **$criteria_satisfied** flag is equal to "yes."

```
shift (@fields);
```

If **$criteria_satisfied** is equal to "yes," then the value of the calculation is calculated. If this value has a percent sign, then the value is calculated based on the subtotal that was passed to this routine. Otherwise, the actual value is considered to be the new calculated value.

```
if ($criteria_satisfied eq "yes") {

    if ($fields[0] =~ /%/) {
        $fields[0] =~ s/%//;
```

```
        $general_value = $subtotal * $fields[0] / 100;
      } else {
        $general_value = $fields[0];
      }
    }

  } # End of foreach loop through shipping logic
```

Now that the shipping logic has been calculated, it is returned as a formatted value to the calling subroutine.

```
  return(&format_price($general_value));
} # End of calculate_general_logic
```

Calculate_sales_tax Subroutine

The **calculate_sales_tax** routine takes the current subtotal as a parameter and calculates the sales tax on the basis of that value plus any configuration variables that affect sales tax in the Setup file.

```
sub calculate_sales_tax {
  local($subtotal) = @_;
```

$sales_tax is defined as a local variable and initialized to **0** before the script performs any processing on it.

```
  local($sales_tax) = 0;
```

If the sales tax is dependent on a form variable, then the routine checks the value of that form variable against the possible values that have been designated in the **@sc_sales_tax_form_variable** array. A successful match results in the sales tax being calculated.

```
  if ($sc_sales_tax_form_variable ne "") {
    foreach $value (@sc_sales_tax_form_values) {
      if ($value =~
          /$form_data{$sc_sales_tax_form_variable}/i) {
        $sales_tax = $subtotal * $sc_sales_tax;
```

```
      }
    }
```

If the sales tax is not form variable-dependent, then the sales tax is always calculated.

```
  } else {
    $sales_tax = $subtotal * $sc_sales_tax;
  }
```

The routine ends by returning the formatted sales tax value.

```
  return (&format_price($sales_tax));
} # End of calculate sales tax
```

Compare_logic_values Subroutine

The **compare_logic_values** subroutine takes a value and checks whether it falls within the range or is equal to a comparison value. These two variables are the parameters to this subroutine (**$input_value** and **$value_to_compare**). The routine returns a **1** if the value is in the range or a **0** if the value does not match the value/range to compare.

```
sub compare_logic_values {
  local($input_value, $value_to_compare) = @_;
```

$lowrange and **$highrange** are declared as local variables. They will be used to break the comparison value into the lower limit and upper limit of a range of values to compare if the comparison value is a range of numbers rather than a straight value. An example of a range value is **10-20**, which would mean that the input value has to be between 10 and 20. In this case, **$lowrange** would be set equal to **10** and **$highrange** would be set equal to **20**.

```
  local($lowrange, $highrange);
```

If the value to compare is a range of values signified by having a hyphen, then a range comparison is done with the input value.

```
if ($value_to_compare =~ /-/) {
```

The low and high end of the range are split by the hyphen into the **$lowrange**
and **$highrange** variables respectively.

```
($lowrange, $highrange) = split(/-/,
$value_to_compare);
```

If the low range does not have a value, it means that the range is open-ended,
so the routine assumes that the high range was entered and it only compares
against this high-range value. An example of an open-ended range that looks
like this is **-10**.

```
if ($lowrange eq "") {
  if ($input_value <= $highrange) {
    return(1);
  } else {
    return(0);
  }
```

Alternatively, the high range could be missing instead of the low range. In this case,
the match is still considered open-ended, but the low range is compared instead of
the high range. An example of an open-ended range that looks like this is **5-**.

```
} elsif ($highrange eq "") {
  if ($input_value >= $lowrange) {
    return(1);
  } else {
    return(0);
  }
```

If both the low and high range have values, then the value is compared against
both ranges.

```
} else {
  if (($input_value >= $lowrange) &&
      ($input_value <= $highrange)) {
    return(1);
  } else {
    return(0);
  }
}
```

The last case that arises is when the value to compare is not a range. Thus, a straight pattern match compare is done with the values.

```
  } else {
   if (($input_value =~ /$value_to_compare/i) ||
       ($value_to_compare eq "")) {
     return(1);
   } else {
     return(0);
   }
  }
} # End of compare_logic_values
```

CHAPTER SIXTEEN

THE LOG ANALYSIS SCRIPT

Global Variable Definition

First, we will define some **global Setup** variables that will govern the usage of this script. The reason that we do not include these variables in the general **web_store.setup** file is that there is the potential that on some servers, because the Setup file must be readable by the Web server, the Setup file is insecure.

Thus, we would not want to include the password there. Instead, you will hardcode the password in the script to provide the highest degree of security. At the same time, we will define other script specific variables as well.

NOTE

Consider what would happen if a sneaky competitor studied up on this application and used her own Web browser to access a **log_analysis.setup** file (if one existed). If you left this file with the default filename, they would easily be able to type in a URL such as:

```
http://www.yourdomain.com/cgi-bin/Web_store/Library/
log_analysis.setup
```

If they did that, the Web server might serve up the Setup file as plain text (if your Web server is configured to allow that). With the Setup file in their browser window, they could easily scan down to determine the password. Then they could use your log analysis scripts to check up on your sales and customers!

Though it makes customizing the application a little less obvious, by placing the password in the script itself we make it impossible for a hacker to glean the password, because when she calls the script from the location window, she will execute the script rather than see its contents displayed.

- **$sc_password** is the password that you will need to enter on the Web form in order to receive a log analysis.

- **$sc_log_file_directory** is the path location of the directory containing the log files.

- **$sc_error_log_path** is the entire path name of the error log.

- **$sc_access_log_path** is the entire path name of the access log.

- **$sc_cgi_lib_path** is the location of **cgi-lib.pl**.

- **$sc_db_lib_path** is the location of **web_store_db_lib.pl**.

- **@sc_db_query_criteria** is the array of search string options you will use for searching the log files. For this default example, we will just allow string equality searching on every environment variable field and will use a text input field in the HTML form using **NAME = "keywords"**.

NOTE

If you do not understand the search definitions, you might want to read through the discussion of keyword searching in Chapter 5.

```
$sc_password = "selena";
$sc_log_file_directory = "./Admin_files";
$sc_error_log_path = "$sc_log_file_directory/error.log";
$sc_access_log_path = "$sc_log_file_directory/access.log";

$sc_cgi_lib_path = "./Library/cgi-lib.pl";
$sc_db_lib_path = "./Library/web_store_db_lib.pl";

@sc_db_query_criteria = ("keywords|0,1,2,3,4,5,6,7,8,9,10,11,12,13,
                14,15,16,17,18,19,20,21,22|=|string");
```

Main Routine

First, Perl is told to bypass its own buffer so that the information generated by this script will be sent immediately to the browser.

```
$| = 1;
```

Then, the HTTP header is sent to the browser. This is done early for two reasons. First, it will be easier to debug the script while making modifications or customizing because we will be able to see exactly what the script is doing. Secondly, the HTTP header is sent out early so that the browser will not "time out" in case the script takes a long time to complete its work.

```
print "Content-type: text/html\n\n";
```

Next, both of the supporting files are read in. **cgi-lib.pl** will be used for reading and parsing incoming form data and **web_store_db_lib.pl** will be used to search the log files for keywords.

```
require "$sc_cgi_lib_path";
require "$sc_db_lib_path";
```

Then, the incoming form data is read and parsed by **cgi-lib.pl** and **$log_file_in** and **$password_in** are defined according to the values coming in as form data. **$log_file_in** will be equal to the name and location of the log file that the script has been requested to analyze. **$password_in** will be equal to the password submitted via the form.

```
&ReadParse(*form_data);
$log_file_in = "$sc_log_file_directory/$form_data{'which_log'}";
$password_in = "$form_data{'password'}";
```

Display Search Results

Now the script determines if the client submitting the password and log files has entered the correct values, because it will only display the correct error and access logs and will do so only if the client submits the right password.

```
if (($password_in eq "$sc_password") && (
    $log_file_in eq "$sc_error_log_path") ||
    ($log_file_in eq "$sc_access_log_path"))
  {
```

If the incoming form data passed the security check, the script opens the log file requested for reading and begins displaying the HTML response page using **log_analyzer_return_header** located at the end of this file.

```
open (LOG_FILE, "$log_file_in") || &CgiDie("Sorry,
      could not open the requested log file.  Please
      check the permissions and the path.");
&log_analyzer_return_header;
```

Next, the script goes through the log file one line at a time, splitting each line into its fields (every log file database row is pipe-delimited and each is separated by a newline). **$not_found** will also be set to zero so that we will be able to check at the end of this routine if we have actually found some hits in the log file, based on the client-submitted keywords.

```
while (<LOG_FILE>)
  {
  @fields = split (/\|/, $_);
```

We start off stating that no criteria were found.

```
$not_found = 0;
```

The information in the fields is then compared to the keywords submitted by the client. Each criteria in the **@sc_db_query_criteria** array is specifically applied to the database row for searching.

In the loop below, if any criteria is not found, the result is an incrementing of **$not_found**.

```
foreach $criteria (@sc_db_query_criteria)
  {
  $not_found += &flatfile_apply_criteria(
              $exact_match,
              $case_sensitive,
              *fields,
              $criteria);
    }
```

If the script found some hits, it displays them in table format.

```
    if ($not_found == 0)
      {
      print "<TR>";
      foreach $field (@fields)
        {
        print "<TD>$field</TD>";
        }
      print "</TR>";
      }
  }
```

Then, the script displays the HTML footer and exits.

```
&log_analyzer_return_footer;
close (LOG_FILE);
}
```

Display Query Form

If the client-supplied information does not pass the security check, or the script is being accessed for the first time, the script displays the form that can be used to submit keywords, a password, and a log file to analyze.

```
else
  {
  &log_analyzer_query_form;
  }
```

log_analyzer_query_form Subroutine

log_analyzer_query_form is used to generate the form used by the administrator to select which log file to view and which keywords to filter with. It is called with no arguments:

```
sub log_analyzer_query_form
  {
  print qq~
  <HTML>
  <HEAD>
```

```
<TITLE>Web Store Log File View</TITLE>
</HEAD>
<BODY BGCOLOR = "FFFFFF" TEXT = "000000">
<CENTER><H2>Basic Log Analyzer</H2></CENTER>
<BLOCKQUOTE>
<FORM ACTION = "web_store_log_analysis.cgi"
      METHOD = "post">
<TABLE>
<TR>
<TH ALIGN = "left">Password (Required)</TH>
<TD><INPUT TYPE = "text" SIZE = "20" MAXLENGTH = "20"
          NAME ="password"></TD>
</TR>
<TR>
<TH ALIGN = "left">Log File to View</TH>
<TD><SELECT NAME = "which_log">
    <OPTION VALUE = "error.log">Error Log
    <OPTION VALUE = "access.log">Access Log
    </SELECT></TD>
</TR>
<TR>
<TH ALIGN = "left">Search Term
                   (None for entire file)</TH>
<TD><INPUT TYPE = "text" SIZE = "20" MAXLENGTH = "20"
          NAME ="keywords"></TD>
</TR>
</TABLE>
<CENTER>
<INPUT TYPE = "submit" NAME = "submit"
       VALUE = "View Log">
</CENTER>
</FORM>
</BLOCKQUOTE>
</BODY>
</HTML>~;
}
```

log_analyzer_return_header Subroutine

log_analyzer_return_header is used to display the HTML header for the
Log File View page. It is also called with no arguments:

```
sub log_analyzer_return_header
  {
  print qq!
<HTML>
<HEAD>
<TITLE>Web Store Log File View</TITLE>
</HEAD>
<BODY BGCOLOR = "FFFFFF" TEXT = "000000">
<TABLE BORDER = "1">!;
  }
```

log_analyzer_return_footer Subroutine

log_analyzer_return_footer is used to display the HTML footer for the Log File View page. It is called with no arguments:

```
sub log_analyzer_return_footer
  {
  print "</TABLE></BODY></HTML>";
  }
```

CHAPTER SEVENTEEN

THE SETUP CHECKING SCRIPT

The Setup Checking script (**web_store_check_setup.cgi**) was programmed so that a check would be performed on all the Setup file path and file location variables in order to make sure they exist and that their permissions were set correctly. Although you can run this script from the command line of UNIX, the benefit comes from running it through the Web browser as a CGI application. By running the script as a CGI application, the permissions that are checked on the directories and paths are your Web server's permissions rather than your own. This is a true test of your setup and how the main Web store script will react when it is executed by a customer. A discussion of how this script is used and its sample output can be found in Chapter 2.

Global Variable Definition and Setup

The first thing that the CGI script does is tell the Web server to run the script using the Perl executable located in **/usr/local/bin/perl**. If the executable is not located there, however, you will need to change the following line to reflect the real location of where it is located.

```
#!/usr/local/bin/perl
```

The next thing that the script must do is figure out which setup file is being checked. In the case below, **web_store.setup.frames** (The Frames Web store) is the Setup file that will be checked by this script. If you are using a different Setup file, you must change this variable to reflect the new filename.

```
$sc_setup_file = "./Library/web_store.setup.frames";
```

Since this is a script that checks for errors in the Setup, buffering of the output is turned off so that if the script crashes, we make sure that all the output is flushed constantly to the Web browser so that you will know exactly where the problem occurred. In addition, the HTTP header, **"Content-type: text/html\n\n"**, is printed immediately so that all subsequent output will be sent to the Web browser as HTML text.

```
$| = 1;
print "Content-type: text/html\n\n";
```

First, an HTML header is printed to the user's Web browser telling them that this is a script that checks the Web store Setup. The use of **qq!** which is used throughout the Web store indicates that everything between the exclamation points (!) is to be printed and that double-quotes do not need to be escaped with a backslash character (\).

```
print qq!
<HTML>
<HEAD>
<TITLE>Check HTML</TITLE>
</HEAD>
<BODY>
<H1>Checking Web Store Setup</H1>
<HR>!;
```

Perl Version and Current Working Directory

For diagnostic purposes, the script checks to see which version of PERL is being used. The special **$]** variable contains the current Perl version. If Perl 4 is being used, the **getcwd.pl** that comes with the standard Perl 4 distribution is required by this script so that it can be used to check what the current working directory is. If Perl 5 is being used, then the **Cwd** package is used instead.

The current working directory is very important for diagnostic purposes. It lets you know where the Web server thinks your script is running, so if the Web store mysteriously cannot find files or require the necessary libraries, you can see whether this problem is being caused by the Web server thinking that the script is actually in another subdirectory.

```
print "<B>You are using version $] of Perl.<P>";
if ($] >= 5) {
  print "<B>We are about to \"use\" the Cwd package to obtain
    the current working directory</B><P>";
  use Cwd;
  $cwd = getcwd();
} else {
  print "<B>We are about to \"require\" getcwd.pl library to obtain
    the current working directory</B><P>";
  require "getcwd.pl";
  $cwd = getcwd();
}

print "<B>The current working
        directory is: <I>$cwd</I></B><P>";
```

NOTE If the Check Setup script dies before displaying the current working directory, then this means that your distribution of Perl is missing some pieces of the standard installation. Your ISP should have installed the current working directory libraries when they installed Perl on your Web server.

Check the Setup File and Load It

Next, the Setup file is checked to see whether it exists and is readable by the Web server. If it is, then it is loaded into memory using the **require** command. If the Setup file does not satisfy this criteria, an error message is printed and the program exits. **$dieflag** indicates whether the error checking should result in the program exiting or not, if an error is encountered in the **Check_path** subroutine.

$dieflag is then set to "off" for dealing with the rest of the file and directory checking through the script. If the Setup file cannot be loaded, this would result in the script exiting anyway, so the **$dieflag** is on for that check. Once the Setup file is loaded, however, the setup check does not exit after every test because if there are multiple problems with the Setup file, the script should inform the user of as many of them that it is able to check.

```
print qq!
<HR>
<H2>Checking: $sc_setup_file</H2>
!;
$dieflag = "on";
&Check_path($sc_setup_file, "sc_setup_file",
"exists,read");
$dieflag = "off";

print "<B>Now, we will load the setup file.</B><P>";
require "$sc_setup_file";
print "<B>Setup File Loaded.</B><HR>";
```

Check the Variables in the Setup File

The following lines in the script check all the variables that were read in
from the Setup file using the **Check_path** function. **Check_path** accepts
the filename/path variable, a descriptive name of this variable, and a
comma-delimited list of permissions that should be checked. The list of
possible permissions and attributes to check are **"exists"**, **"read"**,
"execute", and **"write"**.

```
&Check_path($sc_cgi_lib_path,
  "sc_cgi_lib_path", "exists,read");
&Check_path($sc_mail_lib_path,
  "sc_mail_lib_path", "exists,read");
&Check_path($sc_html_search_routines_library_path,
  "sc_html_search_routines_library_path", "exists,read");
&Check_path($sc_db_lib_path,
  "sc_db_lib_path", "exists,read");
&Check_path($sc_order_lib_path,
  "sc_order_lib_path","exists,read");
&Check_path($sc_pgp_lib_path,
  "sc_pgp_lib_path", "exists,read");
&Check_path($sc_html_setup_file_path,
  "sc_html_setup_file_path", "exists,read");

&Check_path($sc_user_carts_directory_path,
  "sc_user_carts_directory_path", "exists,read,execute,write");

&Check_path($sc_data_file_path,
  "sc_data_file_path", "exists,read");
$data_path = &get_path_from_full_filename(
```

```
  $sc_data_file_path);
&Check_path($data_path, "path from sc_data_file_path",
  "exists,read,execute");

&Check_path($sc_options_directory_path,
  "sc_options_directory_path", "exists,read,execute");
&Check_path($sc_html_product_directory_path,
  "sc_html_product_directory_path", "exists,read,execute");
&Check_path($sc_html_order_form_path,
  "sc_html_order_form_path", "exists,read");
&Check_path($sc_store_front_path,
  "sc_store_front_path", "exists, read");

&Check_path($sc_counter_file_path,
  "sc_counter_file_path", "exists,read,write");
$data_path = &get_path_from_full_filename(
  $sc_counter_file_path);
&Check_path($data_path, "path from sc_counter_file_path",
  "exists,read,execute,write");

&Check_path($sc_error_log_path,
  "sc_error_log_path", "exists,read,write");
$data_path = &get_path_from_full_filename(
  $sc_error_log_path);
&Check_path($data_path, "path from sc_error_log_path",
  "exists,read,execute,write");

&Check_path($sc_access_log_path,
  "sc_access_log_path", "exists,read,write");
$data_path = &get_path_from_full_filename(
  $sc_access_log_path);
&Check_path($data_path, "path from sc_access_log_path",
  "exists,read,execute,write");
```

The order log path and file information is only checked if the **$sc_send_order_to_log** variable is set to "yes". The same check is done to see if PGP is being used before the PGP-related paths are checked.

```
if ($sc_send_order_to_log =~ /yes/i) {
  &Check_path($sc_order_log_file,
    "sc_order_log_file","exists,read,write");
  $data_path = &get_path_from_full_filename(
    $sc_order_log_file);
```

```
&Check_path($data_path, "path from sc_order_log_file",
    "exists,read,execute,write");
}

        # If PGP is on, then we will check the
        # pgp related variables
if ($sc_use_pgp =~ /yes/i) {
    &Check_path($sc_pgp_temp_file_path,
        "sc_pgp_temp_file_path", "exists,read,execute,write");
}

&Check_path($sc_root_web_path, "sc_root_web_path",
    "exists,read,execute");
```

Finally, the HTML footer is displayed to the user. This ends the script processing.

```
print qq!
</BODY>
</HTML>!;
```

Check_path Subroutine

The **Check_path** subroutine checks to see if a given path satisfies the attributes/permissions list that was passed to it. If it does not, then the script prints an error. If the criteria is satisfied, then the script tells the user the variable is working properly. **Check_path** takes the actual path (including filename), descriptive variable name (**$varname**), and a comma-delimited list of permissions to check (**$rights**).

```
sub Check_path {
    local($path, $varname, $rights) = @_;
```

If **$rights** has the word **exist** inside its comma-delimited list, the routine checks to see if the file or path actually does exist before checking any other permissions.

```
    if ($rights =~ /exist/i) {
        if (!(-e $path)) {
```

```
    &HTMLDie("<P>Web server thinks $path specified
        in $varname does not exist. <BR>
            <I>This is bad. YOU NEED TO CORRECT
THIS.</I></B><P>\n");
    } else {
    &HTMLMsg("<B>$path specified in $varname exists.<BR>
            <I>This is good.</I></B><P>\n");
    }
}
```

Next, if the permissions list has the word **read** in it, the file/path is checked to see if it is readable.

```
    if ($rights =~ /read/i) {
        if (!(-r $path)) {
            &HTMLDie("<P>Web server cannot read from $path
            specified in $varname.<BR>
                <I>This is bad. YOU NEED TO CORRECT
THIS.</I></B><P>\n");
        } else {
            &HTMLMsg("<B>The web server can read from $path
                    specified in $varname.<BR>
                    <I>This is good.</I></B><P>\n");
        }
    }
```

If the permissions list has **write** in it, then the file/path is checked to see if the Web server can write to the directory or file.

```
    if ($rights =~ /write/i) {
        if (!(-w $path)) {
            &HTMLDie("<P>Web server cannot write to $path
            specified in $varname.<BR>
                <I>This is bad. YOU NEED TO CORRECT
THIS.</I></B><P>\n");
        } else {
            &HTMLMsg("<B>The web server can write to $path
                    specified in $varname. <BR>
                    <I>This is good.</I></B><P>\n");
        }
    }
```

Finally, if **$rights** contains the word **execute**, then the file/path is checked to see if it is executable.

```
    if ($rights =~ /execute/i) {
      if (!(-x $path)) {
        &HTMLDie("<P>Web server cannot execute $path
        specified in $varname.<BR>
          <I>This is bad. YOU NEED TO CORRECT
THIS.</I></B><P>\n");
      } else {
        &HTMLMsg("<B>The web server can execute $path
                  specified in $varname.<BR>
                  <I>This is good.</I></B><P>\n");
      }
    }
```

The subroutine then prints a horizontal row delimiter (**<HR>**) to the user's Web browser and the subroutine ends.

```
    print "<HR>\n";
} # End of Check_path
```

HTMLMsg Subroutine

HTMLMsg takes a message as an argument and then outputs it in HTML form for this script. This means that the message is changed to have the bold attribute and a paragraph break printed after every message.

```
sub HTMLMsg {
  local($msg) = @_;

  print "<B>$msg</B><P>";
} # End of HTMLMsg
```

HTMLDie Subroutine

HTMLDie does the same thing as **HTMLMsg** except that it also stops the script processing and exits if the **$dieflag** is set to "on".

```
sub HTMLDie {
  local($msg) = @_;
```

```
print "<B>$msg</B><P>";
if ($dieflag =~ /on/i) {
  exit;
}
} # End of HTMLDie
```

get_path_from_full_filename Subroutine

The **get_path_from_full_filename** subroutine takes a full path and filename reference and strips the filename out of it. This is done because anytime there is a file that is being checked in this script, we also generally want to make sure that the directory that it is in has similar permissions. For example, if we check that the error log file is writable, we also want to check that the directory that it is in is writable as well.

```
sub get_path_from_full_filename {
  local($file) = @_;
```

The last **"/"** character is searched in the full filename. If there is one, then the filename is stripped off by truncating the filename variable after the last **/"** in the full filename.

```
if (rindex($file, "/") > 0) {
  $file = substr($file,0,rindex($file, "/") + 1);
}

return($file);
} # end of get_path_from_full_filename
```

Chapter Eighteen

The PGP, Mail, and CGI Libraries

The PGP (**pgp-lib.pl**), mail (**mail-lib.pl**), and CGI (**cgi-lib.pl**) libraries are general libraries that support Web-store-specific functions. For example, since the Web store needs to understand how to process CGI form variables, we use a commonly available library to handle this.

First, the PGP interface library will be discussed in detail. Next, the mail and CGI libraries will be discussed. However, rather than discuss the mail and CGI libraries in depth, this chapter will instead cover the major functions in those libraries that are called. Detailed explanations of the inner workings of these two scripts can be found in our book, *Instant Web Scripts with CGI/Perl* also published by M&T Books (1996).

PGP Interface Library

The purpose of the PGP interface library (**pgp-lib.pl**) is to provide a set of routines that will encrypt orders using the PGP utility. There is just one subroutine in this library, since it only performs one basic duty: encrypting text. The actual use of the PGP Library is discussed in greater detail in Chapter 9.

PGP Library Variables

First, the library defines a set of variables that reflect how PGP is configured on your system. These variables are **$pgp_path**, **$pgp_options**, **$pgp_public_key_user_id**, and **$pgp_config_files**.

- **$pgp_path** is the path to the PGP-executable. This variable includes both the path and filename for the PGP-executable on your system.

  ```
  $pgp_path = "/usr/local/bin/pgp";
  ```

- **$pgp_options** are the command-line options that will be passed to PGP when it is encrypting the text. The options below configure PGP to accept a file as input (**f**), encrypt the data (**e**), make the encrypted output compatible with ASCII (**a**), store the file in a cross-platform manner with regards to text (**t**), and suppress nearly all informational messages from the program (**+VERBOSE=0**).

  ```
  $pgp_options = "-feat +VERBOSE=0";
  ```

- **$pgp_public_key_user_id** tells PGP which public key to use for encrypting the text. In the code below, whatever you change **$pgp_public_key_user_id** to becomes your public key for encrypting ordering data in the Web store.

  ```
  $pgp_public_key_user_id = "yourpublickeyid";
  ```

- **$pgp_config_files** is the path where the PGP configuration files are located. These configuration files include the actual key ring that holds the public key to be used to encrypt ordering information in the Web store.

  ```
  $pgp_config_files = "/home/gunther/public_html/Web_store/
                       Pgpfiles";
  ```

make_pgp_file Subroutine

The **make_pgp_file** subroutine takes a string (text buffer containing the order) and then returns the encrypted version of that text. It is called by passing it the string along with the path and filename of a directory and filename. This temporary file will hold the encrypted data before it is read back into text variable for returning to the caller of the subroutine.

```
sub make_pgp_file {
  local ($output_text, $output_file) = @_;
  local ($pgp_output);
```

The first thing that must be done in the subroutine is that the **PGPPath** environment variable is set. This environment variable tells the PGP program where to find the configuration files such as the key ring that holds the public key for encrypting data.

```
$ENV{"PGPPATH"} = $pgp_config_files;
```

Next, the actual full PGP command is constructed using the **$pgp_path** variable plus the **$pgp_options**, **$pgp_public_key_user_id**, and a redirection of the output to **$output_file**.

```
$pgp_command =  "$pgp_path $pgp_options ";
$pgp_command .= "$pgp_public_key_user_id ";
$pgp_command .= ">$output_file";
```

The command is opened up as a file using the pipe (|) operator. This tells Perl to actually execute the command but make the command accept input as print statements to the resulting file handle. The output text that must be encrypted is then sent to the command using the **print** statement. Then, the command is closed.

```
open (PGPCOMMAND, "|$pgp_command");
print PGPCOMMAND $output_text;
close (PGPCOMMAND);
```

The resulting output file is then opened and read into the **$pgp_output** variable. The resulting output file basically consists of the encrypted text. When this process is complete, the file is closed and then deleted using the **unlink** command.

```
open(PGPOUTPUT, $output_file);

while (<PGPOUTPUT>) {
    $pgp_output .= $_;
}
close (PGPOUTPUT);

unlink($output_file);
```

Finally, the PGP encrypted text is returned to the caller of the subroutine, and the subroutine as well as the library file is completed.

```
return($pgp_output);
} # End of make_pgp_file
```

E-Mail Library

The email interface library distributed with the Web store actually consists of one of two different files: **smtpmail-lib.pl** or **sendmail-lib.pl**. The UNIX version of Web store uses **sendmail-lib.pl** (renamed **mail-lib.pl** by default) because the most reliable way of sending email on UNIX is through the sendmail program. The Windows NT/Windows 95 version of the Web store uses **smtpmail-lib.pl** instead. This file should be copied over **mail-lib.pl** if you are using a Windows NT or Windows 95 Web server. Both of these files have the same exact *interface* (same function calls), so copying one over the other does not result in a change in the program.

The reason the Windows NT/95 Web servers cannot use the sendmail version of the library is that there is no sendmail equivalent distributed with those operating systems. Thus, instead of interfacing with sendmail, **smtp-mail-lib.pl** is programmed to open up "sockets" directly to SMTP (Simple Mail Transfer Protocol) servers on the Internet and send email using the raw, low-level Internet mail protocol.

Unfortunately, using the SMTP version of the library has a downside. The "sendmail" program is a program that does a lot more than just send mail. It has evolved over the years and has a lot of email error-checking built in to itself. The SMTP version of the mail library on the other hand, while it works, has not seen the same distribution level as the standard UNIX sendmail utility. In addition, using the SMTP version of mail means that the email addresses that you provide to the Web Store configuration must have host names that are the actual Internet names (DNS) of the servers that handle the email directly.

Normally, your Internet address will have a host name after the at symbol (@), which is the actual server that is physically handling the email. However, there are occasions where the host name is actually an alias to another server that is actually handling the mail. The UNIX sendmail program handles this situation automatically. The SMTP library does not. If your email address is **you@yourdomain.com** but the actual hostname of the machine that really handles your email is called **mailserver.yourdomain.com**, then you must put **you@mailserver.yourdomain.com** as your email address in the Web store Setup file.

Other than the difference in handling names, though, the mail libraries are basically identical with regards to the interface to the outside world. There are two main function calls in each library: **send_mail** and **real_send_mail**.

Send_mail Subroutine

The **send_mail** subroutine is the main function that is used by programs when they want to send email. It accepts the "from" address, "to" address, subject, and body of the messages to send, and then sends them. That's all there is to it. The following is an example call to the subroutine assuming that **smith@zzz.org** is emailing to **jones@yyy.org**.

```
&send_mail("smith\@zzz.org", "jones\@yyy.org",
    "Subject". "This is the message\ntosend.\n\n");
```

Real_send_mail Subroutine

The **real_send_mail** subroutine does the same thing as **send_mail** except that it takes more parameters. In fact, **real_send_mail** is called by **send_mail** after **send_mail** breaks down the few parameters it was given in order to fill out the more complex parameters of **real_send_mail**. The basic difference between the routines is that **real_send_mail** needs to have the host names sent separately from the actual email addresses. This is done so that if the SMTP version of the library is being used, then the programmer will have the option of specifying the real email address in the "from" and "to" areas of the email while still sending email to the correct real hosts that house the actual SMTP server. The equivalent **real_send_mail** call using the data from above appears below in case the **yyy.org** email server is actually physically located at **mail.yyy.org** instead.

```
&real_send_mail("smith\@zzz.org", "zzz.org",
"jones\@yyy.org", "mail.yyy.org", "Subject",
"This is the message\nto send.\n\n");
```

CGI Library

There are certain tasks that every CGI (Common Gateway Interface) program must be capable of doing in order to perform CGI functions. For example, form variables must be read into the program, and specially formatted information must be communicated back to the server. Although there are several good libraries of CGI-related routines, the Web store uses **cgi-lib.pl** because it is small, efficient, Perl 4–compatible, and well supported throughout the CGI and Perl programming community.

cgi-lib.pl was written by Steven Brenner and is the de facto standard library of CGI programming routines for Perl 4 and above. The library is short and simple, and it does 99 percent of what a CGI programmer needs to accomplish with regard to the Common Gateway Interface specification.

The main thing that **cgi-lib.pl** does is to read all the form-variable input into an associative array for picking out the values. It also has the capability of printing standard HTML headers and footers along with the magic **Content-type: text/html\n\n** header. This header is absolutely necessary and printing it is generally the first thing every CGI programmer does in a script. CGI-LIB also has small routines to do general housekeeping, such as printing error messages as HTML output, printing associative arrays, and returning URLs and certain environmental variables related to CGI. Advanced features, such as the ability to support file uploads, have also recently been added.

The Web store itself only uses a few of the core features of **cgi-lib.pl**. As such, we will only go over those calls that the Web Store actually uses as part of its operation. The operations that the CGI library performs for the Web Store are the processing of form variables and the printing of diagnostic error messages.

Reading and Parsing Form Variables

The **&ReadParse** function is used to read the form variables whether the form was called via a GET or POST method. If **&ReadParse** is called without a parameter, by default the form variables are read into an associative array called **%in**. You can use your own associative array if you pass it by reference to **&ReadParse**. The Web store uses **%form_data** as the associative array name. Thus, **&ReadParse** is called with the following syntax:

```
&ReadParse(*form_data);
```

NOTE Normally, when a variable is passed to a subroutine in Perl, only a copy of its value is passed. By replacing the $, @, or % symbol with a * in front of a normal scalar, list array, and associative array variables respectively, you are telling it to copy the location into memory where the variable exists. This way, when the variable is changed in the subroutine, that change is simultaneously done to the originally passed variable instead of to a mere copy of the value of the variable.

Printing CGI Errors

&CgiError and **&CgiDie** accept an error message as a parameter, convert the error message to HTML, and print it so that users can see the error on a Web browser. **&CgiDie** behaves exactly like **&CgiError** except that **&CgiDie** exits the program with the **DIE** command.

Most Perl programs use the plain **DIE** command in case of a system failure. Using **&CgiDie** is much better in the case of CGI programs, because the **DIE** message frequently never gets sent to the browser, making problems difficult to troubleshoot. The following code gives an example of how you would use **&CgiDie** to trap an error if a file does not open correctly.

```
open(TESTFILE, ">test.file") ||
&CgiDie("The file: test.file could not be opened.");
```

For the code above, you could also have used **CgiError** to report the problem. However, opening a file is usually a crucial step in a program so you want the script to end cleanly instead of attempting to go on when the file could not be opened. Throughout the Web store, **CgiDie** is used instead of **CgiError** for this reason.

APPENDIX A

ABOUT THE CD-ROM

Overview

The companion CD-ROM includes all the scripts discussed in this book, ready to use for both UNIX and Windows NT/Windows 95 Web servers. Since there are a variety of Web server environments in which the scripts can run, certain assumptions discussed below relate to how the scripts are distributed on the CD. Figure A.1 shows the basic directory structure of the Web store distribution.

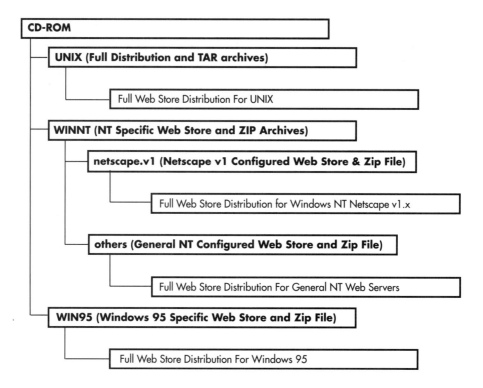

Figure A.1 Basic directory structure of the CD-ROM.

The UNIX directory contains all the scripts discussed in the book. For every platform (UNIX/NT/95), there is a separate directory that contains the CGI scripts, data files, and their subdirectories. In addition, the scripts related to each platform are also archived using a format suitable to that platform: TAR for UNIX and ZIP for Windows NT/Windows 95.

The Windows NT–based Web server versions of the Web store are stored under the WINNT subdirectory. Since there are several different ways that Windows NT Web servers treat CGI/PERL scripts, there is a subdirectory under WINNT to suit each type of major Web server that we have ported the Web store to. This includes Netscape v1.x (Commerce/Communication server), Netscape v2.x (FastTrack/Enterprise), Microsoft IIS v1/v2, and O'Reilly's WebSite server. There is one subdirectory for Netscape v1.x servers and another subdirectory for all the other Web server types since they are configured the same way.

In addition, there is a WIN95 directory that contains a sample Windows 95 Web server distribution of the Web store. Since the difference between the distributions for Windows 95 are not as varied as the ones for Windows NT, only one Web store implementation is provided under the WIN95 directory. This is basically similar to the "others" directory under the WINNT implementation except that **smtpmail-lib.pl** has had some modifications, done to make this library work on Windows 95.

NOTE The applications discussed in this book use long filenames. You will need to unzip the files using a program, such as WinZip95, that recognizes long filenames. Programs for dearchiving the applications on the CD can be found at http://www.shareware.com/.

Finally, if your machine does not recognize long filenames (such as MS-DOS 6.x and below), short filename versions of the script packages can be found at http://www.eff.org/~erict/Scripts/.

The instructions in the first section of Chapter 1 can be used to retrieve the short filename script packages.

NOTE The filenames inside the ZIP and TAR files will still be long filenames, but this procedure will allow you to download the archive to a machine that does not support long filenames and then transfer it to your UNIX or Windows NT/95 machine later.

UNIX Specifics

The UNIX directory on the CD-ROM contains all the applications discussed in the book. The instructions and comments listed below will help you install them.

Installation

To transfer an application to your system, you have two choices. First, the directories and files related to the application can be copied directly to the Web server directory. You can also copy the TAR file to the UNIX server and then use the TAR command to expand the application into its constituent directories and files. For example, if you were unpacking the Web store script (**web_store.tar**), you would issue the following command:

```
tar xvfp web_store.tar
```

Once the scripts are copied onto your server, follow the guidelines in Chapters 1 and Chapter 2 to configure the sample Web store. The guidelines contained in these chapters will help you with the rest of the process of setting up the Web store, such as setting permissions on the files and directories.

Assumptions

First, all the scripts have been written with the assumption that the Perl executable is in the **/usr/local/bin** directory. Second, scripts that do mailing use the **SEND-MAIL-LIB.PL** library (renamed to **MAIL-LIB.PL**) discussed in Chapter 8. In addition, this library has been configured to look for the UNIX sendmail program in the **/usr/lib** directory by default. If your UNIX system is different, you may need to change these defaults. You should read Chapter 1 and Chapter 2 thoroughly to get an idea of how to install and customize the scripts to your Web server environment.

Windows NT/Windows 95 Specifics

The Windows NT/Windows 95 versions of the Web store are stored under the WINNT and WIN95 directories on the CD-ROM respectively. The installation process is similar to that of the UNIX versions of the scripts. You can copy the files directly off the CD-ROM or you can use the provided zip files for the various distributions. In addition, each application comes with a **README.NT** or **README.95** file that briefly outlines what was changed in each CGI application to make it work on the specific Windows NT or Windows 95 Web servers that were tested with the Web store.

Installation

We recommend that you install the NT/95 scripts by copying the application files and directories directly off of the CD-ROM onto your Windows NT/Windows 95 Web server. However, if you must use the zip files instead, there is one thing you need to be aware of. Since the Web store uses long filenames, you will need to unzip the files using a zip program that is aware of long filenames.

Assumptions

First, the scripts have been tested using a variety of different Web servers available for Windows NT/Windows 95. However, they have all been tested with the same version of Perl (Perl 5 for Win32 (build 110) available from http//www.hip.com/. The key points covered in Chapter 1 under installing Windows NT/Windows 95 versions of the Web store are all relevant to installing the Web store on your server. For example, the Netscape server v1.x version of the Web store has been converted to run with batch file wrappers instead of directly using the **.CGI** extension script names.

> There are security issues involved with running batch files on your Web server. For a list of these concerns, you may want to read the WWW Security FAQ located at http://www-genome.wi.mit.edu/WWW/faqs/www-security-faq.html.

N O T E

The batch files on the CD-ROM assume that the **perl.exe** file is located in the path of the Web Server. The following is an example of a batch file that calls the Web store script:

```
@echo off
perl web_store.cgi
```

If your Web server is not configured so that **perl.exe** is included in the Web server path, then you will need to modify the batch file accordingly. The following is an example of the above batch file modified to have a path set to the perl executable file located in the **d:\perl5** directory:

```
@echo off
set OLDPATH=%PATH%
PATH=d:\perl5\;%PATH%
perl web_store.cgi
PATH=%OLDPATH%
```

README.NT/README.95

As a final note, The Windows NT or Windows 95 readme files (README.NT/README.95) for each Web store version contains information about how we took the UNIX versions of the scripts and converted them to the various Windows NT/Windows 95 servers. Generally, there were only three changes that had to be made to the majority of the scripts:

1. In the case of Netscape v1.x servers, the **.CGI** references were replaced with **.BAT** and a batch file was created to call the actual **.CGI** script.

2. **web_store.cgi** had to be edited to include a change directory (**chdir**) command in order to run on Web servers that changed the current working directory of the script.

3. The SMTP version of the email library (**smtpmail-lib.pl**) was copied over the default UNIX-specific **mail-lib.pl**.

If you find yourself in need of modifying any of the UNIX scripts to suit your particular NT/Windows 95 server (or even another operating system's Web server), the various **README.NT** and **README.95** files should point you in the right direction to make the scripts function properly.

APPENDIX B

CGI PROGRAMMING
TECHNIQUES IN PERL

Perl (Practical Extraction and Reporting Language) is not a CGI-specific programming language. In fact, it is a powerful language with many applications far beyond the needs of CGI. Thus, as a CGI programmer, your mastery of Perl initially need only extend to a small subset of the Perl universe.

In this appendix, we will try to identify the most commonly appearing Perl functions used with the CGI applications in this book to give the beginner a quick-and-dirty, but by no means all-inclusive, introduction to Perl. If you are a beginner to Perl as well as to CGI, this appendix should give you the very basic foundation you will need in order to understand the scripts in this book. However, intermediate and advanced readers should only selectively browse this appendix as needed. Most of the information here should already be familiar to you.

If you would like more than a cheat-sheet, we strongly recommend that find *Learning Perl* by Randall Schwartz and *Programming Perl* by Randall Schwartz and Larry Wall, both of which are published by O' Reilly and Associates Inc. Both these books outline Perl completely and, as such, are invaluable resources for the CGI programmer.

In the meantime, let this appendix be your guide.

Discussion

Sending Text to the Web Browser

Every CGI application must output information. For example, both the HTTP header and the HTML code necessary to generate whatever graphical user interface (GUI) the client will be using to navigate must be sent to the Web browser.

USING THE PRINT FUNCTION

The most basic method for sending text to the Web browser is the **print** function in Perl. The print function uses the following syntax:

```
print "[string to print]";
```

By default, the **print** function outputs data to standard output "<STDOUT>" which, in the case of a CGI application, is the Web browser. Thus, whatever you tell Perl to print will be sent to the Web browser to be displayed.

For example, the following line sends the phrase, "Hello Universe" to the Web browser:

```
print "Hello Universe";
```

 Of course, in order to comply with HTTP protocol, you must first send the HTTP header when communicating with a browser using the following syntax:

NOTE
```
print "Content-type: text/html\n\n";
```

However, **print** does have some limitations. For example, it is limited in its ability to handle Perl special characters within an output string. For example, suppose we want to print the following HTML code:

```
<A HREF = "mailto:selena@foobar.com">selena@foobar.com</A>
```

You might extrapolate from the syntax above that you would use the following Perl code to display the hyperlink:

```
print "<A HREF = "mailto:selena@foobar.com">selena@foobar.com</A>";
```

Unfortunately, this would yield a syntax error. Additionally, because this is a very common line of HTML, it is a common source of Perl CGI customization errors. The problem lies in the incorporation of the at sign (@) and double-quote (") characters within the code.

As it so happens, these characters are "special" Perl characters. In other words, each haas a special meaning to Perl and, when displaying them, you must take precautions so that Perl understands what you are asking for. For example, consider the double quote marks in the "mailto" hyperlink. How would Perl know that the double quote marks in the "mailto" hyperlink are supposed to be part of the string to be printed and not actually the end of the string to be printed? Recall that we use the double quote marks to delineate the beginning and the ending of a text string to be printed. Similarly, the at sign (@) is used by Perl to name list arrays.

Many other "special" characters exist and are discussed in other Perl references.

NOTE

One solution to this problem is to escape the Perl special characters with a backslash (\). The backslash character tells Perl that whatever character follows should be considered a part of the string and not a special character. Thus, the correct syntax for the **mailto** hyperlink would be

```
print "<A HREF =
\"mailto:selena\@foobar.com\">selena\@foobar.com</A>";
```

USING "HERE DOCUMENTS"

Unfortunately, much of what your CGI applications will be sending to the Web browser will include the double-quote mark special character. It becomes tedious, especially for long blocks of HTML code, to make **print** statements for every line of HTML and to escape every occurrence of a double-quote with a backslash. Consider the following table definition:

```
print "<TABLE BORDER = \"1\" CELLPADDING = \"2\"
          CELLSPACING = \"2\">";
print "<TR>";
print "<TD ALIGN = \"center\">Email</TD>";
```

```
print "<TD ALIGN = \"center\">
        <A HREF = \"mailto:selena\@foobar.com\">
        selena\@foobar.com</A></TD>";
print "</TR>";
print "</TABLE>";
```

If any one of those backslashes is missing, the whole script breaks down. And this is a very small block of code!

One solution to the sending of large blocks of HTML code that incorporate the double-quote is to use the "here document" method of printing. The "here document" method tells Perl to print everything within a certain block of boundaried code. The "here document" uses the generic format:

```
print <<[TEXT_BOUNDARY_MARKER];
[Text to be printed]
[TEXT_BOUNDARY_MARKER]
```

For example, this code will print out the basic HTML header:

```
print <<end_of_html_header;
<HTML>
<HEAD>
<TITLE>My Title</TITLE>
</HEAD>
<BODY>
end_of_html_header
```

In short, the "here document" method of printing tells the Perl interpreter to print out everything it sees (**print <<**) from the **print** line until it finds the text boundary marker specified in the print line (**end_of_html_header**). The text boundary marker can be anything you like, of course, but it is useful to make the flag descriptive.

Further, the ending flag must be *exactly* the same as the flag definition. Thus, the following code will fail because the final flag is not indented correctly:

```
print <<"    end_of_header";
  <HTML><HEAD><TITLE>$title</TITLE></HEAD><BODY>
  end_of_header
```

The final **end_of_header** tag should have been indented four spaces, but it was only indented two.

NOTE

Though the "here document" method of printing does avoid having to escape double quotes within the block to print, the at sign (@) and other special Perl characters still need escaping.

USING QQ

qq is another Perl trick that helps a programmer solve the double-quote problem by allowing her to change the double-quote delimiter in a print statement.

Normally, as we said, double-quotes (") are used to delimit the characters in a print statement. However, by replacing the first quote with two *q*s followed by another character, that final character becomes the new print statement delimiter. Thus, by using **qq!**, we tell Perl to use an exclamation point (!), also known as "bang," to delimit the string instead of the double quotes.

For example, without using **qq**, a print statement that outputs, "She said, 'hi'." would be written as:

```
print "She said, \"hi\".";
```

But with the **qq** making bang (!) the new delimiter, the same statement can be written as:

```
print qq!She said, "hi"!;
```

Why would we do this? Readability. If the print statement was surrounded with the normal double quotes, then every double-quote would have to be escaped with a backslash whenever it was used within a string. The backslashes clutter the readability of the string. Thus, we choose a different character to delimit the string in the print statement so that we do not have to escape the double-quotes with backslashes.

USING THE PRINTF AND SPRINTF FUNCTIONS

The Perl **printf** is much like the **printf** function in C and awk in that it takes a string to be formatted and a list of format arguments, applies the formatting to the string, and then typically prints the formatted string to standard output, which in our case, is the Web browser.

The **printf** syntax uses a double-quoted string that includes special format markers followed by a comma-delimited list of arguments to be applied to those markers. The format markers are typically in the form of a percent sign followed by a control character.

For example, the generic format of **printf** might look like the following code:

```
printf ("[some text] %[format] [other text]", [argument to be formatted]);
```

In use, we might use the **%s** formatting argument specifying a string and the **%d** formatting argument specifying a digit using the following syntax:

```
$name = "Selena Sol";
$age = 27;
printf ("My name is %s and my age is %d.\n", $name, $age);
```

The code above would produce the following output in the Web browser window:

```
My name is Selena Sol and my age is 27.
```

In reality, the **printf** function is rarely used in Perl CGI since, unlike C which almost demands the use of **printf**, Perl has much easier ways of printing. However, the **printf** routines are essential for another, more useful (to CGI developers) function, **sprintf.**

Unlike **printf, sprintf** takes the formatted output and assigns it to a variable, rather than outputting it to standard output (<STDOUT>), using the following generic syntax:

```
$variable_name = sprintf ("[some text] %[format] [other text]",
[string to be formatted]);
```

A good example of using **sprintf** comes from the **format_price** subroutine in **web_store.cgi**. In this subroutine, we need to format subtotals and grand totals to two decimal places so that prices come out to numbers like "$99.00" or "$98.99" rather than "99" or "98.99876453782". Below is a snippet of code that uses **sprintf** to format the price string to two decimal places.

```
$formatted_price = sprintf ("%.2f", $round_price);
```

In this example, the variable, **$round_price** is formatted using the **"%.2f"** argument which formats (%) the string to two decimal places (.2f) and assigned to the **$formatted_price** string.

There are a multitude of formatting arguments besides "**%s**", "**%d**", and "**%f**", however. Table B.1 lists several useful ones.

Table B.1 printf and sprintf Formats

Format Character	Description
c	Character
s	String
d	Decimal Number
x	Hexadecimal Number
o	Octal Number
f	Floating Point Number

Scalar Variables, List Arrays, and Associative Arrays

WHAT IS A SCALAR VARIABLE?

You can think of a variable as a place holder or a name that represents one or more values. The generic syntax for defining scalar variables (also known as *variables* for short) is as follows:

```
$variable_name = value;
```

Thus, for example, we might assign the value of 27 to the scalar variable named "age" with the syntax:

```
$age = 27;
```

The dollar sign (**$**) is used to let Perl know that we are talking about a scalar variable. From then on, unless we change the value of **$age**, the script will translate it to **27**.

So if we then say:

```
print "$age\n";
```

Perl will send the value **27** to standard output, which in our case, will be the Web browser.

If we are assigning a word or a series of words to a scalar variable rather than just a number, we must mark the boundary of the value with single or double quotes so that Perl will know exactly what should be assigned to the scalar variable.

We use single quotes to mark the boundary of a plain text string and we use double quotes to mark the boundary of a text string that can include scalar variables to be "interpolated." For example, we might have the following lines:

```
$age = 27;
$first_name = 'Selena';
$last_name = 'Sol';
$sentence = "$first_name $last_name is $age";
print "$sentence\n";
```

The routine would print the following line to standard output:

```
Selena Sol is 27
```

Notice that the scalar variable **$sentence** is assigned the actual values of **$first_name** and **$last_name**. This is because they were "interpolated" since we included them within double quotes in the definition of **$sentence**. There is no interpolation inside single quotes. Thus, if we had defined **$sentence** using single quotes as follows:

```
$sentence = '$first_name $last_name is $age';
```

Perl would print the following to standard output:

```
$first_name $last_name is $age
```

USING SCALAR VARIABLES

The benefit of substituting a scalar variable name for a value is that we can then manipulate its value. For example, you can autoincrement a scalar variable using the **++** operator:

```
$number = 1;
print "$number\n";
$number++;
print "$number\n";
```

Perl would send the following to standard output:

```
1
2
```

You can also perform arithmetic such as:

```
$item_subtotal = $item_price * $quantity;
$shipping_price = 39.99 * $quantity;
$grand_total = $item_subtotal + $shipping_price;
```

Scalar variables are the meat and potatoes of CGI. After all, translating between the client and the Web server is essentially the formatting and the reformatting of variables. Be prepared to see them used a lot.

USING THE DOT OPERATOR

Another cool Perl trick is the use of the "dot" (.) operator, which "appends" a value to an already existing scalar variable. Thus, the following code would print out **Selena Sol**:

```
$name = "Selena" . " Sol";
print "$name";
```

An alternative shorthand for appending to scalar variables is using the .= operator. For example, the following code does the same thing as the code above:

```
$name = "Selena";
$name .= " Sol";
print "$name\n";
```

CROPPING SCALAR VARIABLES WITH THE CHOP FUNCTION

Sometimes, you do not want the entire value that has been assigned to a scalar variable. For example, it is often the case that the lines you retrieve from a data file will incorporate a newline character at the end of the line. In this book, data files often take advantage of the newline character as a "database row delimiter." That is, every line in a database file is a new database item. For example, here is a snippet from sample Cart data file:

```
3|0011|Vowels|12.98|The letter E|12.98|100
2|0010|Vowels|15.98|The letter A|15.98|101
```

When the script reads each line, it also reads in the newline information. Thus, the first line is actually represented as:

```
3|0011|Vowels|12.98|The letter E|12.98|100\n
```

The final **\n** is a new line. Since we do not actually want the **\n** character included with the last database field, we use the chop function. The chop function chops off the very last character of a scalar variable using the syntax:

```
chop ($variable_name);
```

Thus, we would take off the final newline character as follows:

```
$database_row = "3|0011|Vowels|12.98|The letter
                E|12.98|100\n";
chop ($database_row);
```

FINDING THE LENGTH OF A SCALAR VARIABLE WITH THE LENGTH FUNCTION

Finding the length of a scalar variable is incredibly easy using the **length** function. The syntax of length is as follows:

```
length ([$variable_name]);
```

Thus, if the scalar variable **$name** equals "Selena," then the scalar variable **$length_of_name** will be assigned the value of **6** in the following line:

```
$length_of_name = length ($name);
```

MANIPULATING SUBSTRINGS WITH THE SUBSTR FUNCTION

Sometimes, you want to work with just part of a string that has been assigned. The **substr** function can be used for that and follows the syntax:

```
$substring = substr([string you want to extract from],
                    [beginning point of extraction],
                    [length of the extracted value]);
```

For instance, to assign **Sol** to the scalar variable **$last_name** you would use the following code:

```
$name = "Selena Sol";
$last_name =  substr ($name, 7, 3);
```

The **substr** function takes the scalar variable **$name**, and extracts three characters beginning with the seventh:

As in array indexing, the substr function counts from zero, not from one. Thus, in the string **Gunther**, the letter *t* is actually referenced as **3** not **4**.

WARNING

The final number (length of extracted value) is not necessary when you want to grab everything "after" the beginning character. Thus, the following code will do just what the previous did since we are extracting the entire end of the variable $name:

NOTE

```
$last_name =  substr ($name, 7);
```

List Arrays

WHAT IS A LIST ARRAY?

List arrays (also known simply as *arrays* for short) take the concept of scalar variables to the next level. Whereas scalar variables associate one value with one variable name, list arrays associate one array name with a "list" of values.

A list array is defined with the following syntax:

```
@array_name = ("element_1", "element_2"..."element_n");
```

For example, consider the following list array definition:

```
@available_colors = ("red", "green", "blue", "brown");
```

As you might have guessed, the at sign (@) is used to communicate to Perl that a list array is being named much as the dollar sign ($) is used to denote a scalar variable name.

NOTE

In this example, the list array **@available_colors** is filled with four color "elements" in the specific order: red, green, blue, brown. It is important to see that the colors are not simply dumped into the list array at random. Each list element is placed in the specific order in which the list array was defined. Thus list arrays are also considered to be *ordered*.

USING A LIST ARRAY

The benefit of ordering the elements in a list array is that we can easily grab one value out of the list on demand. To do this, we use Perl's subscripting operator using the format:

```
$array_name[list_element_number]
```

When pulling an element out of a list array, we create a scalar variable with the same name as the array, prefixed with the usual dollar sign denoting scalar variables.

For example, the first element of the array **@available_colors** is accessed as:

```
$available_colors[0].
```

Notice that the first element is accessed with a zero. This is important. List arrays begin counting at zero, not one. Thus, **$available_colors[0]** is a variable place holder for the word *red*. Likewise, **$available_colors[1]** equals *green* and **$available_colors[2]** equals *blue*.

FIGURING OUT HOW MANY ELEMENTS ARE IN AN ARRAY

Fortunately, Perl provides an easy way to determine how many elements are contained in an array. When used as a scalar, the list array name will be equal to the number of elements it contains. Thus, if the list array **@available_colors** contains the elements: red, green, blue, and brown, then the following line would set **$number_of_colors** equal to 4:

```
$number_of_colors = @available_colors;
```

WARNING

Be careful when using this value in your logic. The number of elements in an array is a number counting from 1. But when accessing an array, you must access starting from 0. Thus, the last element in the array **@available_colors** is not **$available_colors[@available_colors]** but rather **$available_colors[@available_colors - 1]**.

ADDING ELEMENTS TO A LIST ARRAY

Likewise, you can add to or modify the values of an existing array by simply referencing the array by number. For example, to add an element to **@available_colors**, you might use the following line:

```
$available_colors[4] = "orange";
```

Thus, **@available_colors** would include the elements: red, green, blue, brown, and orange.

You can also use this method to overwrite an element in a list array. To change a value in **@available_colors**, you might use the syntax:

```
$available_colors[0] = "yellow";
```

Now, the elements of **@available_colors** would be: yellow, green, blue, brown, orange.

DELETING AND REPLACING LIST ELEMENTS WITH THE SPLICE FUNCTION

The splice function is used to remove or replace elements in an array and uses the following syntax:

```
splice ([array to modify], [offset], [length],
        [list of new elements]);
```

The **array** argument is the array to be manipulated. **offset** is the starting point where elements are to be removed. **length** is the number of elements from the offset number to be removed. The **list** argument consists of an ordered list of values to replace the removed elements with. Of course, if the **list** argument is null, the elements accessed will be removed rather than replaced.

Thus, for example, the following code will modify the **@numbers** list array to include the elements, ("1" , "2", "three", "four", "5").

```
@numbers = ("1", "2", "3", "4", "5");
splice (@numbers, 2, 2, "three", "four");
```

A more common usage of the splice is simply to remove list elements by not specifying a replacement list. For example, we might modify **@numbers** to include only the elements "1", "2", and "5" by using the following code:

```
splice (@numbers, 2, 2);
```

ADVANCED LIST ARRAY MANIPULATION WITH THE PUSH, POP, SHIFT, AND UNSHIFT FUNCTIONS

Of course, once we have created a list array, we can do much more than just access the elements. We can also manipulate the elements in many ways. Throughout this book, list arrays are most often manipulated using the operators **push**, **pop**, **shift**, and **unshift**:

push is used to add a new element on the right-hand side of a list array.

Thus, the following code would create a list array of ("red", "green", "blue"):

```
@colors = ("red", "green");
push (@colors, "blue");
```

In other words, the **push** operator adds an element to the end of an existing list. **pop** does the exact same thing as push, but in reverse. It extracts the right-side element of a list array using the following syntax:

```
$popped_variable_name = pop (@array_name);
```

Thus, we might pop out the value blue from **@colors** with the following syntax:

```
$last_color_in_list = pop (@colors);
```

Thus, the **@colors** array now contains only "red" and "green" and the variable **$last_color_in_list** is equal to "blue".

unshift does the exact same thing as **push**, but it performs the addition to the left side of the list array instead of to the right. Thus, we would create the list ("blue", "red", "green") with the following syntax:

```
@colors = ("red", "green");
unshift (@colors, "blue");
```

Similarly, **shift** works the same as **pop**, but to the left side of the list array. Thus, we reduce **@colors** to just "red" and "green" by shifting the first element blue with the following syntax:

```
$first_color_in_list = shift(@colors);
```

Thus, **@colors** again contains only "red" and "green" and **$first_color_in_list** equals blue.

Though **push**, **pop**, **shift**, and **unshift** are the most common list array manipulation functions used in this book, there are many others covered in more complete references. Table B.3 Summarizes some of the common array manipulating operators.

Table B.2 Array Manipulation Operators

Operator	Description
shift(@array)	Removes the first element in **@array**
unshift (@array, $element)	Adds **$element** to the beginning of **@array**
pop (@array)	Removes the last element of **@array**
push (@array, $element)	Adds $element to the end of **@array**
sort (@array)	Sorts the elements in **@array**
reverse(@array)	Reverses the order of the elements in **@array**
chop (@array)	chops off the last character of every element in **@array**
split (/delimiter/, string)	Creates an array by splitting a string
join (delimiter, @array)	Creates a scalar of every element in **@array** joined by the delimiter.

Associative Arrays

WHAT IS AN ASSOCIATIVE ARRAY?

Associative arrays add the final degree of complexity allowing ordered lists to be associated with other values. Unlike list arrays, associative arrays have index values that are not numbers. You do not reference an associative array as **$associative_array_name[0]** as you did for the list array. Instead, associative arrays are indexed with arbitrary scalar variables. Consider the following associative array definition:

```
%CLIENT_ARRAY = ('full_name', 'Selena Sol',
                 'phone', '213-456-7890',
                 'age', '27');
```

In this example, we have defined the associative array %CLIENT_ARRAY to have three sets of associations.

the percent sign (%) denotes the associative array name just as the dollar sign ($) did for variables and the at sign (@) did for list arrays.

NOTE

Thus, **full_name** is associated with **Selena Sol** as **age** is associated with **27**. This association is discussed in terms of **keys** and **values**. Each key is associated with one value. Thus, we say that the key **full_name** is associated with the value **Selena Sol**.

ACCESSING AN ASSOCIATIVE ARRAY

If we want to extract a value from the associative array, we reference it with the following syntax:

```
$variable_equal_to_value = $ASSOCIATIVE_ARRAY_NAME{'[key]'};
```

Thus, to pull out the value of the **name** key from **%CLIENT_ARRAY**, we use the following syntax:

```
$full_name = $CLIENT_ARRAY{'full_name'}
```

The variable **$full_name** would then be equal to **Selena Sol**. Think of it as using a **key** to unlock a **value**.

When accessing an associative array using a scalar variable as a key, you should not surround the key with single quotes because the scalar variable will not be interpolated. For example, the following syntax generates the value for the age key:

NOTE

```
$key_name = "age";
$age = $CLIENT_ARRAY{$key_name};
```

Accessing an associative array is one of the most basic CGI functions and is at the heart of the **ReadParse** routine in **cgi-lib.pl**, which creates an associative array from the incoming form data. By accessing this associative array (usually referred to in this book as **%form_data**), **web_store.cgi** is able to determine what it is that the client has asked of it since HTML form variables are formed in terms of administratively defined NAMES and client-defined VALUES using syntax such as the following:

```
<INPUT TYPE = "text" NAME = "full_name" SIZE = "40">
```

The "key" of the associative array generated by **ReadParse** will be **full_name** and the **value** will be whatever the client typed into the text box.

USING THE KEYS AND VALUES FUNCTIONS

Perl also provides a convenient way to get a list of all the keys or of all the values in an associative array if you are interested in more than just one key/value pair. keys and values are accessed with the keys and values functions using the following formats:

```
@associative_array_keys = keys (%ASSOCIATIVE_ARRAY_NAME);
```

and

```
@associative_array_values = values (%ASSOCIATIVE_ARRAY_NAME);
```

Thus, the keys and values list of the associative array **%CLIENT_ARRAY** defined above can be generated with the following syntax:

```
@client_array_keys = keys (%CLIENT_ARRAY);
@client_array_values = values (%CLIENT_ARRAY);
```

In this example **@client_array_keys** would look like (**full_name, phone, age**) and **@client_array_values** would look like (**Selena Sol, 213-456-7890, 27**).

ADDING TO AND DELETING FROM AN ASSOCIATIVE ARRAY

Like list arrays, associative arrays can be internally modified. The most common function, other than defining an associative array, is adding to it. Adding to an associative array simply involves telling Perl which key and value to add using the format:

```
$ARRAY_NAME{'key'} = "value";
```

or, using our example above:

```
$CLIENT_ARRAY{'favorite_candy'} = "Hershey's with Almonds";
```

%CLIENT_ARRAY now includes **full_name**, **phone**, **age** and **favorite_candy** along with their associated values.

Similarly, you can easily use the delete function to delete a key/value pair in an associative array. The **delete** function follows the syntax:

```
delete ($ASSOCIATIVE_ARRAY_NAME{'key'});
```

or for our %CLIENT_ARRAY example:

```
delete ($CLIENT_ARRAY{'age'});
```

Thus, **%CLIENT_ARRAY** would contain only **full_name**, **phone**, and **favorite_candy**.

Manipulating Strings

Another important function provided by CGI is the manipulation of strings of data. Whether called upon to display or manipulate the contents of a data file, to reformat some text for Web-display, or simply to use in some logical routine or external program, Perl has a diverse array of string modification functions at its disposal.

EQUALITY OPERATORS

One of the most important string manipulation functions is that of matching or testing of equality. It is an important tool because you can use it as the basis of complex logical comparisons necessary for the intelligence demanded of a CGI application.

For example, consider one of the most basic methods of pattern matching, the **ne** operator, which is used as the basis of the decision making process in **web_store.cgi**:

```
if (the user has hit a specific submit button)
  {
  execute a specific routine.
  }
```

Consider this code snippet:

```
if ($return_to_frontpage_button ne "")
  {
  &display_frontpage;
  }
```

NOTE

If you are confused about the usage of the "if" test, it is explained in greater detail in the "Control Structures" section later in this appendix.

The **ne** operator asks if the value of the variable **$return_to_frontpage_button** is not equal to an empty string. This logic takes advantage of the fact that the HTTP protocol specifies that if a FORM Submit button is pressed, its NAME is set equal to the VALUE specified in the HTML code. For example, the Submit button may have been coded using the following HTML:

```
<INPUT TYPE = "submit"
       NAME = "return_to_frontpage_button"
       VALUE = "Return to the Frontpage">
```

Thus, if the NAME in the associative array has a VALUE, the script knows that the client pushed the associated button. The script determines which routines it should execute by following the logic of these pattern matches.

Similarly, you can test for equality using the **eq** operator. An example of the **eq** operator in use is shown below:

```
if ($name eq "Selena")
  {
  print "Hi, Selena\n";
  }
```

When comparing numbers instead of strings however, Perl uses a second set of operators. For example, to test for equality, you use the double equal (==) operator as follows:

```
if ($number == 11)
  {
  print "You typed in 11\n";
  }
```

WARNING   Never use the single equal sign (=) for comparison. Perl interprets the equal sign in terms of assignment rather than comparison. Thus the line:

`$number = 11;`

actually assigns the value of 11 to **$number** rather than comparing **$number** to 11.

There are many other types of comparison operators, but they are better researched in more comprehensive texts. However, we do include several important ones in Table B.5

Table B.3 Numeric and String Comparison Operators

Numeric Operator	String Operator	Description
==	eq	Equal
!=	ne	Not equal
<	lt	Less than
>	gt	Greater than
<=	le	Less than or equal to
>=	ge	Greater than or equal to

REGULAR EXPRESSIONS

Regular expressions are one of the most powerful, and hence, most complicated tools for matching strings. You can think of a regular expression as a "pattern," which can be used to match against some string. Regular expressions are far more versatile than the simple **eq** and **ne** operators and include a wide variety of modifiers and tricks. Other books have detailed chapters focusing on the use of regular expressions, so we will only touch upon a few common uses of regular expressions found this book.

Pattern Matching with //

Perl invokes a powerful tool for pattern matching that gives the program great flexibility in controlling matches. In Perl, a string is matched by placing it between two slashes as follows:

```
/[pattern_to_match]/
```

Thus, **/eric/** matches for the string "eric." You may also match according to whole classes of characters using the square brackets ([]). The pattern match will then match against any of the characters in the class. For example, to match for any single even-numbered digit, you could use the following match:

```
/[02468]/
```

For classes including an entire range of characters, you may use the dash (-) to represent the list. Thus, the following matches any single lower-case letter in the alphabet:

```
/[a-z]/
```

Likewise, you may use the caret (^) character within the square brackets to match every character that is "not" in the class. The following code matches any single character which is not a digit:

```
/[^0-9]/
```

Matching Operators

Further, the // operator can be modified to include complex pattern matching routines. For example, the period (.) matching operator is used to stand for "any" character. Thus, **/eri./** would match any occurrences of "eric" as well as "erik."

Another commonly used matching operator is the asterisk (*). The asterisk matches zero or more occurrences of the character preceding it. Thus, **/e*ric/** matches occurrences of "eeeeeric" as well as "eric."

Table B.4 includes a list of useful matching operators.

Table B.4 Commonly Used Matching Operators

Operator	Description
\n	Newline
\r	Carriage return
\t	Tab
\d	Digit (same as [0–9])
\D	Any non-digit (same as [^0-9])
\w	A Word Character (same as [0-9a-zA-Z_])
\W	A nonword character
\s	Any whitespace character (\t, \n, \r, or \f)
\S	A nonwhitespace character
*	Zero or more occurrences of the preceding character
+	One or more occurrences of the preceding character
.	Any character
?	Zero or one occurrences of the preceding character

Anchors

Regular expressions also take advantage of anchoring patterns which help match the string in relationship to the rest of the line. For example, the **\b** anchor is used to specify a word boundary. That is, **/\beric\b/** matches "eric", but it does not match **generic**.

Similarly, the caret (^) anchor will match a string to the beginning of the line. Thus, **/^eric/** will match the following line:

```
eric is my name
```

but it will not match:

```
my name is eric
```

 The caret (^) can be confusing since it is used as an anchor when included "outside" of the square brackets ([]) but is used as the **not** operator for a class when used "within."

WARNING

Table B.5 summarizes a few of the most common anchors.

Table B.5 Common Anchors

Anchor	Description
^	Matches the beginning of the string
$	Matches the end of the string
\b	Matches a word boundary (between \w and \W)
\B	Matches on non-word boundary

String Modifiers

Finally, pattern matching can be used to modify strings of text. One of the most common methods of modification is substitution. Substitution is performed using the format:

```
s/[pattern_to_find]/[pattern_to_replace_with]/
```

Thus, for example, the line:

```
s/eric/selena/
```

would change the line

```
eric is my name
```

to

```
selena is my name
```

The substitution function is modified most commonly with the **/i** and the **/g** arguments. The **/i** argument specifies that matching should be done with case insensitivity and the **/g** specifies that the match should occur globally for the entire string of text rather than just for the first occurrence.

Thus, the line:

```
s/eric/selena/gi
```

would change the line:

```
I am Eric, eric I am
```

to:

```
I am selena, selena I am
```

without the **/i**, you would get:

```
I am Eric, selena I am
```

and without **/g** but with the **/i**, you would get:

```
I am selena, eric I am
```

There are many, many different kinds of matching operators, anchors, and string modifiers. If you want a more detailed explanation we recommend that you find a good reference source on regular expressions. Otherwise, the above discussion shouldbe sufficient to explain how we use operators and anchors in this book.

THE =~ OPERATOR

Pattern matching can also be used to manipulate variables. In particular, the scripts in this book take advantage of the **=~** operator in conjunction with the substitution operator using the format:

```
$variable_name =~ s/[string_to_remove]/[string_to_add]/gi;
```

For example, if we want to censor every occurrence of the word *Frack* from the client-defined input field "comment," we might use the line:

```
$form_data{'comments'} =~ s/frack/censored/gi;
```

USING THE SPLIT AND JOIN FUNCTIONS

Finally, regular expressions can be used to split a string into separate fields. To do so, we use the **split** function with the format:

```
@split_array = split (/[pattern_to_split_on]/, [string_to_split]);
```

For example, the applications in this book often use the **split** function to read the fields of database rows. Consider the following code snippet:

```
$database_row = "Selena Sol|213-456-7890|27";
@database_fields = split (/|/, $database_row);
```

Now **@database_fields** will include the elements **Selena Sol, 213-456-7890"** and **27**. Each of these fields can then be processed separately if need be.

The reverse operation is performed with the **join** function, which uses the following format:

```
$joined_string = join ("[pattern_to_join_on]", [list_to_join]);
```

Thus, we might recreate the original database row using:

```
$new_database_row = join ("\|", @database_fields);
```

> Notice that in the above line, the pipe (|) symbol must be escaped with a backslash (\) because the pipe is a special Perl character.

NOTE

Control Structures

Some of the most powerful tools of Perl programming are control structures. Control structures are used to create the basic logic that drives many of the routines used in CGI applications. These control structures use Boolean logic to imbue your script with the intelligence necessary to manage the diverse needs of the clients with the abilities and requirements of the server.

STATEMENT BLOCKS

All control structures are divided into the control statement (which we will explain below) and the statement block. The *statement block* is simply a group of commands that are executed together. This block is grouped by enclosing the commands within curly braces ({}). For example, the following is a simple statement block:

```
{
  statement one
  statement two
  statement three
}
```

Perl will execute each statement in a statement block from beginning to end as a group. When, how, or if the script will execute the commands, however, is determined by the control statement.

USING THE IF, ELSIF, ELSE AND UNLESS CONTROL STATEMENTS

The most common control statement used throughout the scripts in this book is the "if" test. The if test checks to see if some expression is true, and if so, executes the routines in the statement block. Perl uses a simple binary comparison as a test of truth. If the result of some operation is true, the operation returns a one and the statement block is executed. If the result is false, it returns a 0, and the statement block is not executed. For example, consider the following code:

```
if ($name eq "Selena Sol")
  {
  print "Hello Selena.\n";
  }
```

In this example, Perl checks to see if the scalar variable **$name** has the value of **Selena Sol**. If the patterns match, the matching operation will return true and the script will execute the print statement within the statement block. If Perl discovers that **$name** is not equal to **Selena Sol**, however, the print will not be executed.

WARNING

Be careful with your usage of **eq** versus **=.** Within an if test, if you write **$name = Selena Sol**, you will actually be *assigning* **Selena Sol** to the variable **$name** rather than *comparing* it to the value **Selena Sol**. Since this action will be performed successfully, the "if" test will always test to true and the statement block will always be performed even if **$name** did not initially equal **Selena Sol**.

The "if" test also provides for alternatives: the **else** and the **elsif** control statements. The **elsif** alternative adds a second check for truth and the **else** alternative defines a final course of action for every case of failed if or elsif tests. The following code snippet demonstrates the usage of if, **elsif**, and **else:**

```
if ($name eq "Selena Sol")
  {
  print "Hi, Selena.\n";
  }
elsif ($name eq "Gunther Birznieks")
  {
  print "Hi, Gunther\n";
  }
else
```

```
{
print "Who are you?\n";
}
```

Obviously, the else need not perform a match since it is a catch-all control statement.

The **unless** control statement works like an inverse **if** control statement. Essentially it says, "execute some statement block unless some condition is true". The unless control statement is exemplified in the code below:

```
unless ($name eq "Selena")
  {
  print "You are NOT Selena!\n";
  }
```

FOREACH

Another very useful control statement is the **foreach** loop. The **foreach** loop iterates through some list and execute a statement block for each iteration. In this book, the **foreach** loop is most commonly used to iterate through a list array. For example, the following code snippet will print out the value of every element in the list array **@names:**

```
foreach $name (@names)
{
print "$name\n";
}
```

WHILE

The **while** loop also performs iteration and is used in this book primarily for reading lines in a file. The while loop can be used to read and print out every line of a file with the following syntax:

```
open ([FILE_HANDLE_NAME], "[filename]");
while (<[FILE_HANDLE_NAME]>)
  {
  print "$_";
  }
close ([FILE_HANDLE_NAME]);
```

The script would print out every line in the file **filename** because the **$_**, the Perl "default" variable, represents "the current line" in this case.

The process of opening and closing files is covered in the "File Management" section later in this appendix.

NOTE

FOR LOOPS

The **for** loop is another excellent control statement tool. The basic syntax of a **for** loop follows:

```
for ([initial condition]; [test]; [incrementation])
  {
  [action to perform]
  }
```

The **initial condition** defines where the loop should begin. The **test** defines the logic of the loop by letting the script know the conditions that determine the scripts actions. The **incrementation** defines how the script should perform the loop. For example, we might produce a visible countdown with the following for loop:

```
for ($number = 10; $number >= 0; $number-)
  {
  print "$number\n";
  }
```

The script would initially assign 10 to the scalar variables **$number**. It would then test to see if **$number** was greater than or equal to 0. Since 10 is greater than 0, the script would decrement **$number** by subtracting 1 from the value of **$number**.

To decrement, you use **$variable_name—**. To increment, you use **$variable_name++**.

NOTE

Executing the statement block, the script would then print out the number nine. Then, it would go back through the loop again and again, printing each decremented numbers until **$number** was less than zero. At that point, the test would fail and the for loop would exit.

USING LOGICAL OPERATORS (&& AND ||)

Control statements can also be modified with a variety of logical operators that extend the breadth of the control statement truth test using the following syntax:

```
[control statement] ((([first condition])
                       [logical operator]
                      ([second condition]))
{
[action to be performed]
}
```

For example, the **&&** operator can be translated as "and". In usage, it takes the format used in the following example:

```
if (($first_name eq "Selena") && ($last_name eq "Sol"))
{
print "Hello Selena Sol";
}
```

Translating the logic goes something like this: if the first name is Selena AND the last name is Sol, then print **Hello Selena Sol**. Thus, if **$first_name** was equal to "Selena" but **$last_name** was equal to "Flintstone", the control statement would test as false and the statement block would not be executed.

Notice that we use parentheses to denote conditions. Perl evaluates each expression inside the parentheses independently and then evaluates the results for the entire group of conditions. If either returns false, the entire test returns false. The use of parentheses are used to determine precedence. With more complex comparisons, in which there are multiple logical operators, the parentheses help to determine the order of evaluation.

Similarly, you may wish to test using the double pipe (||) operator. This operator is used to denote an **or**. Thus, the following code would execute the statement block if $first_name was Selena *or* Gunther.

```
if (($first_name eq "Selena") || ($first_name eq "Gunther"))
{
print "Hello humble CGI book author!";
}
```

File Management

OPENING AND CLOSING FILES

One of the main resources that your server provides is a file management system. The scripts in this book, for example, use a multitude of supporting files in the server's file system such as temporary files, counter files, user files, data files, setup files, and libraries. Perl includes several excellent tools for working with these files.

First, Perl gives your scripts the ability to open files using the **open** function. The **open** function allows you to create a *filehandle* with which to manipulate a file. A filehandle is another name for a connection between the script and the server. Often, filehandles manage connections between the script and standard input, output, or error, however, in the case of **open**, any file can be read into a filehandle using the syntax:

```
open ([FILE_HANDLE_NAME], "[filename]");
```

For example, we might open a data file for reading using:

```
open (DATA_FILE, "inventory.dat");
```

In this case, all of the lines of **inventory.dat** will be read into the filehandle **DATA_FILE,** which Perl can then use within the program. However, you must also close a file once you are done with it. The syntax for closing a file is as follows:

```
close ([FILE_HANDLE_NAME]);
```

Finally, Perl gives you the ability to execute an error routine if there is a problem opening a file. The logical operator is sometimes discussed in terms of a short circuit. For instance, the logic of the **or** operator is such that if the first expression evaluates to true, there is no need to evaluate the next. On the other hand, if the first expression evaluates to false, the second expression is executed. Thus, using the double pipe (| |) operator, you can specify the default action to perform if an "open" fails. In CGI applications, the alternate action executed is usually something like the subroutine, **CgiDie** located in **cgi-lib.pl**. For example, the following routine would execute the **CgiDie** subroutine if there was a problem opening **data.file**:

```
open (DATA, "data.file") || &CgiDie("Cannot open data.file");
```

Thus, if the script has a problem opening a needed file, the double pipe (||) operator provides a convenient and elegant way to quit the program and report the problem.

READING A FILE LINE BY LINE

An often-used technique in this book for the manipulation of files is the reading of each line of a file. Perhaps we want to check each line for a keyword, or find every occurrence of some marker tag on a line and replace it with some other string. This process is done using a **while** loop as discussed previously. Consider this routine which will print out every line in a data file:

```
open (DATA, "data.file") ||
      &CgiDie ("Cannot open data.file");
while (<ADDRESSES>)
  {
  print "$_";
  }
close (ADDRESSES);
```

Thus, the script would print out every line in the file address.dat because **$_** is Perl's special name for "the current line" in this case:

You can also manipulate the $_ variable in other ways such as applying pattern matching on it or adding it to an array.

N O T E

WRITING AND APPENDING TO FILES

You can do more than just read a file of course. You can also open a filehandle for writing with the greater than sign (>) using the syntax:

```
open ([FILE_HANDLE_NAME], ">[filename]");
```

or for appending using the double-greater-than symbol (>>) with the syntax:

```
open ([FILE_HANDLE_NAME], ">>[filename]");
```

The difference between appending and writing is that when you *write* to a file, you overwrite whatever was previously there. When you append to a file, you simply add the new information to the end of whatever text was already there.

If the file that Perl is asked to write or append to does not already exist, Perl will create the file for you.

N O T E

Typically, when writing to a file, you use the print function. However, instead of printing to standard output, you would specify the filename to print to. Consider the following example:

```
open (TEMP_FILE, ">temp.file") ||
    &CgiDie ("Cannot open temp.file");
print TEMP_FILE "hello there\n";
close (TEMP_FILE);
```

The file **temp.file** will now have the solitary line:

```
hello there
```

DELETING, RENAMING AND CHANGING THE PERMISSIONS OF FILES

Perl also provides you with all the file-management functions typically offered by your operating system. In our experience, the three most utilized functions in CGI scripts are unlink, rename and chmod. unlink is Perl's function for deleting a file from the file system. The syntax is pretty straight forward.

```
unlink ("[filename]");
```

This line of Perl code will delete the file called filename provided that the script has permissions to delete the file.

Your Perl script can also rename a file using the rename function:

```
rename ("[old_filename]", "[new_filename]");
```

In this case, the file's name will be replaced with the new filename specified.

Finally, Perl gives you the ability to affect the permissions of files in the file system using the chmod function. The syntax is also fairly straight forward as follows:

```
chmod (0666, "filename");
```

In this case, "filename" will be made readable and writable by user, group and world.

FILE TESTS

Finally, Perl provides many methods for determining information about files on the file system using "File tests." For the purposes of this appendix, there are too many types of file tests to cover them all in depth. Further, they are covered extensively elsewhere. However, we will note the most frequent syntax of file tests used in this book, which follows the form:

```
if ([filetest] [filename] && [other filetest] [filename])
  {
  do something
  }
```

Consider the following example which checks to see if a file exists (**-e**) and is writable (**-w**) by us, and if so deletes it:

```
if ((-e "temp.file") && (-w "temp.file"))
{
unlink ("temp.file");
}
```

Table B.6 lists several common file tests.

Table B.6 Common File Tests

Test	Description
-r	File or directory is readable
-w	File or directory is writable
-x	File or directory is executable
-o	File or directory is owned by user
-e	File or directory exists
-z	File exists and has zero size
-s	File or directory exists and has non-zero size
-f	Entry is a plain file
-d	Entry is a directory
-T	File is text
-B	File is binary
-M	Modification age in days
-A	Access age in days

OPENING, READING, AND CLOSING DIRECTORIES

As with files, Perl gives you the ability to manage directories. Specifically, Perl allows you to open a directory as a directory handle, read in the current contents of the directory, and then close it again .

To open a directory, you use the following syntax:

```
opendir ([FILE_HANDLE_NAME], "[directory_location]") || &CgiDie
("Can't open [directory_location]");
```

Thus, for example, you might open the directory **/usr/local/etc/www/** with the syntax:

```
opendir (WWW, "/usr/local/etc/www/") || &CgiDie ("Can't open www");
```

As you can see, as with opening files, Perl allows the program to die elegantly in case there is a problem opening the directory. Also, as with file manipulation, you must close a directory after you are through with it using the syntax:

```
closedir ([FILE_HANDLE_NAME]);
```

For example, to close the directory opened above, you use the command:

```
closedir(WWW);
```

Once you have opened a directory, you can also read the contents of the directory with the **readdir** function. For example, the following code snippet assigns all of the filenames in the **WWW** directory to **@filenames**:

```
opendir (WWW, "/usr/local/etc/www/") ||
        &CgiDie ("Can't open www");
@filenames = readdir (WWW);
closedir (WWW);
```

NOTE   If you want to avoid including the "." (current directory) and ".." (root directory) files you can use the **grep** function to avoid including them in the **readdir** function using the syntax:

```
@filenames = grep (!/^\.\.?$/, readdir (FILE_HANDLE_NAME);
```

INDEX